AF819881

QUE Bee

From Doubts to **Distinction**

Your ICSE 2026 Exams Partner

GIST OF THE TEXTBOOK

Crisp & Complete Theory - No need to go back to textbooks!

ALL TYPES OF LATEST PATTERN QUESTIONS

MCQs | Case-based | Assertion-Reason | Fill ups ; All in one place!

KEY WORDS HIGHLIGHTED

Important points and formulae neatly highlighted never miss what matters

COUNCIL-STYLE ANSWERS

Write responses like an examiner expects

SAMPLE QUESTION PAPER

Practice in real-exam mode. Perfect your timing, strategy, and confidence.

arihant
SUCCESS AND NOTHING LESS

ARIHANT PRAKASHAN
(School Division Series)

ADMINISTRATIVE & PRODUCTION OFFICES
Regd. Office
'Ramchhaya' 4577/15, Agarwal Road, Darya Ganj, New Delhi -110002
Tele: 011- 47630600, 43518550; Fax: 011- 23280316

Head Office
Kalindi, TP Nagar, Meerut (UP) - 250002, Tel: 0121-7156203, 7156204

SALES & SUPPORT OFFICES
Agra, Ahmedabad, Bengaluru, Bareilly, Chennai, Delhi, Guwahati, Hyderabad, Jaipur, Jhansi, Kolkata, Lucknow, Nagpur & Pune.

PO No : TXT-XX-XXXXXXX-X-XX

Published By Arihant Publications (India) Ltd.
For further information about the books published by Arihant, log on to www.arihantbooks.com or e-mail at info@arihantbooks.com
Follow us on

PRICE ₹200.00

PRODUCTION TEAM

Publishing Manager
Keshav Mohan

Project Head
Akansha Tomar

Cover Designer
Bilal Hashmi

Inner Designer
Ankit Tyagi

Page Layouting
Nishar Khan

Proof Reader
Nisha Verma,
Sarthak Sharma

QUE Bee

ICSE
CHEMISTRY
Class 9

Types of Questions & their Respective Number

Types of Questions	Total Number
Multiple Choice Questions (MCQs)	146
Assertion-Reason (A-R)	42
Fill in the Blanks	84
Correct the Incorrect Statement	42
Matching Type Questions	16
Identify the following	83
Short Answer Type I Questions (SA-I)	156
Short Answer Type II Questions (SA-II)	122
Long Answer Type Questions (LA)	105
Case Based Questions	20
TOTAL NO. OF QUESTIONS	**816**

Created by

Rafat Naseer

M.Sc. (Physical, Organic & Inorganic Chemistry), B.Ed.
HOD Chemistry, St. Mary's Academy, Meerut

Contributor

Tamanna Sharma

From Learner to Leader

Step-Into the Spotlight

QUE Bee is more than just a book - it's a platform for young achievers like you to guide future toppers. If you've cracked the code to smart study or have insights that can make learning easier for others, this is your moment to shine!

What Can You Share?

- Your study techniques, time management tips, or motivation hacks
- Feedback or suggestions to make QUE Bee even better
- Real experiences that can guide other students through the exam maze

What's in It for You?

- Your name will be featured in our exclusive Student Panel in the next edition
- Win exciting & surprise rewards for impactful suggestions
- **Get published** - your photo, Ideas-or even interviews can be featured in the book
- **Become a student icon** - recognized and followed by peers across schools

Let your learning become someone else's ladder.
Be remembered. Be featured. Be the guide.

SCAN TO SHARE YOUR IDEA

QUE Bee

Index

Latest
Course Structure

There will be one paper of **two hours** duration of 80 marks and Internal Assessment of practical work carrying 20 marks.

Note: All chemical Processes/Reactions should be studied with reference to the reactants, products, conditions, observations and the (balanced) equations and diagrams.

1. The Language of Chemistry

(i) Symbol of an element; valency; formulae of radicals and formulae of compounds. Balancing of simple chemical equations.

- Symbol – definition; symbols of the elements used often.
- Valency - definition; hydrogen combination and number of valence electrons of the metals and non-metals; mono, di, tri and tetra valent elements.
- Radicals – definition; formulae and valencies.
- Compounds – name and formulae.
- Chemical equation – definition and examples of chemical equations with one reactant and two or three products, two reactants and one product, two reactants and two products and two reactants and three or four products; balancing of equations. (by hit and trial method).

(ii) Relative Atomic Masses (atomic weights) and Relative Molecular Masses (molecular weights): either - standard H atom or $1/12^{th}$ of carbon 12 atom.

- Definitions
- Calculation of Relative Molecular Mass and percentage composition of a compound.

2. Chemical Changes and Reactions

(i) Types of chemical changes.

- Direct combination
- Decomposition
- Displacement
- Double decomposition

(The above to be taught with suitable chemical equations as examples).

(ii) Energy changes in a chemical change.

Exothermic and endothermic reactions with examples – evolution/absorption of heat, light and electricity.

3. Water

(i) Water as a universal solvent.

- Solutions as 'mixtures' of solids in water; saturated solutions.
- Qualitative effect of temperature on solubility (e.g. solutions of calcium sulphate, potassium nitrate and sodium chloride in water).

(ii) Hydrated and anhydrous substances.

(a) Hydrated substances:

Water of Crystallisation – meaning and examples.

(b) Anhydrous substances:

Meaning and examples only

(c) Properties:

- Efflorescence
- Deliquescence
- Hygroscopy
- Removal of hardness

(i) By boiling

(ii) By addition of washing soda

(Definition and examples of each of the above).

(iii) Drying and Dehydrating Agents

Meaning and examples only.

(iv) Soft water and Hard water

- Meaning, (in terms of action of soap)
- Advantages and disadvantages of soft water and hard water.
- Types and causes of hardness.

4. Atomic Structure and Chemical Bonding

(i) Structure of an Atom, Mass Number and Atomic number, Isotopes and Octet Rule.

- Definition of an atom
- Constituents of an atom - nucleus (protons, neutrons) with associated electrons; mass number, atomic number.
- Electron distribution in the orbits - $2n^2$ rule, Octet rule. Reason for chemical activity of an atom.
- Definition and examples of isotopes (hydrogen, carbon, chlorine).

(ii) Electrovalent and Covalent Bonding, Structures of Various Compounds – Orbit Structure

(a) Electrovalent Bond
- Definition
- Atomic orbit structure for the formation of Electrovalent compounds (e.g. NaCl, $MgCl_2$, CaO);

(b) Covalent Bond
- Definition
- Atomic orbit structure for the formation of Covalent molecules on the basis of duplet and octet of electrons (examples: hydrogen, chlorine, oxygen, nitrogen, hydrogen chloride, water, ammonia, carbon tetrachloride, methane.)

5. The Periodic Table

Dobereiner's Triads, Newland's law of Octaves, Mendeleev's contributions; Modern Periodic Law, the Modern Periodic Table. (Groups and periods)

- General idea of Dobereiner's triads, Newland's law of Octaves, Mendeleev's periodic law.
- Discovery of Atomic Number and its use as a basis for Modern Periodic law.
- Modern Periodic Table (Groups 1 to 18 and periods 1 to 7).
- Special reference to Alkali metals (Group 1), Alkaline Earth metals (Group 2) Halogens (Group 17) and Zero Group (Group 18).

6. Study of the First Element - Hydrogen

Position of the non-metal (Hydrogen) in the periodic table and general group characteristics with reference to valency electrons, burning, ion formation applied to the above mentioned element.

(i) Hydrogen from: water, dilute acids and alkalis.

(a) Hydrogen from water:
- The action of cold water on sodium potassium and calcium.
- The action of hot water on magnesium.
- The action of steam on aluminium, zinc, and iron; (reversibility of reaction between iron and steam).
- The action of steam on non-metal (carbon).

Students can be shown the action of sodium and calcium on water in the laboratory. They must be asked to make observations and write equations for the above reactions.

Application of activity series for the above mentioned reactions.

(b) Displacement of hydrogen from dilute acids:
- The action of dilute sulphuric acid or hydrochloric acid on metals: Mg, Al, Zn and Fe.

(To understand reasons for not using other metals and dilute nitric acid)

(c) Displacement of hydrogen from alkalis:
The action of Alkalis ((NaOH, KOH) on Al, Zn and Pb –unique nature of these elements.

(ii) The preparation and collection of hydrogen by a standard laboratory method other than electrolysis.
In the laboratory preparation, the reason for using zinc, the impurities in the gas, their removal and the precautions in the collection of the gas must be mentioned.

(iii) Industrial manufacture of hydrogen by Bosch process
- Main reactions and conditions.
- Separation of CO_2 and CO from hydrogen.

(iv) Oxidation and reduction reactions
Differences in terms of addition and removal of oxygen / hydrogen.

7. Study of Gas Laws

(i) The behaviour of gases under changes of temperature and pressure; explanation in terms of molecular motion (particles, atoms, molecules); Boyle's Law and Charles' Law; absolute zero; gas equation; simple relevant calculations.
- The behaviour of gases under changes of temperature and pressure; explanation in terms of molecular motion(particles, atoms, molecules).

- Boyle's Law: statement, mathematical form, simple calculations.
- Charles' Law: statement, mathematical form, simple calculations.
- Absolute zero Kelvin scale of temperature.
- Gas equation $p_1 V_1 / T_1 = p_2 V_2 / T_2$; simple relevant calculations based on gas equation.

(ii) Relationship between Kelvin scale and Celsius Scale of temperature; Standard temperature and pressure.

Conversion of temperature from Celsius Scale to Kelvin scale and *vice versa*. Standard temperature and pressure. (Simple calculations).

8. Atmospheric Pollution

(a) Acid rain – composition, cause and its impact.

Sulphur in fossil fuels giving oxides of sulphur when burnt. High temperatures in furnaces and internal combustion engines produce oxides of nitrogen. (Equations to be included). Acid rain affects soil chemistry and water bodies.

(b) Global warming: Greenhouse gases – their sources and ways of reducing their presence in the atmosphere.

(Water vapour, carbon dioxide, methane and oxides of nitrogen)

(c) Ozone depletion

- Formation of ozone – relevant equations
- Function in the atmosphere.
- Destruction of the ozone layer – chemicals responsible for this to be named but reactions not required.

INTERNAL ASSESSMENT OF PRACTICAL WORK

Candidates will be asked to observe the effect of reagents and/or of heat on substances supplied to them. The exercises will be simple and may include the recognition and identification of certain gases listed below.

Gases Hydrogen, Oxygen, Carbon dioxide, Chlorine, Hydrogen chloride, Sulphur dioxide, Hydrogen sulphide, Ammonia, Water vapour, Nitrogen dioxide.

Candidates are expected to have completed the following minimum practical work.

Simple Experiments on:

1. Action of heat on the following compounds:
   (a) copper carbonate, zinc carbonate
   (b) washing soda, copper sulphate crystals
   (c) zinc nitrate, copper nitrate, lead nitrate
   (d) ammonium chloride, iodine, ammonium dichromate

   Make observations, identify the products and make deductions where possible.

2. Action of dilute sulphuric acid on the following substances. (warm if necessary)
   (a) a metal
   (b) a carbonate
   (c) a sulphide
   (d) a sulphite

   Make observations, identify the gas evolved and make deductions

3. Apply the flame test to identify the metal in the unknown substance.
   (a) a sodium salt
   (b) a potassium salt
   (c) a calcium compound

4. Simple experiments based on hard water and soft water – identification of hardness – simple softening – by heating the temporary hard water, using washing soda and advantage of using detergents over soap in hard water.

5. Find out the sources of pollution of water bodies in the locality. Suggest preventive steps to control it.

01

THE LANGUAGE OF CHEMISTRY

Chemical Symbols

- A **chemical symbol** represents the abbreviation for the full names of the element. In another words, it is the short form for the atom of an element.
- When the first letter of more than one element is same then the symbol of elements incorporates first two letters or any two letters. The **first letter** is written in **capital**, while the **second** one is written in **small**.

  e.g. – Carbon is denoted by C. – Calcium is denoted by Ca – Cadmium is denoted by Cd.
- The symbol of an element has qualitative as well as quantitative significance as explained below.
  - **Qualitatively**, symbol represents name of the element.
  - **Quantitatively**, symbol represents one atom of the element.

  e.g. The symbol C represents

  Qualitatively, (a) Carbon

  Quantitatively, (b) One atom of carbon (c) 12 parts by weight of carbon
- In most cases, the **first letter** of the name of an element was taken as the symbol for that element and written in capitals.
- In some cases, the **initial letter** of the name in capital along with its second letter in small is used.

Name	Symbol
Carbon	C
Nitrogen	N
Hydrogen	H

Name	Symbol
Calcium	Ca
Aluminium	Al
Silicon	Si

- The symbols for some elements were derived from their Latin names.

English name of the element	Latin name of the element	Symbol
Sodium	**Na**trium	Na
Potassium	**K**alium	K
Iron	**Fe**rrum	Fe
Copper	**Cu**prum	Cu
Silver	**A**r**g**entum	Ag

English name of the element	Latin name of the element	Symbol
Gold	**Au**rum	Au
Mercury	**H**ydra**g**yrum	Hg
Lead	**P**lum**b**um	Pb
Tin	**S**ta**n**num	Sn

- The symbols of elements used today are first suggested by the Swedish chemist **Berzelius**.

Valency

- The combining power (or capacity) of an element is called its **valency**. The modern definition of valency is that valency is the number of electrons that atom can gain, lose or share during a chemical reaction.
- The electrons that are present in the outermost shell are known as **valence electrons**.
- The loss or gain of electrons by an atom depends upon **valence shell electrons**.

REVISION NOTES

- Elements that have one, two or three electrons present in their outermost shell (valence shell), are known as **metals** (except hydrogen).
- **Metals** form univalent, divalent, trivalent and tetravalent **cation** (positive ions) by losing their valence electrons.

e.g. $\underset{(2,8,1)}{Na} - e^- \longrightarrow \underset{2,8}{Na^+}$ *(univalent)* $\underset{(2,8,2)}{Mg} - 2e^- \longrightarrow \underset{2,8}{Mg^{2+}}$ *(divalent)* $\underset{(2,8,3)}{Al} - 3e^- \longrightarrow \underset{2,8}{Al^{3+}}$ *(trivalent)*

- Elements that have five, six or seven electrons present in their outermost (valence) shell are known as **non-metals** except hydrogen which has one valence electron but still it is a **non-metal.** They form univalent, divalent, trivalent and tetravalent **anion** (negative ions) by gaining electrons.

e.g. $\underset{(2,8,7)}{Cl} + e^- \longrightarrow \underset{2,8,8}{Cl^-}$ *(univalent)* $\underset{(2,6)}{O} + 2e^- \longrightarrow \underset{2,8}{O^{2-}}$ *(divalent)* $\underset{(2,5)}{N} + 3e^- \longrightarrow \underset{2,8}{N^{3-}}$ *(trivalent)*

- Valency in terms of hydrogen is defined as the number of hydrogen atoms that are attached with the element. e.g.

(i) One atom of hydrogen is attached with one atom of chlorine to form a molecule of hydrogen chloride (HCl). So, the **valency of chlorine is one.**

H—Cl

(ii) Two atoms of hydrogens are attached with one atom of oxygen to form a molecule of water (H_2O). So, the **valency of oxygen is two.**

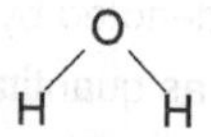

(iii) Three atoms of hydrogens are attached with one atom of nitrogen to form a molecule of ammonia (NH_3). So, the **valency of nitrogen is three.**

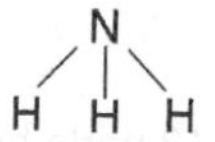

Ions

An ion is an atom or a group of atoms of same or different elements which behave as a single unit having positive or negative charges. The valency of an ion is equal to the charge on it.

Names, Symbols and Valency of Some Ions

Valency	Ion of metallic element	Symbol	Ion of non-metallic element	Symbol	Polyatomic ions	Symbol
1	Sodium	Na^+	Hydrogen	H^+	Ammonium	NH_4^+
	Potassium	K^+	Hydride	H^-	Hydroxide	OH^-
	Silver (I)* (argentous)	Ag^+	Chloride	Cl^-	Nitrate	NO_3^-
	Copper (I)* (cuprous)	Cu^+	Bromide	Br^-	Hydrogen carbonate (bicarbonate)	HCO_3
			Iodide	I^-		
2	Magnesium	Mg^{2+}	Oxide	O^{2-}	Carbonate	CO_3^{2-}
	Calcium	Ca^{2+}	Sulphide	S^{2-}		
	Zinc	Zn^{2+}				
	Iron (II)* (ferrous)	Fe^{2+}				
	Copper (II)* (cupric)	Cu^{2+}				
3	Aluminium	Al^{3+}				
	Iron (III)* (ferric)	Fe^{3+}				
4	Lead (IV)*	Pb^{4+}	Carbide	C^{4-}		

* These elements show more than one valency, i.e. **variable valency.**

Chemical Formula

- The shortest way to represent a compound with the help of symbols and valency of elements is known as **chemical formula.** It shows constituent elements and the number of atoms of each combining element.
- In ionic compounds, the charge on each ion is used to determine the chemical formula of a compound.

- A chemical formula is also known as **molecular formula** as it denotes the molecule of an element or of a compound. e.g. 2NaCl represents two molecules of sodium chloride and each molecule contains one atom of sodium and one atom of chlorine.
- To write the chemical formula for simple compound, **criss-cross method** is used, in which valencies or charges of the constituents are criss-crossed to balance the negative and positive charges to get a neutral compound.

Naming Chemical Compounds

Following rules are followed while naming the chemical compound from chemical formula.

- In **binary compounds** with one **metal** atom and a **non-metal** atom, the **metal** is named **first** and non-metal is named at the end with suffix '*ide*'.

  e.g. $Na_2O \rightarrow$ Sodium oxide $\quad$ $Ca_3N_2 \rightarrow$ Calcium nitride
- The compounds containing two **non-metals** are named by using prefix **mono**, **di**, **tri**, etc.

  e.g. $PCl_3 \rightarrow$ Phosphorus trichloride $\quad$ $PCl_5 \rightarrow$ Phosphorus pentachloride
- The prefix **'hypo'** is used, if the number of oxygen atoms is less than 2. The suffix **'ite'** is used, if the number of oxygen atom is 2.
- The suffix **'ate'** is used if the number of oxygen is 3. The prefix **'per'** is used if the number of oxygen atom is more than 3.

  e.g. $NaClO \rightarrow$ Sodium hypochlorite $\quad$ $NaClO_2 \rightarrow$ Sodium chlorite

  $NaClO_3 \rightarrow$ Sodium chlorate $\quad$ $NaClO_4 \rightarrow$ Sodium perchlorate
- The acids containing **two elements** where one atom is **hydrogen** that combines with one **non-metal** are named by adding prefix **'hydro'** and suffix **'ic'** to the name of second element.
- The bases are named as hydroxides after the name of the metal or radical.

  $HCl \rightarrow$ Hydrochloric acid (acid) $\quad$ $NH_4OH \rightarrow$ Ammonium hydroxide (base)

Radicals

Radical is an **atom** or **group of atoms** of the same or of different elements having a **charge** (positive or negative). It behaves as a single unit in chemical reaction. Radicals have their own valencies and chemical formulae.

e.g. In Na_2CO_3, sodium radical (Na^+), combining power is 1 and carbonate (CO_3^{2-}), combining power is 2.

Types of Radicals

There are four types of radicals

(i) **Acid radicals** Radicals having negative charge on them are called acid radicals. e.g. F^-, CO_3^{2-}, SO_4^{2-}, etc.
Those acidic radicals which carry a negative charge are also called **electronegative radicals** or **anions**.

(ii) **Basic radicals** Radicals having positive charge on them are called basic radicals. e.g. Na^+, NH_4^+, Zn^{2+}, etc.
Those basic radical that carry a positive charge are also called **electropositive radicals** or **cations**.

(iii) **Simple radicals** These are made up of only one kind of atoms. e.g. F^-, Na^+, K^+, etc.

(iv) **Compound radicals** These are made up of two or more type of atoms (polyatomic). e.g. CO_3^{2-}, OH^-, NH_4^+, etc.

Chemical Equation

A chemical equation is the symbolic representation of a chemical reaction. In this equation, the symbols and formulae of the **reactant substances** are written on the **left hand side** of the arrow and **product substances** are written on the **right hand side** of the arrow.

e.g. The reaction of burning of methane gas can be written in words as

$$\underbrace{\text{Methane} + \text{Oxygen}}_{\text{(Reactants)}} \xrightarrow{\Delta} \underbrace{\text{Carbon dioxide} + \text{Water}}_{\text{(Products)}}$$

This equation is called **word equation**. The word equation can be changed into a **chemical equation** by writing symbol and formulae of the substance in place of their name.

$$\underset{\text{Methane}}{CH_4(g)} + \underset{\text{Oxygen}}{2O_2(g)} \xrightarrow{\Delta} \underset{\text{Carbon dioxide}}{CO_2(g)} + \underset{\text{Water}}{2H_2O(g)}$$

Balanced Chemical Equation

A balanced chemical equation is that in which the total number of atoms of each element are equal on both (reactant and product) sides of the arrow.

e.g. Balanced equation, $CaCO_3 \xrightarrow{\Delta} CaO + CO_2$

In this reaction, the number of Ca, O and C on both sides is the same.

Information Conveyed by a Balanced Chemical Equation

- The chemical nature of the reactants and products participating in a chemical reaction.
- The nature of elements and radicals involved.
- Chemical composition of the respective molecules.
- The direction of the reaction, i.e. whether the reaction is irreversible ($\rightarrow$) or reversible ($\rightleftharpoons$).
- The physical states of matter, i.e. whether the substances are present in the solid (*s*), liquid (*l*) or gaseous (*g*) state.

Limitations of Chemical Equation

- A chemical equation does not tell us about the feasibility of a chemical reaction. It means we cannot predict whether a particular reaction will take place or not.
- It does not tell us whether a particular reaction will proceed at a slow, moderate or fast speed or rate.

Relative Atomic Mass (Atomic Weight)

It is defined as "the number of times a given atom is heavier than $\frac{1}{12}$th of mass of 1 atom of carbon-12 (C-12)" or it is the average mass of the atom as compared to $\frac{1}{12}$th the mass of one carbon-12 atom.

Thus, **relative atomic mass** (RAM) $= \dfrac{\text{mass of 1 atom of the element}}{\frac{1}{12}\text{ th the mass of one C-12 atom}}$

Atomic Mass Unit

It is defined as "the mass unit equal to exactly 1/12th of the mass of one atom of C-12 isotope". Earlier, it was abbreviated as **amu** but according to latest recommendation of IUPAC, it is now written as '*u*'–unified mass.

$$1 \text{ amu or u} = 1.6605 \times 10^{-24} \text{ g}$$

Relative Molecular Mass (Molecular Weight)

It is defined as the "ratio of the average mass of one molecule of an element or compound to 1/12th of the mass of an atom of carbon-12 isotope".

Relative molecular mass (RMM) of a compound is the sum of relative atomic masses of the atomic species as given in the chemical formula.

Percentage Composition

Percent composition of a compound is the percentage by weight of each element present in it. It is obtained by dividing mass of that element in the compound by the total mass of the compound and multiplying by 100. i.e.

$$\text{Percentage composition of element} = \frac{\text{Total mass contributed by the element in a compound}}{\text{Total molecular mass of compound}} \times 100$$

Empirical Formula of a Compound

- Empirical formula of a compound gives us an idea about the elements present in compound and also the ratio in which the elements are combined.
- The empirical formula of a compound is defined as the formula which gives the simplest whole number ratio of atoms of different elements present in one molecule of the compound.

  e.g. The molecular formula of glucose is $C_6H_{12}O_6$ and its empirical formula is CH_2O.

  From this empirical formula of glucose, it is clear that glucose consist of carbon, hydrogen and oxygen combined in the ratio 1 : 2 : 1.
- There are certain compounds whose empirical formula and molecular formula are same. e.g. Empirical formula and molecular formula of water is same H_2O.

REVISION NOTES

EXAM ORIENTED QUESTIONS

TYPE - 1 01 Mark

Multiple Choice Questions

Q.1 The symbol of tin is
(a) Sn (b) Tn (c) Ti (d) S

Ans. (a) The symbol of tin is **Sn**.

Q.2 The valency of iron in Fe_2O_3 is
(a) 1 (b) 2
(c) 3 (d) Both (b) and (c)

Ans. (c) By criss-cross method. Valency of oxygen is 2 covalency of Fe in that compound is **3**.

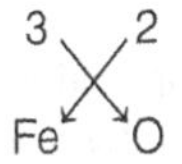

Fe_2O_3

Q.3 Valency of P in PCl_3 and in PCl_5 are
(a) 5, 5 (b) 3, 5 (c) 5, 5 (d) 5, 3

Ans. (b) 3, 5

Q.4 Oxygen, nitrogen and platinum are respectively
(a) trivalent, trivalent, tetravalent
(b) divalent, trivalent, trivalent
(c) divalent, tetravalent, trivalent
(d) divalent, trivalent, tetravalent

Ans. (d) Oxygen is divalent (O^{2-}), nitrogen is trivalent (N^{3-}) and platinum is tetravalent (Pt^{4+}).

Q.5 Which of the following pairs correctly represent a divalent and a trivalent cation, respectively?
(a) Mg^{2+}, Fe^{3+} (b) Na^+, Al^{3+}
(c) Ca^{2+}, K^+ (d) Zn^{2+}, Cu^+

Ans. (a) Mg^{2+} is divalent cation, Fe^{3+} is trivalent cation.

Q.6 List of some common electrovalent positive ions are given below. Which of the following correctly represent about the nature of ion.

	Monovalent	Divalent	Trivalent
(a)	Stannous	Ferric	Ferrous
(b)	Sodium	Mercurous	Mercuric
(c)	Zinc	Stannous	Stannic
(d)	Cuprous	Ferrous	Ferric

Ans. (d) Since, cuprous is Cu^+ (monovalent), ferrous is Fe^{2+}(divalent) and ferric is Fe^{3+} (trivalent). Therefore, based on the table, the option (d) correctly represents the nature of the ion.

Q.7 The correct chemical formula of aluminium oxide is
(a) AlO (b) AlO_3 (c) Al_2O_3 (d) Al_3O_2

Ans. (c) Formula for aluminium oxide:

Symbol Al O

Charge +3 −2

Formula : Al_2O_3

Q.8 What is the correct chemical formula of boric acid?
(a) H_2BO_3 (b) H_3BO_3
(c) H_3BO_2 (d) H_3BO_4

Ans. (b) The chemical formula of boric acid is $\mathbf{H_3BO_3}$.

Q.9 The number of carbon atoms in a hydrogen carbonate radical is
(a) one (b) two (c) three (d) four

Ans. (a) Hydrogen carbonate radical is represented by the formula $\mathbf{HCO_3^-}$. So number of carbon atoms is **1**.

Q.10 In sodium sulphite, the acidic radical is:
(a) SO_4^{2-} (b) SO_3^{2-} (c) Cl^- (d) PO_4^{3-}

Ans. (b) The chemical formula of sodium sulphite is Na_2SO_3. So the acidic radical is $\mathbf{SO_3^{2-}}$.

Q.11 Identify *a, b, c, d, e* in the following:

$$aNH_4Cl + bCa(OH)_2 \longrightarrow cCaCl_2 + dNH_3 + eH_2O$$

	a	b	c	d	e		a	b	c	d	e
(a)	1	2	1	2	2	(b)	2	2	1	1	2
(c)	2	1	1	2	2	(d)	1	2	2	2	1

Ans. (c) $2NH_4Cl + 1Ca(OH)_2 \longrightarrow 1CaCl_2 + 2NH_3 + 2H_2O$

$a = 2, b = 1, c = 1, d = 2, e = 2$

Q.12 An equation is show.

$$xNa + yCl_2 \longrightarrow zNaCl$$

Which numbers will correctly balance this equation?

	x	y	z
(a)	1	1	2
(b)	1	2	2
(c)	2	1	1
(d)	2	1	2

Ans. (d) The number of sodium and chlorine atoms need to be the same on both sides of the equation for it to be balanced.

Q.13 What is the relative molecular mass of ammonia (NH_3)?
[Given that the relative atomic mass of N = 14, H = 1]
(a) 14 amu (b) 17 amu
(c) 18 amu (d) 15 amu

Ans. (b) Relative molecular mass of ammonia (NH_3)
$$= 14 + (3 \times 1) = 14 + 3 = 17 \text{ amu}$$

TYPE - 2 01 Mark

Assertion-Reason Questions

Directions (Q. Nos. 1-5) In the following questions statement are given Assertion and Reason.
(a) Both (A) and (R) are true and (R) is the correct explanation of (A).
(b) Both (A) and (R) are true but (R) is not the correct explanation of (A).
(c) (A) is true but (R) is false.
(d) (A) is false but (R) is true.

Q.1 Assertion (A) The molecular formula of glucose is $C_6H_{12}O_6$.
Reason (R) Glucose is composed of six carbon atoms, twelve hydrogen atoms and six oxygen atoms.

Ans. (a) Both (A) and (R) are true and (R) is the correct explanation of (A).
The molecular formula of glucose is $C_6H_{12}O_6$. The molecular formula gives the exact number of each element present in one molecule of the compound.

Q.2 Assertion (A) The valency of sulphur is 2.
Reason (R) Sulphur can form bonds by sharing two electrons, but in certain compounds, it may show a valency of 6.

Ans. (b) Both (A) and (R) are true but (R) is not the correct explanation of (A).
The outermost shell of the sulphur atom contains six electrons. So, it requires two electrons to attain noble gas electronic configuration.

Q.3 Assertion (A) Balancing chemical equation involves adjusting the coefficient of the reactants and products.
Reason (R) A chemical equation must be balanced in order to follow the law of conservation of matter.

Ans. (b) Both (A) and (R) are true but (R) is not the correct explanation of (A).
A chemical equation must be balanced to find the chemical nature of the reactants and products participating in the reaction elements and radicals involved, direction of the reaction, and physical states of matter involved.

Q.4 Assertion (A) The molecular mass of water (H_2O) is 18 amu.
Reason (R) The relative atomic mass of hydrogen is 1 and that of oxygen is 16.

Ans. (a) Both (A) and (R) are true and (R) is the correct explanation of (A).
The molecular mass of water is indeed the sum of the atomic masses of hydrogen and oxygen. Water (H_2O) has 2 hydrogen atoms and 1 oxygen atom.
So, molecular mass of H_2O
$$= (2 \times 1) + (1 \times 16) = 2 + 16 = 18.$$
The reason correctly states that the relative atomic mass of hydrogen is 1 and oxygen is 16.

Q.5 Assertion (A) The percentage composition of hydrogen in water is 11.1%.
Reason (R) Percentage composition of a compound is the percentage by weight of each element present in it.

Ans. (b) Both (A) and (R) are true but (R) is not the correct explanation of (A).
The percentage composition of hydrogen in water is 11.1% because 2 g of hydrogen is contained in 18 g of water by mass.

TYPE - 3 01 Mark

Fill in the Blanks

Q.1 Usually .... represents one atom of an element. (symbol, formula)
Ans. symbol

Q.2 Ammonium ion (NH_4^+) is a ...... radical. (acidic, basic)
Ans. basic

Q.3 Formula of iron (III) carbonate is .... (Fe_2CO_3, $Fe_2(CO_3)_3$)
Ans. $Fe_2(CO_3)_3$

Q.4 The formula of caustic potash is .... (KOH, NaH)
Ans. KOH

Q.5 Cl^-, F^-, CO_3^{2-} and SO_4^{2-} are .... radicals. (acidic, basic)
Ans. acidic

Q.6 .... does not tell about the light related changes during chemical reactions. (chemical equation, physical equation)
Ans. Chemical equation

Q.7 $2NaHCO_3 \longrightarrow$ .... + H_2O + CO_2 (Na_2CO_3, $2NaCO_3$)
Ans. Na_2CO_3

Q.8 $2H_2O + 2Cl_2 \longrightarrow$ .... + O_2 (4HCl, 5HCl)
Ans. 4HCl

TYPE - 4 — 01 Mark

Correct the Incorrect Statement

Q.1 An atom is the smallest particle that has the capability to exit independently.

Ans. A **molecule** is the smallest particle that has the capability to exist independently.

Q.2 The formula of an element is a measure of its combining power with other elements.

Ans. The **valency** of an element is a measure of its combining power with other elements.

Q.3 A molecule of an element is always monoatomic.

Ans. A molecule of an **inert gas** is always monoatomic.

Q.4 A balanced equation obeys the law of conservation of energy while unbalanced equation does not.

Ans. A balanced equation obeys the law of conservation of **mass** while unbalanced equation does not.

Q.5 The molecular formula of water (H_2O) represents 9 parts by mass of water.

Ans. The molecular formula of water (H_2O) represents **18** parts by mass of water.

TYPE - 5 — 01×05=05 Marks

Match the Columns

Q.1 Match the following columns.

Column I (Name of the compound)		Column II (Formula)
A. Sodium carbonate	1.	Na_2SO_4
B. Sodium chlorate	2.	Na_2CO_3
C. Sodium sulphate	3.	$NaClO_3$
D. Sodium nitrate	4.	$NaNO_2$
E. Sodium nitrite	5.	$NaNO_3$

Ans. A → (2), B → (3), C → (1), D → (5), E → (4)

Q.2 Match the following columns.

Column I (Name of radicals)		Column II (Formula of radicals)
A. Phosphite	1.	$[Fe(CN)_6]^{4-}$
B. Ferrocyanide	2.	$C_2O_4^{2-}$
C. Oxalate	3.	$P_2O_7^{4-}$
D. Pyrophosphate	4.	PO_3^{3-}
E. Phosphate	5.	PO_4^{3-}

Ans. A → (4), B → (1), C → (2), D → (3), E → (5)

TYPE - 6 — 01 Mark

Identify the Following

Q.1 Name the smallest particle of an element which may or may not exist independently but can take part in a chemical reaction.

Ans. Atom

Q.2 What is number of atoms in a molecule of an element called?

Ans. Atomicity

Q.3 What do you call a short form that stands for the atom of a specific element.

Ans. Symbol

Q.4 State the term for the combining capacity of an element with other elements.

Ans. Valency

Q.5 If an element *X* has its valency equal to 3, what will be its formula with carbonate ion?

Ans. X ↖↗ CO_3; 3 ✕ 2 $= X_2(CO_3)_3$

Q.6 What is the chemical formula of ammonium phosphate?

Ans. NH_4 ↖↗ PO_4; 1 ✕ 3 $= (NH_4)_3PO_4$

Q.7 Give the chemical name of Mg_3N_2.

Ans. Magnesium nitride

Q.8 What are the cation and anion present in the CH_3COONa?

Ans. Cation : Na^+

Anion : CH_3COO^-

Q.9 State the term for "An atomic group of atoms of the same or of different elements that behave as a single unit with positive or negative charge".

Ans. Radical

Q.10 What do you call the number of times one atom of an element is heavier than 1/12 times of the mass of an atom of carbon-12.

Ans. Relative atomic mass.

Q.11 State the term for 1/12 of mass of one atom of carbon – 12 isotope.

Ans. Atomic mass unit

Q.12 Give the term for the number of times, one molecule of a substance is heavier than 1/12 of mass of one atom of carbon 12.

Ans. Relative molecular mass

Q.13 What do you name the percentage by weight of each element present in a compound?

Ans. Percentage composition

Q.14 Name the formula of a compound which gives the simplest whole number ratio of atoms of different elements present in one molecule of the compound.

Ans. Empirical formula

Q.15 What is the sum of the atomic mass of various elements present in the empirical formula called?

Ans. Empirical formula mass

TYPE - 7 — 02 Marks

Short Answer Type I Questions

Q.1 Give the letter names of the following elements Copper, sodium, potassium, mercury.

Ans. Copper-cuprum
Sodium-natrium
Potassium-kalium
Mercury-hydrargyrum $\left(\frac{1}{2}\times 4=2\right)$

Q.2 Name two metals and two non-metals that show variable valency.

Ans. Metals-Iron and copper
Non-metals -Phosphorus and nitrogen **(2)**

Q.3 Give a suitable reason for the following assertion. $AlCl_3$ is called aluminium chloride whereas PCl_3 is called phosphorus trichloride.

Ans. Aluminium shows only one valency, i.e. three. Therefore, its chloride is known as aluminium trichloride or aluminium chloride, whereas phosphorus exhibit variable valency, i.e. 3 and 5, thus PCl_3 is known as phosphorus trichloride (valency of P is 3) and PCl_5 as phosphorus pentachloride (valency of P is 5). **(2)**

Q.4 Write the formulae and valency of the following radicals or ions.
(i) Oxalate (ii) Bicarbonate

Ans. (i) Oxalate : $C_2O_4^{2-}$ (Valency = 2)
(ii) Bicarbonate : HCO_3^- (Valency = 1) **(1 × 2 = 2)**

Q.5 Write the formula of the following compounds.
(i) Magnesium chloride (ii) Potassium dichromate

Ans. (i) Magnesium chloride = $MgCl_2$
(ii) Potassium dichromate = $K_2Cr_2O_7$ **(1 × 2 = 2)**

Q.6 'Methane burns in oxygen to form carbon dioxide and water'. Write the chemical equation for the given chemical reaction and balance it.

Ans. Methane burns with oxygen to form carbon dioxide and water.
The balanced equation is
$$CH_4 + 2O_2 \longrightarrow CO_2 + 2H_2O$$ **(2)**

Q.7 Write chemical equations for the following word equations.
(i) Magnesium reacts with sulphuric acid to form magnesium sulphate and hydrogen gas
(ii) Calcium reacts with nitrogen to form calcium nitride
(iii) Nitrogen reacts with oxygen to form nitrogen monoxide
(iv) Phosphorous reacts with nitric acid to form nitrogen dioxide, water and phosphoric acid.

Ans. (i) $Mg(s) + H_2SO_4(aq) \longrightarrow MgSO_4(aq) + H_2(g)$
(ii) $3Ca + N_2 \longrightarrow Ca_3N_2$
(iii) $N_2 + O_2 \longrightarrow 2NO$
(iv) $P + 5HNO_3 \longrightarrow H_3PO_4 + H_2O + 5NO_2$ $\left(\frac{1}{2}\times 4=2\right)$

Q.8 Balance each of the chemical equations given below:
(i) $FeCl_3 + NH_4OH \longrightarrow NH_4Cl + Fe(OH)_3$
(ii) $KI + Cl_2 \longrightarrow KCl + I_2$

Ans. (i) $FeCl_3 + 3NH_4OH \longrightarrow 3NH_4Cl + Fe(OH)_3$
(ii) $2KI + Cl_2 \longrightarrow 2KCl + I_2$ **(1 × 2 = 2)**

Q.9 Write balanced equations of the following:
(i) Aluminium sulphate + Sodium hydroxide ⟶ Aluminium hydroxide + Sodium sulphate
(ii) Silver nitrate ⟶ silver + nitrogen dioxide + oxygen

Ans. (i) $Al_2(SO_4)_3 + 6NaOH \longrightarrow 2Al(OH)_3 + 3Na_2SO_4$
(ii) $2AgNO_3 \longrightarrow 2Ag + 2NO_2 + O_2$ **(1 × 2 = 2)**

Q.10 Write the significance of *s*, *l*, *g* and *aq* in a chemical equation.

Ans. The symbol (*s*) is used for solid-state. The symbol (*l*) is used to denote the liquid state.
The symbol (*g*) is used to denote the gaseous state and the symbol (*aq*) is used to denote the aqueous solution. **(2)**

Q.11 Give difference between relative atomic mass and relative molecular mass.

Ans. **Relative atomic mass** It is defined as the number of times a given atom is heavier than $\frac{1}{12}$th of mass of 1 atom of carbon-12 or it is the average mass of the atom as compared to $\frac{1}{12}$th mass of one carbon-12 atom. **(1)**

Relative molecular mass It is defined as the ratio of average mass of one molecule of an element or compound to $\frac{1}{12}$th of the mass of an atom of carbon-12 isotope. **(1)**

Q.12 Calculate the molecular mass of ammonium carbonate [$(NH_4)_2CO_3$].

Ans. The molecular mass of ammonium carbonate is

$$N = 2 \times 14 = 28$$
$$H = 8 \times 1 = 8$$
$$C = 1 \times 12 = 12$$
$$O = 3 \times 16 = 48$$
$$\overline{96 \text{ u}}$$

(2)

Q.13 Find the percentage mass of water in epsom salt, $MgSO_4 \cdot 7H_2O$.

Ans. Relative molecular mass of $MgSO_4 \cdot 7H_2O$

$$Mg = 1 \times 24 = 24$$
$$S = 1 \times 32 = 32$$
$$O = 11 \times 16 = 176$$
$$H = 14 \times 1 = 14$$
$$\overline{246 \text{ u}}$$

246 g of epsom salt contains 126 g of water of crystallisation.

Hence, 100 g of epsom salt contains $100 \times \frac{126}{246}$% of

H_2O in $MgSO_4 \cdot 7H_2O = 51.22\%$ **(2)**

Q.14 A compound contains C, H and O in the ratio 1 : 2 : 1. Give its empirical formula.

Ans. C : H : 1 = 1 : 2 : 1

∴ Empirical formula of compound is CH_2O. **(2)**

Q.15 Give two compounds whose molecular and empirical formulae are same.

Ans. H_2O, CO_2 **(2)**

TYPE - 8 — 03 Marks

Short Answer Type II Questions

Q.1 (i) Define poly-atomic ions. Give two examples.
(ii) Name the fundamental law involved in every equation.

Ans. (i) Charged species (or radical) made up of two or more different atoms that behaves as a single unit is called polyatomic ion. e.g. PO_4^{3-}, NH_4^+. **(2)**

(ii) Fundamental law involved in every equation is "the **law of conservation of mass**". **(1)**

Q.2 Identify the difference in the following symbols.
(i) O (ii) O_2 (iii) $2O_2$

Ans. (i) One atom of oxygen.
(ii) One molecule of oxygen.
(iii) Two molecules of oxygen. **(1 × 3 = 3)**

Q.3 An element '*X*' has a valency 1.
(i) Write the chemical formula of its phosphide.
(ii) Write the chemical formula of its chloride.
(iii) Is element '*X*' a metal or a non-metal?

Discuss about the hit and trial method using a chemical equation.

Ans. (i) Symbol *X* ⤫ P
Valency 1 ⤫ 3
Chemical formula : X_3P

(ii) Symbol *X* ⤫ Cl
Valency 1 ⤫ 1
Chemical formula : *X*Cl

(iii) The element *X* is metal. **(1 × 3 = 3)**

Q.4 Valency is simply equal to the number of electrons gained or shared by an atom of an element to achieve the nearest noble gas configuration. *X*[2, 8, 1] and *Y*[2, 8, 7] are two elements.
(i) .... is the valency of *Y*.
(ii) Formula of the compound formed when *X* combines with *Y* is ....
(iii) *X* forms ...... radical.

Ans. (i) 1 (ii) *XY* (iii) Basic **(1 × 3 = 3)**

Q.5 Complete the following table.

Acidic Radicals → Basic Radicals ↓	Chloride	Nitrate	Sulphate
Magnesium	$MgCl_2$	$Mg(NO_3)_2$	*A*
Zinc	*B*	$Zn(NO_3)_2$	$ZnSO_4$
Potassium	KCl	*C*	K_2SO_4

Ans. *A*. $MgSO_4$ *B*. $ZnCl_2$ *C*. KNO_3 **(1 × 3 = 3)**

Q.6 The formula of the chloride of a metal '*M*' is MCl_2. State the formula of its
(i) carbonate (ii) nitrate (iii) hydroxide.

Ans. (i) MCO_3 (ii) $M(NO_3)_2$ (iii) $M(OH)_2$ **(1 × 3 = 3)**

Q.7 Write the chemical formulae, using criss-cross method.
(i) Magnesium bicarbonate (ii) Barium nitrate
(iii) Potassium nitrate

Ans. (i) Mg ⤫ HCO_3
2 ⤫ 1
Formula is $Mg(HCO_3)_2$.

(ii) Ba ⤫ NO_3
2 ⤫ 1
Formula is $Ba(NO_3)_2$.

(iii) K ⤫ NO_3
1 ⤫ 1
Formula is KNO_3. **(1 × 3 = 3)**

Q.8 (i) Write chemical formulae of the following compounds.

(a) Aluminium nitride (b) Ammonium phosphate

(ii) Name an element which shows a variable valency. Write the formulae of its two chlorides.

Ans. (i) (a) AlN (b) $(NH_4)_3PO_4$ **(2)**

(ii) Iron (Fe), it forms $FeCl_2$ and $FeCl_3$ with chlorine. **(1)**

Q.9 Give the chemical name of the following.

(i) $Al_2(SO_4)_3$ (ii) $CaCl_2$ (iii) K_2SO_4 (iv) KNO_3
(v) $CaCO_3$ (vi) $CaZnO_2$

Ans. (i) Aluminium sulphate (ii) Calcium chloride
(iii) Potassium sulphate (iv) Potassium nitrate
(v) Calcium carbonate (vi) Calcium zincate **($\frac{1}{2} \times 6 = 3$)**

Q.10 Write the essential or necessary requirements of a chemical equation.

Ans. (i) Chemical equation should represent a true chemical change.

(ii) Chemical equation should be balanced, i.e. number of atoms of each element should be equal on both sides of the equation.

(iii) Chemical equation should be molecular, i.e. all the substances present in the chemical equation should be represented in their molecular forms. **(1 × 3 = 3)**

Q.11 Write the balanced equation of the following:

(i) Ammonia + Oxygen → Nitric oxide + Water

(ii) Barium chloride + Sulphuric acid → Barium Sulphate + Hydrochloric acid

(iii) Zinc sulphide + Oxygen → Zinc oxide + Sulphur dioxide

Ans. (i) $4NH_3 + 5O_2 \longrightarrow 6H_2O + 4NO$

(ii) $BaCl_2 + H_2SO_4 \longrightarrow BaSO_4 + 2HCl$

(iii) $2ZnS + 3O_2 \longrightarrow 2ZnO + 2SO_2$ **(1 × 3 = 3)**

Q.12 (i)

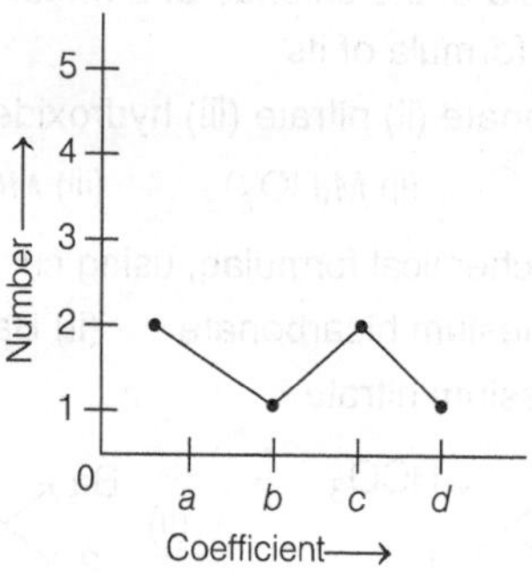

After studying the above graph, balance the given equation.

$$aKI + bH_2O_2 \longrightarrow cKOH + dI_2$$

(ii) Complete the following equations.

(a) $CaCO_3 + 2HCl \longrightarrow \ldots + \ldots + \ldots$

(b) $\ldots + \ldots \longrightarrow MgSO_4 + H_2$

Ans. (i) The balanced chemical equation is

$$2KI + 1H_2O_2 \longrightarrow 2KOH + 1I_2$$

Therefore, a, b, c, d are 2, 1, 2, 1 respectively. **(1)**

(ii) (a) $CaCO_3 + 2HCl \longrightarrow CaCl_2 + H_2O + CO_2$ **(1)**

(b) $Mg + H_2SO_4 \longrightarrow MgSO_4 + H_2$ **(1)**

Q.13 Calculate the percentage of water molecules in hydrated calcium sulphate.
[Ca = 40; S = 32; O = 16; H = 1]

Ans. Relative molecular mass of hydrated calcium sulphate; $CaSO_4 \cdot 2H_2O$

$$Ca = 1 \times 40 = 40$$
$$S = 1 \times 32 = 32$$
$$O = 4 \times 16 = 64$$
$$H_2O = 2 \times 18 = 36$$
$$= 172\ u$$

$$H_2O\ \% = \frac{36}{172} \times 100 = 20.93\%$$ **(3)**

Q.14 Calculate the percentage composition of nitrogen in urea, NH_2CONH_2.
[At. mass N = 14, C = 12, O = 16, H = 1.

Ans.
$$N = 2 \times 14 = 28$$
$$H = 4 \times 1 = 4$$
$$C = 1 \times 12 = 12$$
$$O = 1 \times 16 = 16$$
$$= 60\ u$$

Percentage composition of nitrogen

$$= \frac{\text{Total mass contributed by N}}{\text{Total molecular mass of } NH_2CONH_2} \times 100$$

$$= \frac{28}{60} \times 100 = 46.67\%$$ **(3)**

Q.15 Calculate the percentage of boron [B] in $Na_2B_4O_7.10H_2O$. (H = 1, B = 11, O = 16, Na = 23)

Ans. Molecular mass of $Na_2B_4O_7 \cdot 10H_2O$

$$Na = 2 \times 23 = 46$$
$$B = 4 \times 11 = 44$$
$$O = 17 \times 16 = 272$$
$$H = 20 \times 1 = 20$$
$$= 382\ u$$

So, % of boron in $Na_2B_4O_7 \cdot 10H_2O$

$$= \frac{44}{382} \times 100$$
$$= \frac{22 \times 100}{191}$$

% of B = 11.518% **(3)**

Q.16 Calculate the percentage of water molecules of crystallisation in blue vitriol ($CuSO_4.5H_2O$).
(At. mass Cu = 64, O = 16 , S = 32, H = 1)

Ans.
$Cu = 1 \times 64 = 64$
$S = 1 \times 32 = 32$
$O = 4 \times 16 = 64$
$H_2O = 5 \times 18 = 90$
$= 250$

$\% \text{ of } H_2O = \frac{90}{250} \times 100 = 36\%$ **(3)**

TYPE - 9 04/05 Marks

Long Answer Type Questions

Q.1 Write the valency of elements by using the concept of criss-cross method.

(i) Carbon in CH_4 (ii) Phosphorus in PH_3 (iii) Sulphur in SF_6 (iv) Fluorine in CaF_2

Ans. (i) The valency of carbon in CH_4 is '4'.
(ii) The valency of phosphorus in PH_3 is '3'.
(iii) The valency of sulphur in SF_6 is '6'.
(iv) The valency of fluorine in CaF_2 is '1'. **(1 × 4 = 4)**

Q.2 Complete the following table.

Acid radicals → Basic radicals ↓	Phosphate	Hydroxide	Carbonate	Sulphate	Nitrate	Chloride
Magnesium	$Mg_3(PO_4)_2$	$Mg(OH)_2$	$MgCO_3$	$MgSO_4$	$Mg(NO_3)_2$	$MgCl_2$
Potassium						
Iron (II)						
Calcium						
Ammonium						
Silver (I)						
Zinc						
Sodium						

Ans.

Acid radicals → Basic radicals ↓	Phosphate	Hydroxide	Carbonate	Sulphate	Nitrate	Chloride
Magnesium	$Mg_3(PO_4)_2$	$Mg(OH)_2$	$MgCO_3$	$MgSO_4$	$Mg(NO_3)_2$	$MgCl_2$
Potassium	K_3PO_4	KOH	K_2CO_3	K_2SO_4	KNO_3	KCl
Iron (II)	$Fe_3(PO_4)_2$	$Fe(OH)_2$	$FeCO_3$	$FeSO_4$	$Fe(NO_3)_2$	$FeCl_2$
Calcium	$Ca_3(PO_4)_2$	$Ca(OH)_2$	$CaCO_3$	$CaSO_4$	$Ca(NO_3)_2$	$CaCl_2$
Ammonium	$(NH_4)_3PO_4$	NH_4OH	$(NH_4)_2CO_3$	$(NH_4)_2SO_4$	NH_4NO_3	NH_4Cl
Silver (I)	Ag_3PO_4	AgOH	Ag_2CO_3	Ag_2SO_4	$AgNO_3$	AgCl
Zinc	$Zn_3(PO_4)_2$	$Zn(OH)_2$	$ZnCO_3$	$ZnSO_4$	$Zn(NO_3)_2$	$ZnCl_2$
Sodium	Na_3PO_4	NaOH	Na_2CO_3	Na_2SO_4	$NaNO_3$	NaCl

(½ × 8 = 4)

Q.3 Balance the following equations.

(i) $P + HNO_3 \longrightarrow NO_2 + H_2O + H_3PO_4$
(ii) $HNO_3 + H_2S \longrightarrow NO_2 + H_2O + S$
(iii) $H_2O + Cl_2 \longrightarrow HCl + O_2$
(iv) $Pb_3O_4 + HCl \longrightarrow PbCl_2 + H_2O + Cl_2$

Ans. (i) $P + 5HNO_3 \longrightarrow 5NO_2 + H_2O + H_3PO_4$
(ii) $2HNO_3 + H_2S \longrightarrow 2NO_2 + 2H_2O + S$
(iii) $2H_2O + 2Cl_2 \longrightarrow 4HCl + O_2$
(iv) $Pb_3O_4 + 8HCl \longrightarrow 3PbCl_2 + 4H_2O + Cl_2$ **(1 × 4 = 4)**

Q.4 Write the balanced chemical equation of the following reactions.

(i) Sodium chloride + manganese dioxide + sulphuric acid $\longrightarrow$ Sodium hydrogen sulphate + Manganese sulphate + Water + Chlorine

(ii) Sulphur + nitric acid $\longrightarrow$ Sulphuric acid + Nitrogen dioxide + Water

(iii) Potassium dichromate + hydrochloric acid $\longrightarrow$ Potassium chloride + chromium chloride + water + chlorine

(iv) Aluminium sulphate + Sodium hydroxide $\longrightarrow$ Sodium sulphate + Sodium meta aluminate + Water

Ans. (i) $2NaCl + MnO_2 + 3H_2SO_4 \longrightarrow 2NaHSO_4 + MnSO_4 + 2H_2O + Cl_2$

(ii) $S + 6HNO_3 \longrightarrow H_2SO_4 + 6NO_2 + 2H_2O$

(iii) $K_2Cr_2O_7 + 14HCl \longrightarrow 2KCl + 2CrCl_3 + 7H_2O + 3Cl_2$

(iv) $Al_2(SO_4)_3 + 8NaOH \longrightarrow 3Na_2SO_4 + 2NaAlO_2 + 4H_2O$ **(1 × 4 = 4)**

Q.5 Sodium chloride reacts with silver nitrate to produce silver chloride and sodium nitrate.

(i) Write the chemical equation.

(ii) Check whether it is balanced, if not then balance it.

(iii) Calculate the weights of reactants and products.

(iv) Write the law which satisfies this chemical equation.

Ans. (i) $NaCl + AgNO_3 \longrightarrow AgCl + NaNO_3$

(ii) It is a balanced chemical equation.

(iii) Total weight of reactants = 58.5 + 170 = 228.5
Total weight of products = 143.5 + 85 = 228.5

(iv) It is based upon the **law of conservation of mass**, i.e. in a chemical reaction total mass of the reactants must be equal to the total mass of the products. **(1 × 4 = 4)**

Q.6 How are the limitations or drawbacks of a chemical equation removed or how we can make a chemical equation more informative?

Ans. Some of the drawbacks of chemical equation can be removed as follows

(i) The physical states of the reactants and products can be indicated by using the symbol, i.e. (*s*) for solids, (*l*) for liquids, (*g*) for gases and (*aq*) for aqueous solutions.

e.g. $Zn(s) + 2HCl(aq) \longrightarrow ZnCl_2(aq) + H_2(g)$

(ii) The conditions necessary for the reaction to occur are represented by the arrow between the reactants and products.

e.g. $Fe(s) + S(s) \xrightarrow{\text{Heat}} FeS(s)$

(iii) The concentration of the solution of reactants can be shown by writing dil. for dilute and conc. for concentrated solution. e.g.

$$Cu(s) + 2H_2SO_4(\text{conc.}) \xrightarrow{\Delta} CuSO_4(aq) + SO_2(g) + 2H_2O(l)$$

(iv) The heat changes during a reaction are indicated by writing + Q kJ or − Q kJ along with the products for exothermic and endothermic reactions respectively.

e.g. $2H_2(g) + O_2(g) \longrightarrow 2H_2O(l) + 572\ kJ$ **(1 × 4 = 4)**

Q.7 Calculate the relative molecular mass of the following compounds.

(i) Lead sulphate (ii) Calcium phosphate

(Given, atomic masses of various elements, Ca = 40 u, S = 32 u, O = 16 u, Pb = 207 u and P = 31 u)

Ans. (i) Relative molecular mass of lead sulphate ($PbSO_4$)

Pb = 1 × 207 = 207
S = 1 × 32 = 32
O = 4 × 16 = 64
303 u **(2)**

(ii) Relative molecular mass of calcium phosphate [$Ca_3(PO_4)_2$]

Ca = 3 × 40 = 120
P = 2 × 31 = 62
O = 8 × 16 = 128
310 u **(2)**

Q.8 Calculate the relative molecular mass of the following (i) H_2SO_4 (ii) $(NH_4)_2SO_4$
[Given, atomic mass of N = 14 u, H = 1 u, S = 32 u, O = 16 u]

Ans. (i) Relative molecular mass of H_2SO_4

H = 2 × 1 = 2
S = 1 × 32 = 32
O = 4 × 16 = 64
98 u **(2)**

(ii) Relative molecular mass of $(NH_4)_2SO_4$

N = 2 × 14 = 28
H = 8 × 1 = 8
S = 1 × 32 = 32
O = 4 × 16 = 64
132 u **(2)**

Q.9 Calculate the relative molecular masses of the following: (N = 14, H = 1, S = 32, O = 16, Cr = 52, K = 39, Mg = 24, Cl = 35.5)

(i) $(NH_4)_2SO_4$ (ii) $(NH_4)_2Cr_2O_7$

(iii) $MgSO_4.7H_2O$ (v) $KClO_3$

Ans. (i) $N = 2 \times 14 = 28$
$H = 8 \times 1 = 8$
$S = 1 \times 32 = 32$
$O = 4 \times 16 = 64$
$= \overline{132}$ u

(ii) $N = 2 \times 14 = 28$
$H = 8 \times 1 = 8$
$Cr = 2 \times 52 = 104$
$O = 7 \times 14 = 98$
$= \overline{238}$ u

(iii) $Mg = 1 \times 24 = 24$
$S = 1 \times 32 = 32$
$O = 11 \times 16 = 176$
$H = 14 \times 1 = 14$
$= \overline{246}$ u

(iv) $K = 1 \times 39 = 39$
$Cl = 1 \times 35.5 = 35.5$
$O = 3 \times 16 = 48$
$= \overline{122.5}$ u

(1 × 4 = 4)

Q.10 Calculate the percentage of phosphorus in:
(i) Calcium hydrogen phosphate, $Ca(H_2PO_4)_2$
(ii) Calcium phosphate, $Ca_3(PO_4)_2$

Ans. (i) Relative molecular mass of $Ca(H_2PO_4)_2$

$Ca = 1 \times 40 = 40$
$H = 4 \times 1 = 4$
$P = 2 \times 31 = 62$
$O = 8 \times 16 = 128$
$\overline{234}$ u

$$P\% = \frac{62}{234} \times 100 = 26.49\%$$ **(2)**

(ii) Relative molecular mass of $Ca_3(PO_4)_2$

$Ca = 3 \times 40 = 120$
$P = 2 \times 31 = 62$
$O = 8 \times 16 = 128$
$\overline{310}$ u

$$P\% = \frac{62}{310} \times 100 = 2\%$$ **(2)**

Q.11 Calculate the percentage of calcium in calcium nitrate and percentage of phosphorus in phosphoric acid. (At. mass Ca = 40, P = 31, O = 16)

Ans. Calcium nitrate $Ca(NO_3)_2$

$Ca = 1 \times 40 = 40$
$N = 2 \times 14 = 28$
$O = 6 \times 16 = 96$
$\overline{164}$ u

$$Ca\% = \frac{40}{164} \times 100 = 24.39\% \approx 24.4\%$$ **(2)**

H_3PO_4 (phosphoric acid)

$H = 3 \times 1 = 3$
$P = 1 \times 31 = 31$
$O = 4 \times 16 = 64$
$\overline{98}$ u

$$\%P = \frac{31}{98} \times 100 = 31.6\%$$ **(2)**

Q.12 The valency of an element '*X*' is 2. Give the formula of its chloride sulphate, borate, zincate, aluminate, *meta*-aluminate.

Ans.

Criss-cross	Formula
2 ╳ 1 ; X, Cl	XCl_2
2 ╳ 3 ; X, BO_3	$X_3(BO_3)_2$
2 ╳ 2 ; X, ZnO_2	$XZnO_2$
2 ╳ 3 ; X, AlO_3	$X_3(AlO_3)_2$
2 ╳ 1 ; X, AlO_2	$X(AlO_2)_2$

(1 × 5 = 5)

Q.13 Find the valency of the underlined element.
(i) <u>Cu</u>O (ii) <u>C</u>H_4 (iii) <u>S</u>F_6
(iv) <u>P</u>Cl_3 (iv) <u>K</u>Cl

Ans. (i) CuO
Valency of oxygen is 2.
$(CuO)_2 = Cu_2O_2$
2 ╳ 2 ; Cu, O
∴ Valency of Cu = 2

(ii) CH_4
Valency of C is 4.

(iii) SF_6
Valency of F is 1.
6 ╳ 1 ; S, F
∴ Valency of S is 6.

(iv) PCl_3
Valency of Cl is 1.
3 ╳ 1 ; P, Cl
∴ Valency of P is 3.

(v) KCl
Valency of Cl is 1
1 ╳ 1 ; K, Cl
∴ Valency of K is 1. **(1 × 5 = 5)**

Q.14 Give the acidic radical and basic radical of the following and then give their chemical formulae.

Potassium manganate, chromium (III) sulphate, potassium permanganate, ferrous sulphide, sodium thiosulphate.

Ans.

	Acidic radical	Basic radical	Chemical formulae
Potassium manganate	MnO_4^{2-}	K^+	K_2MnO_4
Chromium (III) sulphate	SO_4^{2-}	Cr^{3+}	$Cr_2(SO_4)_3$
Potassium permanganate	MnO_4^-	K^+	$KMnO_4$
Ferrous sulphide	S^{2-}	Fe^{2+}	FeS
Sodium thiosulphate	$S_2O_3^{2-}$	Na^+	$Na_2S_2O_3$

(1 × 5 = 5)

Q.15 Write the basic and acidic radicals in the following compounds.

(i) $ZnSO_4$ (ii) $(NH_4)_2SO_4$

(iii) $Al_2(SO_4)_3$ (iv) $MgCO_3$ (v) $Mg(OH)_2$

Ans.

S.No.	Compound	Basic radicals	Acidic radicals
(i)	$ZnSO_4$	Zn^{2+}	SO_4^{2-}
(ii)	$(NH_4)_2SO_4$	NH_4^+	SO_4^{2-}
(iii)	$Al_2(SO_4)_3$	Al^{3+}	SO_4^{2-}
(iv)	$MgCO_3$	Mg^{2+}	CO_3^{2-}
(v)	$Mg(OH)_2$	Mg^{2+}	OH^-

(1 × 5 = 5)

Q.16 Split the following into acidic and basic radicals and given their chemical names.

(i) $K_4[Fe(CN)_6]$ (ii) $Mn_3(BO_3)_2$

(iii) $Ba(ClO_3)_2$ (iv) $Al_2(SO_4)_3$

(v) $(NH_4)_2CO_3$ (vi) $K_2Cr_2O_7$

Ans.

(i)	$K_4[Fe(CN)_6]$	K^+	$[Fe(CN)_6]^{4-}$	Potassium ferrocyanide
(ii)	$Mn_3(BO_3)_2$	Mn^{2+}	BO_3^{3-}	Manganese borate
(iii)	$Ba(ClO_3)_2$	Ba^{2+}	ClO_3^{3-}	Barium chlorate
(iv)	$Al_2(SO_4)_3$	Al^{3+}	SO_4^{2-}	Aluminium sulphate
(v)	$(NH_4)_2CO_3$	NH_4^+	CO_3^{2-}	Ammonium carbonate
(vi)	$K_2Cr_2O_7$	K^+	$Cr_2O_7^{2-}$	Potassium dichromate

(1 × 5 = 5)

Q.17 The formula of phosphate of a compound '*X*' *is* $X_3(PO_4)_2$. Give the formula of its oxide, hydroxide, sulphate and acetate.

Ans. Valency of *X* is 2 (Criss-cross method) **(1)**

2 ╳ 2 : X, O → XO

2 ╳ 1 : X, OH → $X(OH)_2$

2 ╳ 2 : X, SO_4 → XSO_4

2 ╳ 1 : X, CH_3COO → $(CH_3COO)_2X$

(4)

Q.18 Identify the different elements and give the numbers of each type of element in the following compounds. Potassium permanganate, sodium phosphite magnesium nitride, calcium oxalate, magnesium hydroxide.

Ans.

Compound	Elements	No. of atoms
Potassium permanganate ($KMnO_4$)	K (Potassium)	1
	Mn (Manganese)	1
	O (Oxygen)	4
Sodium phosphite (Na_3PO_3)	Na (Sodium)	3
	P (Phosphorus)	1
	O(Oxygen)	3
Magnesium nitride (Mg_3N_2)	Mg (Magnesium)	3
	N(Nitrogen)	2
Calcium oxalate [$Ca(C_2O_4)_2$]	Ca (Calcium)	1
	C (carbon)	4
	O (Oxygen)	8
Magnesium hydroxide [$Mg(OH)_2$]	Mg (Magnesium)	1
	O (Oxygen)	2
	H (Hydrogen)	2

(1 × 5 = 5)

Q.19 Balance the following equations.

(i) $Fe + H_2O \longrightarrow Fe_3O_4 + H_2$

(ii) $PbO + NH_3 \longrightarrow Pb + H_2O + N_2$

(iii) $Zn + KOH \longrightarrow K_2ZnO_2 + H_2$

(iv) $Ca + N_2 \longrightarrow Ca_3N_2$

(v) $Fe_2O_3 + CO \longrightarrow Fe + CO_2$

Ans. (i) $3Fe + 4H_2O \longrightarrow Fe_3O_4 + 4H_2$

(ii) $3PbO + 2NH_3 \longrightarrow 3Pb + 3H_2O + N_2$

(iii) $Zn + 2KOH \longrightarrow K_2ZnO_2 + H_2$

(iv) $3Ca + N_2 \longrightarrow Ca_3N_2$

(v) $Fe_2O_3 + 3CO \longrightarrow 2Fe + 3CO_2$ **(1 × 5 = 5)**

Q.20 Balance the following equations

(i) $KI + H_2O_2 \longrightarrow KOH + I_2$

(ii) $Zn + HNO_3 \longrightarrow Zn(NO_3)_2 + H_2O + NO_2$

(iii) $S + H_2SO_4 \longrightarrow SO_2 + H_2O$

(iv) $MnO_2 + HCl \longrightarrow MnCl_2 + H_2O + Cl_2$

(v) $Fe + H_2O \longrightarrow Fe_3O_4 + H_2$

Ans. (i) $2KI + H_2O_2 \longrightarrow 2KOH + I_2$

(ii) $Zn + 4HNO_3 \longrightarrow Zn(NO_3)_2 + 2H_2O + 2NO_2$

(iii) $S + 2H_2SO_4 \longrightarrow 3SO_2 + 2H_2O$

(iv) $MnO_2 + 4HCl \longrightarrow MnCl_2 + 2H_2O + Cl_2$

(v) $3Fe + 4H_2O \longrightarrow Fe_3O_4 + 4H_2$ **(1 × 5 = 5)**

Q.21 Write chemical equations for the following equations and balance them.

(i) Carbon + Oxygen → Carbon dioxide

(ii) Calcium + Nitrogen → Calcium nitride

(iii) Magnesium + Sulphuric acid → Magnesium sulphate + Hydrogen

(iv) Nitrogen + Oxygen → Nitrogen monoxide

(v) Calcium oxide + Carbon dioxide → Calcium carbonate.

Ans. (i) $2C + O_2 \longrightarrow CO_2$

(ii) $3Ca + N_2 \longrightarrow Ca_3N_2$

(iii) $Mg(s) + H_2SO_4(aq) \longrightarrow MgSO_4(aq) + H_2(g)$

(iv) $N_2 + O_2 \longrightarrow 2NO$

(v) $CaO + CO_2 \longrightarrow CaCO_3$ **(1×5=5)**

Q.22 Write balanced chemical equation for the following word equations.

(i) Sodium reacts with water to form sodium hydroxide and hydrogen.

(ii) Lead sulphide reacts with oxygen to give lead (II) oxide and sulphur dioxide.

(iii) Carbon reacts with sulphuric acid to give carbon dioxide, water and sulphur dioxide.

(iv) Sodium bicarbonate on heating decomposes to give sodium carbonate, carbon dioxide and water.

(v) Nitric acid oxidises hydrogen sulphide to give sulphur, nitrogen dioxide and water.

Ans. (i) $2Na(s) + 2H_2O(l) \longrightarrow 2NaOH(aq) + H_2(g)$

(ii) $2PbS(s) + 3O_2(g) \longrightarrow 2PbO(s) + 2SO_2(g)$

(iii) $C(s) + 2H_2SO_4(aq) \longrightarrow CO_2(g) + 2H_2O(l) + 2SO_2(g)$

(iv) $2NaHCO_3(s) \xrightarrow{\Delta} Na_2CO_3(s) + CO_2(g) + H_2O(g)$

(v) $2HNO_3(aq) + H_2S(g) \longrightarrow S(s) + 2NO_2(g) + 2H_2O(l)$

(1 × 5 = 5)

Q.23 Give a balanced chemical reaction for each of the following, where a reaction involves

(i) One reactant two products.

(ii) One reactant three products.

(iii) Two reactants two products.

(iv) Two reactants three products.

(v) Two reactants four products.

Ans. (i) $\underset{\text{(Acidulated)}}{2H_2O(l)} \longrightarrow 2H_2(g) + O_2(g)$

(ii) $\underset{\text{(White)}}{2Pb(NO_3)_2} \xrightarrow{\Delta} \underset{\text{(Yellow)}}{2PbO\downarrow} + \underset{\text{(Reddish brown)}}{4NO_2\uparrow} + O_2$

Or $\underset{\text{(White)}}{2AgNO_3} \longrightarrow \underset{\text{Silver white}}{2Ag\downarrow} + \underset{\text{(Reddish brown)}}{2NO_2\uparrow} + O_2$

(iii) $NaOH(aq) + HCl(aq) \longrightarrow NaCl(aq) + H_2O(l) + \text{Heat}$

(iv) $Cu(s) + \underset{\text{(Conc.)}}{2H_2SO_4(aq)} \longrightarrow \underset{\text{Blue (Copper sulphate)}}{CuSO_4(aq)} + \underset{\text{(Sulphur dioxide)}}{SO_2(g)\uparrow} + H_2O(l)$

(v) $\underset{\text{Potassium Dichromate}}{K_2Cr_2O_7} + \underset{\text{Hydro-chloric acid}}{14HCl} \longrightarrow \underset{\text{Potassium chloride}}{2KCl} + \underset{\text{Chromium (III) chloride}}{2CrCl_3} + 7H_2O + 3Cl_2$

(1 × 5 = 5)

Q.24 State the information conveyed by the following chemical equation.

$$Zn + 2KOH \longrightarrow K_2ZnO_2 + H_2$$

(At. mass Zn = 65, K = 39, O = 16, H = 1)

Ans. (i) One atom of zinc reacts with two molecules of KOH (potassium hydroxide). **(1)**

(ii) One molecule of potassium zincate is formed and one molecule of H_2 gas is released. **(1)**

(iii) **KOH**

K = 1 × 39 = 39

O = 1 × 16 = 16

H = 1 × 1 = 1

= 56 g **(1)**

K_2ZnO_2

K = 2 × 39 = 78

Zn = 1 × 65 = 65

O = 2 × 16 = 32

= 175 g **(1)**

(iv) 65 g of zinc reacts with 112 g of KOH (56 × 2) to form 175 g of K_2ZnO_2 and 2 g of hydrogen. **(1)**

Q.25 Alum is $K_2SO_4.Al_2(SO_4)_3.24H_2O$ is a double salt commonly used as antiseptic.

(i) Name the different elements present in it.

(ii) Find the number of each element present in it.

(iii) Calculate its molecular mass and percentage of water in it.

Ans. (i) Alum consist of potassium, aluminium, sulphur, oxygen and hydrogen. **(1)**

(ii) Potassium (K) = 2, Aluminium (Al) = 2

Sulphur (S) = 4

Oxygen (O) = 40 (24 atoms in water and 16 atoms in the salts)

Hydrogen (H) = 48 **(1)**

(iii) Molecular mass

K	$2 \times 39 = 78$
Al	$2 \times 27 = 54$
S	$4 \times 32 = 128$
O	$16 \times 16 = 256$
H_2O	$24 \times 18 = 432$
	$= \underline{948}$ u

$$\% H_2O = \frac{432}{948} \times 100 = 45.6\%$$ **(3)**

Q.26 **The following represents the structural formula of an organic compound benzene.**

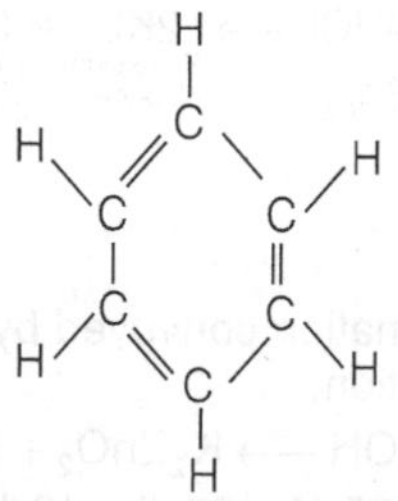

(i) **How many carbon and hydrogen atoms present in the compound?**

(ii) **Give the molecular formula of the compound.**

(iii) **Give the ratio of C:H in the molecular formula.**

(iv) **Also establish the empirical formula of the compound.**

(v) **Calculate the percentage compositions of the C and H in the benzene. (At. mass C = 12, H = 1)**

Ans. (i) C = 6, H = 6 (ii) Molecular formula = C_6H_6

(iii) C : H = 6 : 6 = 1 : 1 (iv) Empirical formula = CH

(v) C_6H_6

$C = 6 \times 12 = 72$

$H = 6 \times 1 = 6$

$= \underline{78}$ u

$$\%C = \frac{72}{78} \times 100 = 92.3\%$$

$$\%H = \frac{6}{78} \times 100 = 7.69\%$$ **(1 × 5 = 5)**

TYPE - 10 — 03 Marks

Case Based Questions

Q.1 In an experiment, a student is working with sodium (Na) and sulphur (S) to form the ionic compound sodium sulphide. Sodium has a valency of 1 and sulphur has a valency of 2.

(i) **Write the chemical formula for sodium sulphide.**

(ii) **Write the chemical formula of sodium sulphite.**

(iii) **Identify the acidic and basic radical in sodium sulphide.**

Ans. (i) Sodium has a Na^+ ion with a charge of + 1, and sulphur has an S^{2-} ion with a charge of − 2. To balance the charges, two sodium ions are needed for one sulphur ion, so the formula is **Na_2S**.

Symbol Na S

Charge + 1 − 2

Formula : Na_2S **(1)**

(ii) By using criss cross method.

1 2

Na SO_3

Formula : Na_2SO_3 **(1)**

(iii) Acidic radical = S^{2-}

Basic radical = Na^+ **(1)**

Q.2 **In a laboratory experiment, a student is working with water (H_2O). The student is asked to calculate the molecular mass of water and explain the concept of relative atomic mass to understand how the molecular mass is determined.**

The relative atomic mass of hydrogen (H) is 1, and the relative atomic mass of oxygen (O) is 16. The formula of water is H_2O, which means each molecule of water contains 2 hydrogen atoms and 1 oxygen atom.

Based on the information above, answer the following:

(i) **Calculate the molecular mass of water (H_2O).**

(ii) **Define relative atomic mass and explain its significance in calculating molecular mass.**

(iii) **Explain the significance of relative atomic mass in calculating the molecular mass.**

Ans. (i) The molecular formula of water is H_2O.

The relative atomic mass of hydrogen (H) = 1.

The relative atomic mass of oxygen (O) = 16.

Molecular mass of H_2O = (2× Relative atomic mass of hydrogen) + (1 × Relative atomic mass of oxygen)

Molecular mass of H_2O = (2×1) + (1×16) = 2 + 16 = 18 u (atomic mass units). **(1)**

(ii) **Relative atomic mass** is the ratio of the average mass of an atom of an element to the mass of one atom of carbon-12 (which is assigned a mass of exactly 12 atomic mass units). **(1)**

(iii) It is significant because it allows us to calculate the molecular mass of a compound by adding the relative atomic masses of all the atoms in a molecule. This helps in understanding the mass relationships between elements in compounds. **(1)**

02

CHEMICAL CHANGES AND REACTIONS

Chemical Changes

A chemical change is a permanent change in which one substance reacts with another substance to undergo a change in chemical composition, i.e. a change in which always a new substance is formed with entirely new properties. It involves breaking of chemical bonds of reacting substances and making of new bonds of products. A chemical change take place due to a **chemical reaction**. e.g. Burning of coal, formation of curd from milk, etc.

Following conditions are necessary for a chemical change to occur.

1. Mixing (Close contact)

For a chemical reaction to occur, the reactants has to be in **close proximity**. In some cases, reaction easily occurs even in solid state, while some reactions require a medium or aqueous state.

e.g. Lead nitrate (solid) and potassium iodide (solid) react to make lead iodide.

$$Pb(NO_3)_2(s) + 2KI(s) \longrightarrow 2KNO_3(s) + PbI_2(s)$$

2. Heat

Heating increases the kinetic energy of the molecules of the substance and thus, the substances are able to react with each other easily.

e.g. Iron (Fe) filings and sulphur (S) powder do not react through mixing but they react when this mixture is heated and produce iron sulphide (FeS) as shown below.

$$Fe + S \xrightarrow{\Delta} FeS \quad (\Delta \text{ is the symbol for heating})$$

3. Light

Light is a form of energy that can facilitate certain chemical reactions. Such chemical reactions are called **photochemical reactions** or the process is known as **photolysis**.

e.g. Hydrogen gas (H_2) and chlorine gas (Cl_2) do not react with each other readily but when the mixture of these two gases is exposed to diffused sunlight, they combine to form hydrogen chloride gas (HCl).

$$H_2(g) + Cl_2(g) \xrightarrow{\text{Diffused sunlight}} 2HCl(g)$$

4. Electricity

Few chemical changes or reactions can be brought by supplying electrical energy to the substances. These are **electrochemical reactions.**

e.g. Electrolysis of acidulated water. **Electrolysis** is the process of using electricity to break down a compound or produce chemical change.

$$2H_2O \xrightarrow{\text{Electricity}} 2H_2\uparrow + O_2\uparrow$$

5. Pressure

Pressure plays an important role in carrying out certain reactions, which otherwise do not occur by bringing the particles closer.

e.g. Nitrogen and hydrogen gases usually do not react but when subjected to a high pressure (200 atm) they combine to form ammonia gas (NH_3).

$$N_2(g) + 3H_2(g) \underset{\text{Fe/Mo}}{\overset{\text{200 atm}}{\rightleftharpoons}} 2NH_3(g)$$

6. Catalyst

A catalyst is a substance which alters the rate of a reaction but does not participate in it. Thus, it either increases or decreases the rate of the reaction. The catalysts which **increase** the rate of the reaction are known as **positive catalysts.** The catalysts which **decrease** the rate of reaction are known as **negative catalysts.**

Substances that enhance the activity of a catalyst are called **promoters** while substance that inhibits or decreases the activity of a catalyst are called **poisons**.

Characteristics of Chemical Reactions

In a chemical reaction, the conversion of reactants into products result in some observable changes known as characteristics of chemical reactions.

- **Evolution of gas** Certain chemical reactions in which one or more product is gas, which escapes from the test tube. When sodium sulphite reacts with hydrochloric acid, SO_2 gas is evolved with effervescence.

e.g. $$Na_2SO_3 + 2HCl \longrightarrow 2NaCl + H_2O + SO_2\uparrow$$

- **Formation of precipitate** In some chemical reactions, the formation of insoluble solid substance takes place. This insoluble solid substance is known as **precipitate**.

e.g. $$\underset{\text{Copper sulphate}}{CuSO_4(aq)} + \underset{\text{Sodium hydroxide}}{2NaOH(aq)} \longrightarrow \underset{\text{Sodium sulphate}}{Na_2SO_4(aq)} + \underset{\text{Copper hydroxide (Pale blue precipitate)}}{Cu(OH)_2\downarrow}$$

- **Change in colour** Some chemical reactions are characterised by change in colour.

e.g. $$\underset{\text{Iron}}{Fe(s)} + \underset{\text{Copper sulphate (Blue solution)}}{CuSO_4(aq)} \longrightarrow \underset{\text{Ferrous sulphate (Green solution)}}{FeSO_4(aq)} + \underset{\text{Copper (Reddish brown ppt.)}}{Cu(s)}$$

- **Change in state** Chemical reactions in which a change of state is observed.

e.g. $$\underset{\text{Ammonia}}{NH_3(g)} + \underset{\text{Hydrochloric acid}}{HCl(g)} \rightleftharpoons \underset{\text{Ammonium chloride}}{NH_4Cl(s)}$$

- **Change in temperature** Some chemical reactions are characterised by change in temperature.

e.g. $$\underset{\text{Calcium oxide}}{CaO} + H_2O \longrightarrow \underset{\text{Calcium hydroxide}}{Ca(OH)_2} + \text{Heat}$$

This change is characterised by rise in temperature.

Types of Chemical Reactions

On the basis of chemical changes taking place, reactions can be divided into following types:

1. Combination Reaction

A reaction, in which two or more reactants combine to form a single product, is called combination reaction.
e.g. Reaction between hydrogen gas and oxygen gas to form water.

$$\underset{\text{Hydrogen}}{2H_2(g)} + \underset{\text{Oxygen}}{O_2(g)} \longrightarrow \underset{\text{Water}}{2H_2O(l)}$$

- Two elements combine to form a product.

$$2Mg(s) + O_2(g) \longrightarrow 2MgO(s)$$

- An element and a compound combine to form a new compound.

$$2CO(g) + O_2(g) \longrightarrow 2CO_2(g)$$

- Two or more compounds combine to form a single compound.

$$\underset{\text{Quick lime}}{CaO(s)} + H_2O \longrightarrow \underset{\text{Slaked lime}}{Ca(OH)_2} + \text{Heat}$$

- Photosynthesis is also an example of combination reaction.

2. Decomposition Reaction

A reaction in which a single reactant breaks down to form two or more products is known as decomposition reaction. Decomposition may occur in presence of heat, light or by the passage of electricity.

- Decomposition on heating (Thermal decomposition)

$$\underset{\text{White}}{2Pb(NO_3)_2\ (s)} \xrightarrow{\Delta} \underset{\text{(Yellow)}}{2PbO\ (s)} + 4NO_2\ (g) + O_2(g)$$

- Decomposition in presence of sunlight (Photolytic decomposition)

$$\underset{\text{(White)}}{2AgBr(s)} \xrightarrow{\text{Sunlight}} \underset{\text{Silver grey}}{2Ag(s)} + \underset{\text{Reddish brown}}{Br_2\uparrow}$$

- Decomposition by electricity (Electrolytic decomposition)

$$\underset{\text{(Acidulated)}}{2H_2O(l)} \xrightarrow{\text{Electricity}} 2H_2(g) + O_2(g)$$

3. Displacement Reaction

A reaction in which a more reactive element displaces a less reactive element from its salt solution is called displacement reaction.

e.g. When iron reacts with copper sulphate then iron displaces copper from copper sulphate solution.

$$\underset{\substack{\text{Iron}\\\text{metal}}}{Fe(s)} + \underset{\substack{\text{Copper sulphate}\\\text{solution}\\\text{(Blue)}}}{CuSO_4(aq)} \longrightarrow \underset{\substack{\text{Ferrous sulphate}\\\text{Or Iron (II) sulphate}\\\text{solution (Green)}}}{FeSO_4(aq)} + \underset{\substack{\text{Copper}\\\text{metal}}}{Cu(s)}$$

Displacement in displacement reactions occur on the basis of **activity series**.

4. Double Displacement Reaction

The reaction in which two compounds in their solution, exchange their ions or radicals to form new compounds is called double displacement reaction. These are of two types:

(a) **Precipitation reaction** Reaction in which an insoluble salt (precipitate) is formed as one of the product while the other one remains in the aqueous state.

e.g.

$$\underset{\text{Silver nitrate}}{AgNO_3(aq)} + \underset{\text{Sodium bromide}}{NaBr(aq)} \longrightarrow \underset{\substack{\text{Silver bromide}\\\text{(Yellow ppt.)}}}{AgBr\downarrow} + \underset{\text{Sodium nitrate}}{NaNO_3(aq)}$$

(b) **Neutralisation reaction** Reaction in which an acid and a base react with each other to form salt and water.

$$\underset{\substack{\text{Sodium hydroxide}\\\text{(Base)}}}{NaOH} + \underset{\substack{\text{Hydrogen chloride}\\\text{(Acid)}}}{HCl} \longrightarrow \underbrace{\underset{\substack{\text{Sodium chloride}\\\text{(Salt)}}}{NaCl\ (aq)} + \underset{\text{Water}}{H_2O(l)}}_{\substack{\text{Neutral, neither acidic nor}\\\text{basic solution}}}$$

Activity series

- The series in which the metals are arranged in the decreasing order of their reactivity is called **activity series**. The more reactive element displaces the less reactive element from its salt solution.
- The elements lying above in the activity series can displaces the elements lying below in the activity series from its salt solution.
- Metals present above hydrogen in this activity series, displaces it from mineral acids (HCl, H_2SO_4, etc.) and H_2O.

e.g. $Zn + 2HCl \longrightarrow ZnCl_2 + H_2\uparrow$

(A detailed account of activity series is given in class 10th.)

K	**Potassium**	⟶ Most reactive element
Na	Sodium	Reactivity Decreases ↓
Ca	Calcium	
Mg	Magnesium	
Al	Aluminium	
Zn	Zinc	
Fe	Iron	
Pb	Lead	
H	Hydrogen	
Cu	Copper	
Hg	Mercury	
Ag	Silver	
Au	Gold	⟶ Least reactive element

Energy Change in Chemical Reactions

On the basis of energy changes, the chemical reactions are of following four types

- **Exothermic Reactions** The reactions which are accompanied by the evolution of heat are called exothermic reactions. e.g. Respiration, rusting and burning of coal, petrol, etc.
- **Endothermic Reactions** The reaction occurring by the absorption of heat are called endothermic reactions. e.g. Formation of carbon disulphide, decomposition of $CaCO_3$, etc.
- **Photochemical Reactions** The reaction which occur with the absorption of light energy is called photochemical reaction.

e.g.

$$2AgNO_3 \xrightarrow{\text{Sunlight}} \underset{\text{Silver}}{2Ag\downarrow} + \underset{\text{(Reddish brown)}}{2NO_2} + O_2$$

- **Electrochemical Reaction** A chemical reaction which proceeds in the presence of electricity is known as electrochemical reaction. e.g. Electrolysis of molten NaCl, electrolysis of acidulated water, etc.

EXAM ORIENTED QUESTIONS

TYPE - 1 01 Mark

Multiple Choice Questions

Q.1 A student poured 100 mL of water in a bottle and added 40 mL vinegar to it. A balloon was filled with 20 g baking soda and was fixed at the mouth of the bottle. Slowly the shape of the balloon changed, as shown.

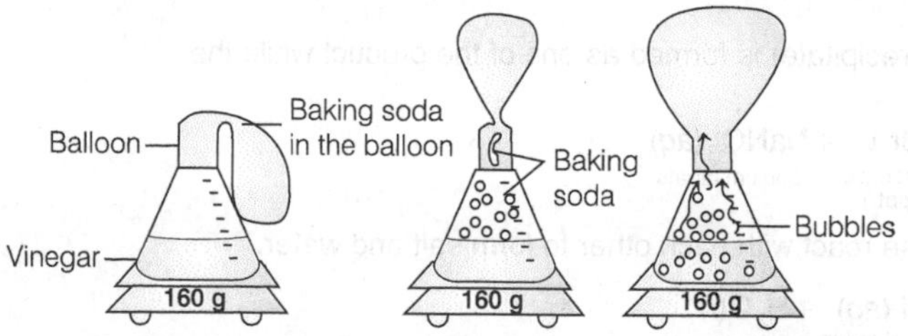

The student claims that a chemical change happened when the two substances were mixed. Is the claim made by the student correct?

(a) Yes, as a new substance was formed in the form of a gas.

(b) No, as the formation of bubbles in the mixture shows a physical change.

(c) Yes, as the mass remains the same throughout the experiment.

(d) No, as the change in the shape and size of the balloon shows a physical change.

Ans. (a) Student's claim was correct as in the reaction of acid (vinegar) and base (baking soda) carbon dioxide gas is released which changed the shape of the balloon.

Q.2 Electrolysis of acidulated water is a decomposition reaction.

The molar ratio of hydrogen and oxygen gas liberated during electrolysis of water is

(a) 2 : 1

(b) 1 : 1

(c) 1 : 2

(d) 4 : 1

Ans. (a) 2 : 1

Electrolytic decomposition of acidulated water follows the reaction

$$2H_2O\,(l) \xrightarrow{\text{Electricity}} 2H_2(g) + O_2(g)$$

Q.3 Consider the following.

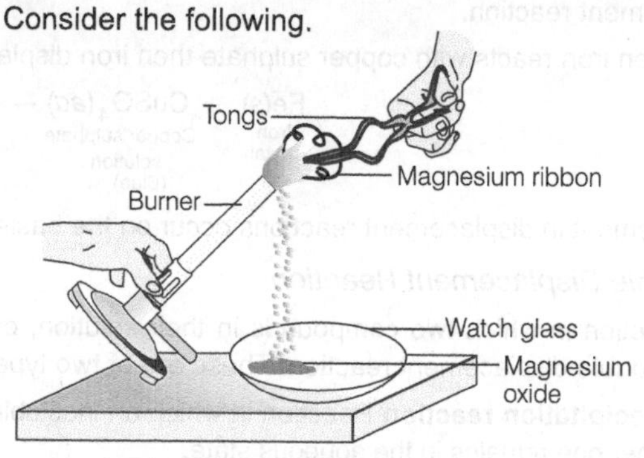

Which of the following is the correct observation of the reaction shown in the above set up?

(a) Brown powder of magnesium oxide is formed.

(b) Colourless gas which turns lime water milky is evolved.

(c) Magnesium ribbon burns with brilliant white light.

(d) Reddish brown gas with a smell of burning sulphur has evolved.

Ans. (c) Magnesium ribbon burns in presence of oxygen with a white dazzling flame.

Q.4 The emission of reddish brown fumes in the given experimental set-up is due to

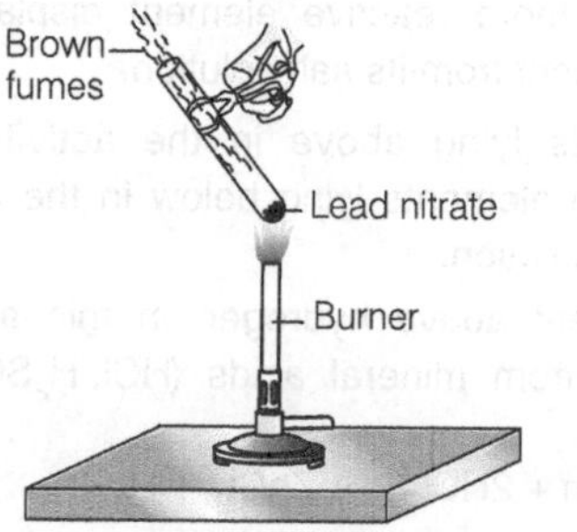

(a) thermal decomposition of lead nitrate which produces brown fumes of nitrogen dioxide

(b) thermal decomposition of lead nitrate which produces brown fumes of lead oxide

(c) oxidation of lead nitrate forming lead oxide and nitrogen dioxide

(d) oxidation of lead nitrate forming lead oxide and oxygen

Ans. (a) Heating of lead nitrate is a decomposition reaction. The reaction takes place as

$$\underset{\text{Lead nitrate}}{2Pb(NO_3)_2(s)} \xrightarrow{\Delta} \underset{\substack{\text{Lead oxide}\\\text{(Yellow)}}}{2PbO\,(s)} + \underset{\substack{\text{Nitrogen dioxide}\\\text{(Brown fumes)}}}{4NO_2(g)} + \underset{\text{Oxygen}}{O_2(g)}$$

The brown fumes is due to nitrogen dioxide.

Q.5 Two gases '*Z*' having suffocating odour are obtained when a green solid '*X*' is heated alongwith a residue '*Y*'. These gases are major air pollutants.

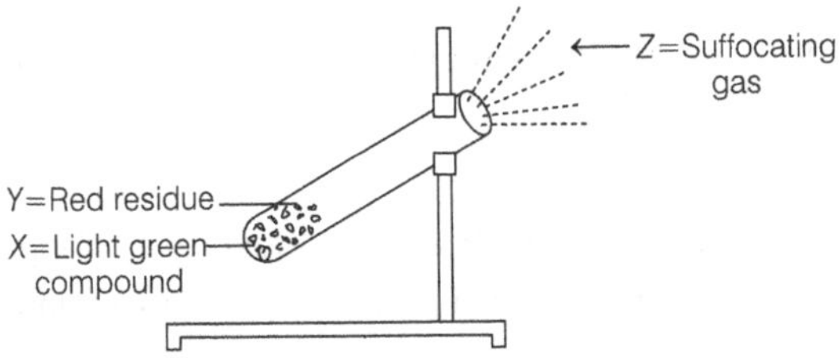

Here *X*, *Y*, *Z* would be

(a) $Pb(NO_3)_2$, PbO_2, $NO_2 + N_2O_4$

(b) $Fe(OH)_2$, FeO, $H_2O + H_2O_2$

(c) $FeSO_4$, Fe_2O_3, $SO_2 + SO_3$

(d) $PbSO_4$, Pb_2O_3, $SO_2 + SO_3$

Ans. (c) $\underset{\text{Green (X)}}{2FeSO_4} \xrightarrow{\Delta} \underset{\text{Reddish brown (Y)}}{Fe_2O_3} + \underbrace{SO_2\uparrow + SO_3\uparrow}_{\text{Suffocating Smell (Z)}}$

Thus, *X* is $FeSO_4$, *Y* is Fe_2O_3 and *Z* are SO_2 and SO_3, which are major air pollutants.

Q.6 Dilute hydrochloric acid is added to granulated zinc taken in a test tube. The following observations are recorded.

Point out the correct observation.

(a) The surface of metal becomes shining.

(b) The reaction mixture turns milky.

(c) Odour of a pungent smelling gas is recorded.

(d) A colourless and odourless gas is evolved.

Ans. (d) A colourless and odourless gas is evolved. When a reactive metal (Zn) reacts with dil. acids (dil.HCl), hydrogen gas is given out.

Q.7 Reema took 5 mL of lead nitrate solution in a beaker and added approximately 4 mL of potassium iodide solution to it. What would she observe?

(a) The solution turned red.

(b) Yellow precipitate was formed.

(c) White precipitate was formed.

(d) The reaction mixture became hot.

Ans. (b) The chemical reaction involved in given statement is

$$\underset{\text{Potassium iodide}}{2KI(aq)} + \underset{\text{Lead nitrate}}{Pb(NO_3)_2(aq)} \longrightarrow \underset{\text{Potassium nitrate}}{2KNO_3(aq)} + \underset{\text{Lead iodide (Yellow)}}{PbI_2\downarrow}$$

This reaction is an example of precipitation and double displacement reaction because of the formation of yellow precipitate of lead iodide.

Q.8 Which one of the following reactions is different from the remaining three?

(a) $NaCl(aq) + AgNO_3(aq) \longrightarrow AgCl(s) + NaNO_3(aq)$

(b) $CaO(s) + H_2O(l) \longrightarrow Ca(OH)_2(aq)$

(c) $KNO_3(aq) + H_2SO_4(aq) \longrightarrow KHSO_4(aq) + HNO_3(aq)$

(d) $ZnCl_2(aq) + H_2S(g) \longrightarrow ZnS(aq) + 2HCl(aq)$

Ans. (b) Among the given reactions, only (*b*) is the combination reaction while others are double displacement reaction.

Q.9 Calcium oxide reacts vigorously with water to produce slaked lime.

$$CaO(s) + H_2O(l) \longrightarrow Ca(OH)_2 + \text{Heat}$$

The reaction can be classified as

(A) Combination reaction (B) Exothermic reaction

(C) Endothermic reaction (D) Oxidation reaction

Which of the following is a correct option?

(a) (A) and (C) (b) (C) and (D)

(c) (A), (C) and (D) (d) (A) and (B)

Ans. (d) (A) and (B)

Q.10 The following reaction is used for the preparation of oxygen gas in the laboratory.

$$2KClO_3(s) \xrightarrow[\text{Catalyst}]{\text{Heat}} 2KCl(s) + 3O_2(g)$$

Which of the following statement(s) is/are correct about the reaction?

(a) It is a decomposition reaction and endothermic in nature.

(b) It is a combination reaction.

(c) It is a decomposition reaction and accompanied by release of heat.

(d) It is a photochemical decomposition reaction and exothermic in nature.

Ans. (a) The given reaction is a decomposition reaction and endothermic in nature because decomposition of $KClO_3$ requires heat for products formation.

TYPE - 2 01 Mark

Assertion-Reason Questions

Directions (Q. Nos. 1-5) In the following questions statement are given Assertion and Reason.

(a) Both (A) and (R) are true and (R) is the correct explanation of (A).

(b) Both (A) and (R) are true but (R) is not the correct explanation of (A).

(c) (A) is true but (R) is false.

(d) (A) is false but (R) is true.

Q.1 Assertion (A) A chemical reaction involves the formation of new substances with new properties.

Reason (R) Chemical reactions involve breaking of chemical bonds of the reacting substances and making new bonds to form a product.

Ans. (a) Both (A) and (R) are true and (R) is the correct explanation of (A).

Q.2 Assertion (A) When zinc is added to copper sulphate solution, zinc sulphate is formed, and copper is displaced.

Reason (R) Zinc is more reactive than copper.

Ans. (a) Both (A) and (R) are true and (R) is the correct explanation of (A).

Q.3 Assertion (A) A precipitate is always formed in a double displacement reaction.

Reason (R) Double displacement reactions always occur between two ionic compounds in solution.

Ans. (d) (A) is false but (R) is true.

A precipitate does not always form in a double displacement reaction. A precipitate forms only if one of the products is insoluble in solution. If both products are soluble, then no precipitate will be observed.

Q.4 Assertion (A) Rusting of iron is a physical change.

Reason (R) Rusting of iron involves the formation of a new substance, iron oxide.

Ans. (d) (A) is false but (R) is true.

Rusting of iron is not a physical change. It is a chemical change, because it involves the formation of a new substance (iron oxide).

Q.5 Assertion (A) Exothermic reactions release heat into the surroundings.

Reason (R) Breaking of bonds in the reactants releases energy during a chemical reaction.

Ans. (c) (A) is true but (R) is false.

Exothermic reactions do release heat into the surroundings. However, breaking of bonds requires energy, it does not release energy. Energy is released when bonds are formed.

TYPE - 3 (01 Mark)

Fill in the Blanks

Q.1 When calcium oxide reacts with water to form calcium hydroxide, the reaction is called .... reaction. (combination, displacement)

Ans. combination

Q.2 Decomposition of substance using heat is called .... decomposition. (thermal, photochemical)

Ans. thermal

Q.3 Calcium carbonate decomposes into calcium oxide and ..... (CO_2 /CO)

Ans. CO_2

Q.4 .... on heating gives potassium nitrite and oxygen. (KO_2/KNO_3)

Ans. KNO_3

Q.5 Colour of conc. H_2SO_4 in a test tube changes to blue on adding a small piece of .... to it (zinc, copper).

Ans. copper

Q.6 Blue solution of copper sulphate changes to .... colour when a piece of iron is added to this solution. (white, green)

Ans. green

Q.7 Reaction between copper sulphate and hydrogen sulphide is an example of .... (reversible reaction/ precipitation reaction).

Ans. precipitation reaction

TYPE - 4 (01 Mark)

Correct the Incorrect Statement

Q.1 A chemical change is a permanent and reversible change.

Ans. A chemical change is a permanent and **irreversible** change.

Q.2 Ammonia and hydrogen both compounds, combine to form a new compound, ammonia chloride.

Ans. Ammonia and **hydrogen chloride** both compounds combine to form a new compound, ammonium chloride.

Q.3 A less reactive metal displaces a more reactive metal from its compound.

Ans. A **more** reactive metal displaces a **less** reactive metal from its compound.

Q.4 When aluminium is added to iron oxide, aluminium does not displaces iron to form aluminium oxide.

Ans. When aluminium is added to iron oxide, aluminium **displaces** iron to form aluminium oxide.

Q.5 Photosynthesis is an example of exothermic reaction.

Ans. Photosynthesis is an example of **endothermic** reaction.

TYPE - 5

01 × 05 = 05 Marks

Match the Columns

Q.1 Match the following columns.

Column I (Process)	Column II (Reactions)
A. Combination	1. $2H_2O(l) \xrightarrow[\text{Current}]{\text{Electric}} 2H_2(g) + O_2(g)$
B. Thermal decomposition	2. $NaOH(aq) + HCl(aq) \longrightarrow NaCl(aq) + H_2O(l)$
C. Electrolysis	3. $CaO(s) + H_2O(l) \longrightarrow Ca(OH)_2(aq) + \text{Heat}$
D. Precipitation	4. $CaCO_3(s) \xrightarrow{\Delta} CaO(s) + CO_2(g)$
E. Neutralisation	5. $Na_2SO_4(aq) + BaCl_2(aq) \longrightarrow BaSO_4(s)\downarrow + 2NaCl(aq)$

Ans. A → (3), B → (4), C → (1), D → (5), E → (2).

Q.2 Match the following columns.

Column I (Reaction)	Column II (Colour of precipitate/ residue)
A. $Pb(NO_3)_2 + 2KI \longrightarrow PbI_2 + KNO_3$	1. Grey
B. $FeSO_4 \cdot 7H_2O \xrightarrow{\Delta} FeSO_4 + 7H_2O \longrightarrow Fe_2O_3 + SO_2 + SO_3$	2. Black
C. $AgNO_3 + NaCl \longrightarrow NaNO_3 + AgCl\downarrow$	3. White
D. $2AgCl \longrightarrow 2Ag + Cl_2$	4. Yellow
E. $CuSO_4(aq) + H_2S(g) \longrightarrow CuS(s) + H_2SO_4(aq)$	5. Brown

Ans. A → (4), B → (5), C → (3), D → (1), E → (2).

TYPE - 6

01 Mark

Identify the Following

Q.1 Some crystals of lead nitrate were heated. The crystals first melt and on further heating reddish brown fumes of a gas were appeared. Name the gas released during the process.

Ans. NO_2 (Brown gas)

Q.2 Name a chemical process in which a solid of insoluble mass is produced.

Ans. Precipitation

Q.3 What is the precipitate formed when sodium sulphate (Na_2SO_4) reacts with barium chloride?

Ans. $BaSO_4$ (White ppt.)

Q.4 Name a type of chemical reaction in which heat is evolved.

Ans. Exothermic reaction

Q.5 Name a type of chemical reaction in which heat is absorbed.

Ans. Endothermic reaction

Q.6 Give the name to a chemical reaction that occurs with absorption of light energy.

Ans. Photochemical reaction

TYPE - 7

02 Marks

Short Answer Type I Questions

Q.1 Give an example of a reaction where the following are involved.

(i) Heat (ii) Light (iii) Electricity (iv) Catalyst

Ans. (i) Example of reaction involving heat is as follows

$$\underset{\text{Copper carbonate}}{CuCO_3(s)} \xrightarrow{\Delta} \underset{\text{Copper oxide}}{CuO(s)} + \underset{\text{Carbon dioxide}}{CO_2(g)}$$

(ii) Example of reaction involving light is as follows

$$\underset{\text{Carbon dioxide}}{6CO_2} + 12H_2O \xrightarrow{\text{Sunlight}} \underset{\text{Glucose}}{C_6H_{12}O_6} + 6O_2 + 6H_2O$$

(iii) On passing current through molten sodium chloride, sodium and chlorine are obtained separately.

$$2NaCl \xrightarrow{\text{Electricity}} 2Na + Cl_2$$

(iv) The rate of decomposition of hydrogen peroxide increases in the presence of manganese dioxide.

$$2H_2O_2 \xrightarrow{MnO_2} 2H_2O + O_2$$

($\frac{1}{2} \times 4 = 2$)

Q.2 Given an example of each of the following chemical changes.

(i) Two gases combine to form a white solid.

(ii) Two solids combine to form a liquid.

Ans. (i) $NH_3(g) + HCl(g) \longrightarrow NH_4Cl(s)$ **(1)**

(ii) $C(s) + 2S(s) \longrightarrow \underset{\text{(Carbon disulphide)}}{CS_2(l)}$ **(1)**

Q.3 Name the products obtained on heating

(i) $Pb(NO_3)_2$ (ii) $(NH_4)_2Cr_2O_7$

Ans. (i) PbO, NO_2, O_2 (ii) Cr_2O_3, N_2, H_2O

$$2Pb(NO_3)_2 \xrightarrow{\Delta} 2Pb + 4NO_2\uparrow + O_2\uparrow$$

$$(NH_4)_2Cr_2O_7 \xrightarrow{\Delta} Cr_2O_3 + 4H_2O + N_2\uparrow$$ **(1 × 2 = 2)**

Q.4 What happens when electricity is passed through

(i) KCl (ii) H_2O

Ans. (i) $2KCl \xrightarrow[\text{current}]{\text{Electric}} 2K + Cl_2\uparrow$ **(1)**

(ii) $2H_2O \xrightarrow[\text{current}]{\text{Electric}} 2H_2 + O_2$ **(1)**

Q.5 (i) Mention a reaction in which nitric oxide gas is evolved.

(ii) Give the reaction to show action of heat on ammonium dichromate.

Ans. (i) $N_2 + O_2 \xrightarrow[3000°C]{\text{Heat}} 2NO(g)$

(ii) $(NH_4)_2Cr_2O_7 \xrightarrow{\Delta} Cr_2O_7 + 4H_2O\uparrow + N_2\uparrow$ **(1 × 2 = 2)**

Q.6 ***Case I*** Hydrogen gas burns in air with a clean blue flame to form water.

Case II When electricity is passed through acidulated water, it gives out hydrogen and oxygen.

Name the type of chemical reactions involved in the above two cases.

Ans. When hydrogen gas is burnt in oxygen to form water, this is a **combination reaction.**

When electricity is passed through acidulated water forming hydrogen and oxygen, this is an example of **electrolytic decomposition reaction.** **(2)**

Q.7 Give reason for each of the following.

(i) Silver chloride is stored in dark coloured bottles.

(ii) Chlorine displaces iodine from KI solution.

Ans. (i) Silver chloride undergoes decomposition in the presence of sunlight. Dark bottles are used to store it to prevent the entry of sunlight and thus preventing the decomposition.

(ii) The more reactive element displaces the less reactive element from its solution. Cl is more reactive than iodine. **(1×2 = 2)**

Q.8 (i) What is displacement reaction?

(ii) $Zn + CuSO_4(aq) \longrightarrow X + Y$

Find is X and Y in the above reaction.

Ans. (i) It is a chemical change in which a more active element displaces a less active element from its salt solution. **(1)**

(ii) $Zn + CuSO_4(aq) \longrightarrow \underset{(X)}{ZnSO_4(aq)} + \underset{(Y)}{Cu\downarrow}$ **(1)**

Q.9 A student takes Cu, Al, Fe and Zn strips, separately in four test tubes labelled as I, II, III and IV respectively. He adds 10 mL of freshly prepared ferrous sulphate solution to each test tube and observes the colour of the metal residue in each case.

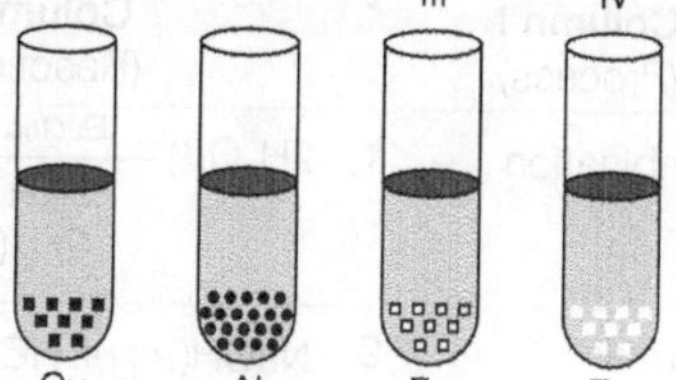

(i) A black residue is observed in which of the following test tube(s)?

(ii) Which type of reaction is illustrated in the test tube?

Ans. (i) Black residue is observed in **test tube (II) and (IV).** **(1)**

(ii) Displacement reaction. **(1)**

Q.10 What is the difference between displacement and double displacement reactions?

Ans.

Displacement reaction	Double displacement reaction
It is a chemical in which a more active element displaces a less active element from its salt solution.	This is a type of chemical change in which two compounds in a solution react to form two new compounds by mutual exchange of radicals.
$AB + C \longrightarrow AC + B$	$AB(aq) + CD(aq) \longrightarrow AD + CB$

(2)

Q.11 What is the difference between the following two reactions?

(i) $Mg + 2HCl \longrightarrow MgCl_2 + H_2$

(ii) $NaOH + HCl \longrightarrow NaCl + H_2O$

Ans. (i) Here, Mg is more reactive than H. Hence, it displaces hydrogen. Therefore, it is a **displacement reaction.** **(1)**

(ii) In this reaction, two different group of atoms are displaced by each other. Hence, it is a **double displacement reaction.** **(1)**

Q.12 What is a precipitate? Give example.

Ans. Insoluble product formed during a chemical reaction is known as a **precipitate.**

e.g. $\underset{\text{Silver nitrate solution}}{AgNO_3(aq)} + \underset{\text{Sodium chloride solution}}{NaCl(aq)} \longrightarrow \underset{\text{Silver chloride (white ppt.)}}{AgCl\downarrow} + \underset{\text{Sodium nitrate solution}}{NaNO_3(aq)}$ **(2)**

Q.13 (i) Why does the colour of copper sulphate solution change when an iron nail is dipped in it?

(ii) Explain neutralisation reaction with an example.

Ans. (i) The colour of copper sulphate solution changes when an iron nail is dipped in it because iron being more reactive than copper, displaces copper metal from aqueous copper sulphate solution.

Thus, blue colour of copper sulphate disappears and green colour of ferrous sulphate is formed. **(1)**

(ii) **Neutralisation reaction** The reaction between an acid and a base that forms salt and water only is called neutralisation reaction.

e.g. $\underset{\text{Acid}}{HNO_3(aq)} + \underset{\text{Base}}{KOH(aq)} \longrightarrow \underset{\text{Salt}}{KNO_3(aq)} + \underset{\text{Water}}{H_2O}$ **(1)**

Q.14 Classify the following reactions as Direct combination, Decomposition, Displacement, Precipitation and Neutralisation.

(i) $Fe + CuSO_4 \longrightarrow FeSO_4 + Cu$

(ii) $2Pb(NO_3)_2 \xrightarrow{\Delta} 2PbO + 4NO_2 + O_2$

Ans. (i) Displacement reaction **(1)**

(ii) Decomposition reaction **(1)**

Q.15 Write the balanced chemical equation for the reactions that take place during respiration.

Identify whether the reaction is exothermic or endothermic.

Ans. $C_6H_{12}O_6 + 6O_2 \longrightarrow 6CO_2 + 6H_2O + \text{Energy}$ **(1)**

It is an **exothermic reaction** because a large amount of heat is released. **(1)**

Q.16 Observe the given reaction and answer the following questions

$$N_2 + X \xrightarrow[3000°C]{Y} 2NO(g)$$

(i) Identify '*X*' and '*Y*' in the above reaction.

(ii) Depending upon the energy change identify the type of chemical reaction.

Ans. (i) $N_2 + O_2 \xrightarrow[3000°C]{\text{Heat}} 2NO(g)$

'X' is O_2 and 'Y' is heat. **(1)**

(ii) This chemical reaction is an **endothermic reaction**. **(1)**

TYPE - 8 03 Marks

Short Answer Type II Questions

Q.1

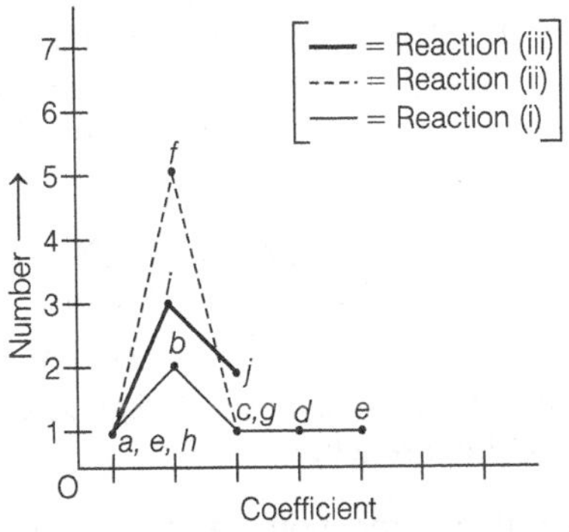

After studying the above graph, balance the given equations.

(i) $aCaCO_3 + bHCl \longrightarrow cCaCl_2 + dH_2O + eCO_2$

(ii) $eCuSO_4 + fH_2O \longrightarrow gCuSO_4 \cdot 5H_2O$

(iii) $hN_2 + iH_2 \longrightarrow jNH_3$

Ans. (i) $CaCO_3 + 2HCl \longrightarrow CaCl_2 + H_2O + CO_2$ **(1)**

(ii) $CuSO_4 + 5H_2O \longrightarrow CuSO_4 \cdot 5H_2O$ **(1)**

(iii) $N_2 + 3H_2 \longrightarrow 2NH_3$ **(1)**

Q.2 Name the gas evolved during the reaction:

(i) Heating of mercuric oxide.

(ii) When electric current is passed through water.

(iii) On heating of ferrous sulphate.

Ans. (i) $2HgO(s) \xrightarrow{\text{Heat}} 2Hg(l) + O_2(g)$

Oxygen gas.

(ii) $2H_2O \xrightarrow{\text{Electricity}} 2H_2(g) + O_2(g)$

Hydrogen and oxygen gas.

(iii) $\underset{\text{White}}{2FeSO_4(s)} \xrightarrow{\text{Heat}} \underset{\text{Brown}}{Fe_2O_3(s)} + SO_2(g) + SO_3(g)$

Sulphur dioxide and sulphur trioxide gases. **(1 × 3 = 3)**

Q.3 A white salt on heating decomposes to give brown fumes and a residue is left behind.

(i) Name the salt.

(ii) Name the type of reaction.

(iii) Write the equation for the decomposition reaction.

Ans. (i) Lead nitrate (ii) Decomposition reaction

(iii) $2Pb(NO_3)_2(s) \xrightarrow{\text{Heat}} 2PbO(s) + 4NO_2(g) + O_2(g)$

Lead nitrate (White salt) — Lead oxide (Residue) — Nitrogen dioxide (Brown fumes) — Oxygen

(1 × 3 = 3)

Q.4 **A yellowish coloured compound *X* is a photosensitive material. On exposure to sunlight, it gives a silver grey substance *Y* and reddish brown fumes of a gas *Z*. Identify *X*, *Y* and *Z*.**

Ans. $2AgBr \xrightarrow{\text{Sunlight}} 2Ag + Br_2\uparrow$

Silver bromide (*X*) — Silver (*Y*) (Greyish) — Bromine (*Z*) (Brown fumes)

Thus, on exposure to sunlight, AgBr undergoes **decomposition reaction**. **(3)**

Q.5 **Balance these reactions and state what type of reactions they are:**

(i) $NaNO_3 \xrightarrow{\Delta} NaNO_2 + O_2$

(ii) $AgNO_3 + Zn \longrightarrow Zn(NO_3)_2 + Ag$

(iii) $NaBr + Cl_2 \longrightarrow NaCl + Br_2$

Ans. (i) $2NaNO_3 \longrightarrow 2NaNO_2 + O_2$

This is thermal decomposition reaction.

(ii) $2AgNO_3 + Zn \longrightarrow Zn(NO_3)_2 + 2Ag$

This is displacement reaction.

(iii) $2NaBr + Cl_2 \longrightarrow 2NaCl + Br_2$

This is displacement reaction. **(1 × 3 = 3)**

Q.6 $KI + Cl_2 \longrightarrow KCl + I_2$

(i) Balance the equation given above.

(ii) Which type of reaction is it?

(iii) Which element is more reactive?

Ans. (i) $2KI + Cl_2 \longrightarrow 2KCl + I_2$

(ii) It is a **single displacement reaction**.

(iii) Chlorine is more reactive than iodine. So, Cl displaces I. **(1 × 3 = 3)**

Q.7 **Observe the two test tubes *A* and *B* in the diagram given below and answer the following questions.**

(i) In which test tube, reaction will take place?

(ii) Name the type of reaction.

(iii) Give another example of this reaction.

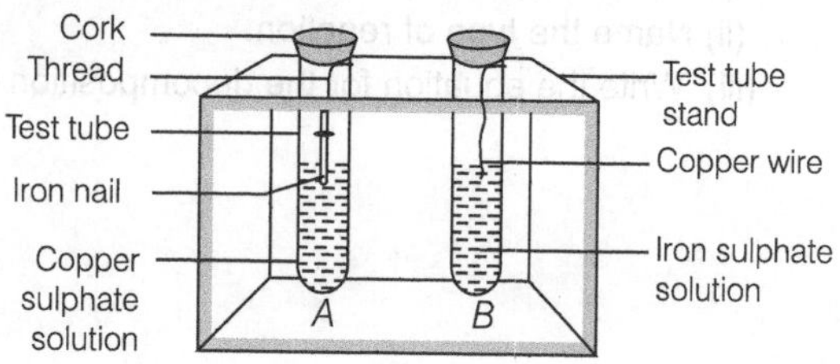

Ans. (i) In **test tube *A***, because Fe more reactive than Cu. So, it displaces Cu from $CuSO_4$ solution.

(ii) Displacement reaction.

(iii) Another example of displacement reaction is

$2KI(aq) + Cl_2(g) \longrightarrow 2KCl + I_2$ **(1 × 3 = 3)**

Q.8 **You are provided with list of elements mentioned below in the box.**

Ag, Cu, Hg, Pt, Au, Zn, Ca, Cl

Choose suitable elements which shows displacement reaction with the solutions given below and write the balanced chemical reaction is each.

(i) Magnesium sulphate

(ii) Dilute sulphuric acid

(iii) Potassium iodide

Ans. (i) **Calcium** displaces magnesium from its solution.

$Ca + MgSO_4 \longrightarrow CaSO_4 + Mg$ **(1)**

(ii) **Zinc** displaces hydrogen from sulphuric acid.

$Zn + H_2SO_4 \longrightarrow ZnSO_4 + H_2$ **(1)**

(iii) **Chlorine** displaces iodine from potassium iodide.

$2KI + Cl_2 \longrightarrow 2KCl + I_2$ **(1)**

Q.9 ***A*, *B* and *C* are three elements which undergo chemical reaction according to the following equations.**

$A_2O_3 + 2B \longrightarrow B_2O_3 + 2A$

$3CSO_4 + 2B \longrightarrow B_2(SO_4)_3 + 3C$

$3CO + 2A \longrightarrow A_2O_3 + 3C$

Answer the following questions with reason.

(i) Which element is the most reactive?

(ii) Which element is the least reactive?

(iii) What is the type of reactions listed above?

Ans. (i) The most reactive element is ***B***. The order of reactivity is $B > A > C$ because in the given reactions, *B* replaced *A* and *C*, and *A* replaced *C*. **(1)**

(ii) The least reactive elements is ***C***. **(1)**

(iii) The type of reactions listed above are **single displacement reactions**. **(1)**

Q.10 **Consider the following reaction,**

(i) (A) + (B) ⟶ (AB)

(ii) (A) + (BC) ⟶ (AC) + (B)

(iii) (AB) + (CD) ⟶ (AD) + (CB)

Identify the types of reaction mentioned above in (i), (ii) and (iii). Give one example for each type in the form of a balanced chemical equation.

Ans. (i) The given reaction is **combination reaction**. The example of this type of reaction is

$$\underset{\text{Calcium oxide (Quick lime)}}{CaO(s)} + H_2O(l) \longrightarrow \underset{\text{Calcium hydroxide (Slaked lime)}}{Ca(OH)_2(aq)}$$ **(1)**

(ii) The given reaction is **displacement reaction**. The examples of this type of reactions is

$$\underset{\text{Iron}}{Fe(s)} + \underset{\text{Copper sulphate}}{CuSO_4(aq)} \longrightarrow \underset{\text{Ferrous sulphate}}{FeSO_4(aq)} + \underset{\text{Copper}}{Cu(s)}$$ **(1)**

(iii) The given reaction is **double displacement reaction**. The example of this type of reaction is

$$\underset{\text{Sodium sulphate}}{Na_2SO_4(aq)} + \underset{\text{Barium chloride}}{BaCl_2(aq)} \longrightarrow \underset{\text{Barium sulphate}}{BaSO_4(s)} + \underset{\text{Sodium chloride}}{2NaCl(aq)}$$ **(1)**

Q.11 A student takes two test tubes labelled as I and II. Test tube I contains barium chloride solution and II contains sodium sulphate solution. She adds barium chloride solution slowly into test tube containing sodium sulphate solution as shown in the diagram below. Observe the diagram and answer the following questions.

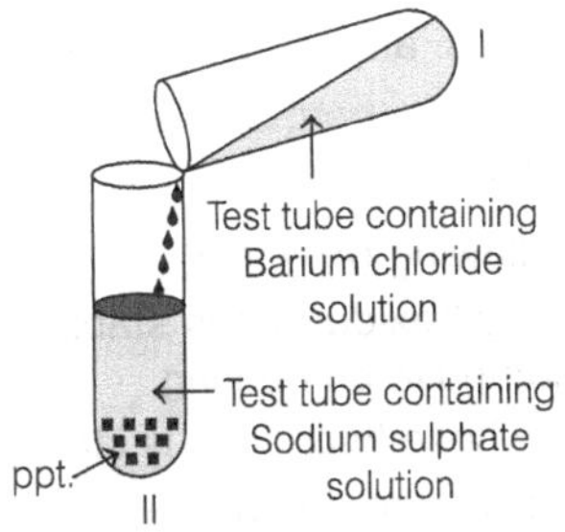

(i) Identify the types of reaction that occur after addition of solution of test tube I to II.

(ii) Write the balanced chemical equation for the reaction that occured after addition.

(iii) Identify the solid product obtained after reaction.

Ans. (i) Double displacement and precipitate reaction. **(1)**

(ii) $BaCl_2(aq) + Na_2SO_4(aq) \longrightarrow \underset{\text{White ppt.}}{BaSO_4(s)} + 2NaCl(aq)$ **(1)**

(iii) The solid product (precipitate) obtained after reaction is barium sulphate ($BaSO_4$). **(1)**

TYPE - 9 — 04/05 Marks

Long Answer Type Questions

Q.1 Complete the following reactions.

(i) $N_2 + O_2 \longrightarrow$ (ii) $Ca(NO_3)_2 \xrightarrow{\Delta}$

(iii) $NO + O_2 \longrightarrow$ (iv) $KNO_3 \xrightarrow{\Delta}$

Ans. (i) $N_2 + O_2 \longrightarrow 2NO$

(ii) $2Ca(NO_3)_2 \xrightarrow{\Delta} 2CaO(s) + 4NO_2(g) + O_2(g)$

(iii) $2NO + O_2 \longrightarrow 2NO_2$

(iv) $2KNO_3(s) \xrightarrow{\Delta} 2KNO_2(s) + O_2(g)$ **(1 × 4 = 4)**

Q.2 Give one observation for each of the following.

(i) Water is added to calcium oxide or quick lime.

(ii) Carbon dioxide is passed through lime water, first in small amount and then in an excess.

(iii) Lead sulphide is heated in a test tube

(iv) A magnesium ribbon is burnt over a flame.

Ans. (i) When water is added to quick lime, large amount of heat is given out, so the temperature rises.

(ii) When carbon dioxide is passed through lime water, it turns milky and when excess of carbon dioxide is passed through lime water, it again turns colourless.

(iii) When lead sulphide is heated in a test tube, it turns white because of formation of lead sulphate, by a combination reaction.

(iv) When a magnesium ribbon is burnt in air, it burns with a dazzling white flame. **(1 × 4 = 4)**

Q.3 Keerti added dilute hydrochloric acid to four metals and recorded her observations as shown in the table given below.

Metal	**Gas evolved** (Observation)
(i) Copper	Yes
(ii) Iron	Yes
(iii) Magnesium	No
(iv) Zinc	Yes

Identify the correct observation(s) and give chemical equation(s) of the reaction involved.

Ans. (i) $\underset{\text{Copper}}{Cu} + \underset{\text{Hydrochloric acid}}{2HCl} \longrightarrow$ No reaction **(1)**

No reaction occurs in this case.

(ii) $\underset{\text{Iron}}{Fe} + \underset{\text{Hydrochloric acid}}{2HCl} \longrightarrow \underset{\text{Ferrous chloride}}{FeCl_2} + \underset{\text{Hydrogen gas}}{H_2\uparrow}$ **(1)**

In this reaction, hydrogen gas evolved.

(iii) $\underset{\text{Magnesium}}{Mg} + \underset{\text{Hydrochloric acid}}{2HCl} \longrightarrow \underset{\text{Magnesium chloride}}{MgCl_2} + \underset{\text{Hydrogen gas}}{H_2\uparrow}$ **(1)**

(iv) $\underset{\text{Zinc}}{Zn} + \underset{\text{Hydrochloric acid}}{2HCl} \longrightarrow \underset{\text{Zinc chloride}}{ZnCl_2} + \underset{\text{Hydrogen gas}}{H_2\uparrow}$ **(1)**

In this reaction of Zn with HCl, H_2 gas evolved. Thus, correct observation are given for iron and zinc.

(ii) **Exothermic reaction**

$$\underset{\text{Quicklime}}{CaO} + H_2O \longrightarrow \underset{\text{Slaked lime}}{Ca(OH)_2} + \text{Heat}$$

Endothermic reaction

$$\underset{\substack{\text{Ammonium}\\\text{chloride}}}{NH_4Cl} + H_2O \longrightarrow \underset{\substack{\text{Ammonium}\\\text{hydrogen}}}{NH_4OH} + HCl$$ **(1)**

(iii) The beaker became hot because the reaction between CaO (quicklime) and water releases a large amount of heat energy. **(1)**

Q.3 **In a chemistry lab, Priya accidentally spilled hydrochloric acid (HCl) on the lab table. Her teacher quickly poured a solution of sodium hydroxide (NaOH) on the spill.**

(i) **What do you think, why teacher quickly poured a solution of NaOH on the spilled HCl?**

(ii) **Write the balanced chemical reaction occurred after addition of NaOH.**

(iii) **Is heat absorbed or evolved during the reaction?**

Ans. (i) The teacher quickly poured a solution of NaOH on the spilled HCl to **neutralise the acid** as sodium hydroxide is a base, so it reacts with HCl to form salt and water. **(1)**

(ii) Balanced chemical equation is as follows

$$\underset{\text{Acid}}{HCl} + \underset{\text{Base}}{NaOH} \longrightarrow \underset{\text{Salt}}{NaCl} + \underset{\text{Water}}{H_2O}$$ **(1)**

(iii) Heat is evolved in this reaction because neutralisation reactions are **exothermic reactions**. **(1)**

03

WATER

- **Molecular formula** of water is H_2O.
- **Chemical name** of water is dihydrogen oxide.

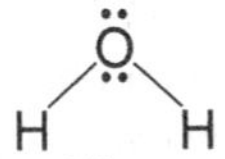

Water

- **Molecular mass** of water = **18 amu**

Occurrence of Water

- Water is the most important natural resource; more than 70% of Earth's surface is occupied with water. However, hardly 2.5% of this water makes up the world's supply of fresh water, including the frozen water in polar ice caps and glaciers.
- It can exist in all three physical states as solid (as ice, snow, etc.), liquid (in lake, river, sea, etc.) or gaseous state (as water vapour). It occurs in both free as well as combined states.
- It constitutes a major part of all the living organisms, e.g. it forms about 65% of human body and almost 95% of some plants body.

Physical Properties of Water

(i) **Nature** Pure water is a **transparent**, **colourless**, **tasteless** and **odourless** substance.

(ii) **Freezing point** The term freezing point means the constant temperature at which a liquid turns into a solid when cooled. Pure water freezes at **0°C** under normal pressure.

(iii) **Boiling point** The constant temperature at which a liquid boils and changes into vapours is called its boiling point. At normal pressure (760 mm Hg) pure water boils at **100°C**.

(iv) **Density** At **4°C** water has its maximum density of $1\ g\ cm^{-3}$ or $10^3\ kg\ m^{-3}$, and minimum volume.

(v) **Anomalous expansion of water** When cooled, water first contracts in volume, as do other liquids, but below 4°C, it starts expanding and continues to do so till the temperature reaches 0°C.

(vi) **Latent heat of fusion** The energy required to change 1g of solid to a liquid at its melting point (without any change in temperature) is called latent heat of fusion. The latent heat of fusion of water is 336 J/g or 80 cal/g.

(vii) **Latent heat of vaporisation** The energy required to change the state of a substance from liquid to its vapour at its boiling point (without any change in temperature) is called latent heat of vaporisation. The value of latent heat of vaporisation of water is 2268 J/g or 540 cal/g.

(viii) **Specific heat capacity** The amount of heat needed to raise the temperature of 1g of a material by 1°C is known as specific heat capacity. The specific heat capacity of water is 4.186 J/g °C.

Water as a Universal Solvent

- Water dissolves many substances, forming aqueous solutions. Not only solids, but also gases and other liquids dissolve in water. Hence, it is difficult to find absolutely pure water in nature. So, water is also called a **universal solvent**.
- **Water has a high dielectric constant**, so it reduces the electrostatic force of attraction between positive and negative ions and dissolves even inorganic compounds, which are usually electrovalent.

Importance of Dissolved Salts in Water

The dissolved solids in water are salts, minerals and impurities.

- Salts and minerals are essential for growth and development of plants.
- They add taste to water.
- They supply the essential minerals needed by our body.

Air Dissolved in Water

Air is present in dissolved state in all the natural sources of water. The composition of air dissolved in water in 33% oxygen, 66% nitrogen and 1% CO_2.

Importance of Air Dissolved in Water

Air dissolved in water is biologically very important.

- Marine life, like fish, use the oxygen dissolved in water for respiration, and thus aquatic life is sustained. 1 dm^3 (1 litre) of water contains nearly 40 cm^3 of dissolved oxygen.
- Aquatic plants make use of dissolved carbon dioxide for photosynthesis, i.e. to prepare their food.

$$6CO_2 + 12H_2O \xrightarrow[\text{Sunlight}]{\text{Chlorophyll}} \underset{\text{Glucose}}{C_6H_{12}O_6} + 6O_2 + 6H_2O$$

Solutions

- A **homogeneous mixture** of two or more substances, whose composition may be changed is called **solution**. e.g. Lemonade, soda water, salt solution, sugar solution, etc.
- A solution in which the size of the solute particles is about 10^{-10} m is called **true solution.** In common use, the term solution actually means true solutions.

There are two main components of a solution.

(i) **Solvent** (Dissolving phase) The component (usually present in larger amount) of the solution that dissolves the other component in it is called the solvent.

(ii) **Solute** (Dissolved phase) The component (usually present in lesser amount) of the solution that is dissolved in the solvent is called the solute.

$$\boxed{\text{Solution} = \text{Solute} + \text{Solvent}}$$

- A solution which is made up of **two** components is a **binary solution**. Solutions which are made up of **three** components are **ternary**. Whereas, the solutions made up of **four** components are called **quaternary solutions**.
- **Depending upon the amount of solute present in comparison to solvent,** *solution can be classified as:*
  (i) **Dilute solution** The solution in which amount of solute is very less as compared to the amount of solvent.
  (ii) **Concentrated solution** The solution in which amount of solute is relatively more for a given amount of the solvent.
- **Depending upon the amount of solute present in a given amount of solvent,** *solution can be classified as*:
  (i) **Saturated solution** A solution in which no more amount of solute can be dissolved at a given temperature.
  (ii) **Unsaturated solution** A solution which can dissolve more amount of solute at a given temperature.
  (iii) **Supersaturated solution** A solution that contain more amount of solute than required to saturate it at that particular temperature.
- **Depending upon the nature of solvent used, solution** can be classified as:
  (i) **Aqueous solution** A solution in which water is the solvent. e.g. Sugar in water.
  (ii) **Non-aqueous solution** A solution in which the solvent is a liquid other than water. e.g. Tincture of iodine (a solution of iodine in alcohol) etc.

Characteristics of a Solution

- The **solute particles** of a solution are about $\mathbf{10^{-10}}$ **m**. Therefore, they cannot be seen by naked eyes.
- Due to very small size of particles, solutions do not scatter the beam of light passing through the solution. So, the path of light is not visible in a solution.
- A solution is stable, i.e. the solute particles do not settle down when left undisturbed.
- The solute particles cannot be separated from the mixture by the process of filtration.
- A solution is clear and transparent.

Concentration of a Solution

Concentration of a solution is the amount of solute dissolved in a given quantity of solution.

- **Mass per cent** The mass of a solute (in gram) present in 100 gram of solution is called mass percent.

$$\text{Concentration of solution (in terms of mass \%)} = \frac{\text{Mass of solute}}{\text{Mass of solution}} \times 100$$

e.g. If 10 g of sodium chloride is added to 90 g of water, the concentration of the solution

$$= \frac{10}{10+90} \times 100 = \frac{10}{100} \times 100 = 10\%$$

- **Volume per cent** The volume of a solute (in mL) present in 100 mL solution is called volume percent.

$$\text{Concentration of solution (in terms of volume \%)} = \frac{\text{Volume of solute}}{\text{Volume of solution}} \times 100$$

e.g. If 30 mL of alcohol is mixed with 70 mL of water to get 100 mL of solution, volume percent

$$= \frac{30}{30+70} \times 100 = \frac{30}{100} \times 100 = 30\%$$

Solubility

- It is defined as the maximum amount of a substance that can be dissolved in a specified amount (100 g) of solvent at a specified temperature to completely saturate it.
- It depends on nature of solute, nature of solvent, temperature and pressure.

Factors Affecting Solubility

The rate of dissolution or rate of solubility of a solid in a liquid depends on the following factors

- **Size of solute particles** Smaller the size of solute particles, greater is the solubility.
- **Stirring** Regular stirring helps to bring more solvent in contact with solute, thus solubility increases.
- **Temperature** The solubility of a gas in a liquid always decreases with rise in temperature. But the solubility of most of the solids in water usually increases with rise in temperature.

Solubility Curves

The curves showing the changes in solubility of a solute in a solvent with changes in temperature, are called solubility curves.

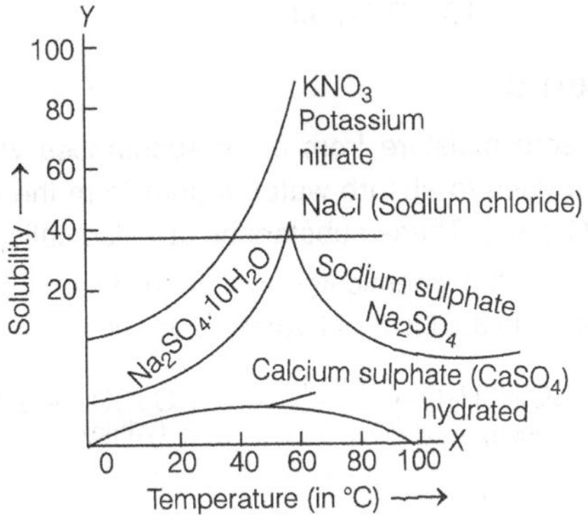

Variation in solubility of some solids with change in temperature

Inferences from Solubility Curves

- Some substances show increase in solubility with increase in temperature. e.g. Potassium nitrate (KNO_3), etc.
- Some substances show only a little increase in solubility with increase in temperature. e.g. Sodium chloride ($NaCl$).
- Some substances show decrease in solubility on further increase in temperature e.g. Hydrated calcium sulphate ($CaSO_4$).
- Some salts show first increase in solubility and then decrease, with increase in temperature. e.g. Glauber's salt ($Na_2SO_4 \cdot 10H_2O$).

Effect of Pressure and Temperature on Solubility of Gases in Water

- **Pressure** An increase in pressure on the surface of water increases the solubility of a gas in water.

  At any given temperature, the mass of gas dissolved by a fixed volume of liquid is directly proportional to the pressure on the surface of the liquid. This law is known as **Henry's law**.
- **Temperature** An increase in temperature of water causes a decrease in solubility of a gas in it.

Hydrated and Anhydrous Substances

- Substances which contain water molecules along with salts are called **hydrated substances**. e.g. $Na_2CO_3 \cdot 10H_2O$, $CuSO_4 \cdot 5H_2O$.
- The fixed amount water that is associated with hydrated crystals (is an integral part of crystal) is said to be **water of crystallisation**.
- A hydrated substance from which water molecule of crystallisation has been removed is known as **anhydrous substance**. e.g. Anhydrous copper sulphate ($CuSO_4$).

Properties of Hydrated and Anhydrous Substances

Efflorescence

The phenomenon in which a hydrated compound loses its water of crystallisation on exposure to dry air is called efflorescence. Substances showing this phenomena are called **efflorescent substances**.

e.g. Washing soda ($Na_2CO_3 \cdot 10H_2O$), Glauber's salt ($Na_2SO_4 \cdot 10H_2O$), Epsom salt ($MgSO_4 \cdot 7H_2O$), etc.

Deliquescence

Some of the water soluble substances, when left exposed to the atmosphere at ordinary temperature, absorb moisture from atmospheric air, lose their crystalline form and get converted into their saturated solutions by dissolving in the absorbed water. Such a substance is called a **deliquescent substance** and the phenomenon is said to be **deliquescency**.

e.g. Caustic soad (NaOH), caustic potash (KOH), calcium chloride ($CaCl_2$), etc.

Hygroscopy

The phenomenon where certain substances absorb moisture (water vapour) from the atmosphere when they are exposed to air is called **hygroscopy**. Such substances are called **hygroscopic substances.**

e.g. Calcium oxide (CaO), silica gel, conc. H_2SO_4, P_2O_5, etc.

Drying and Dehydrating Agents

- The substances that can readily absorb moisture from other substances without chemically reacting with them are called **drying agents**. These are used to absorb water vapour from the air, e.g., anhydrous calcium chloride ($CaCl_2$), phosphorus pentaoxide (P_2O_5), etc. These substances are also called **desiccants** or **desiccating** agents.
- The substances that can remove even the chemically combined water molecules from compounds are called **dehydrating agents**. e.g. Conc. sulphuric acid is a dehydrating agent.

$$\underset{\text{(Blue)}}{CuSO_4 \cdot 5H_2O} \xrightarrow{\text{Conc. } H_2SO_4} \underset{\text{(White)}}{CuSO_4} + 5H_2O$$

Soft and Hard Water

Soft Water

- Water free from soluble salts of calcium and magnesium is called **soft water**.
- It gives lather with soap (sodium or potassium salt of higher fatty acids). It is suitable for use.
- The most common examples of soft water are distilled water and rain water.
- Hardness in water is only because of soluble salts, that reacts with soap and precipitate it.

REVISION NOTES

Hard Water

- It contains soluble salt of calcium or magnesium (bicarbonates, sulphates or chlorides).
- It does not give lather with soap. This is because of the precipitation of soap as insoluble compound (calcium or magnesium stearate).

$$\underset{\substack{\text{Calcium chloride}\\\text{(present in}\\\text{hard water)}}}{CaCl_2} + \underset{\substack{\text{Sodium}\\\text{stearate}\\\text{(soluble soap)}}}{2C_{17}H_{35}CO\bar{O}\overset{+}{Na}} \longrightarrow \underset{\substack{\text{Calcium stearate}\\\text{(insoluble soap)}}}{(C_{17}H_{35}COO)_2Ca\downarrow} + 2NaCl$$

Cause of Hardness

When water flows over beds of limestone ($CaCO_3$) and dolomite ($MgCO_3$), carbon dioxide (CO_2) slowly converts some of these into soluble calcium and magnesium bicarbonates, which gets mixed with the water and makes it hard.

e.g.
$$\underset{\text{(Insoluble)}}{MgCO_3} + CO_2 + H_2O \longrightarrow \underset{\substack{\text{Magnesium bicarbonate}\\\text{(soluble)}}}{Mg(HCO_3)_2}$$

Types of Hardness

- **Temporary hardness** It occurs due to dissolved bicarbonate of calcium and magnesium [$Ca(HCO_3)_2$ and $Mg(HCO_3)_2$], so it is also called **bicarbonate hardness**. This type of hardness is temporary because it can be easily removed by just boiling and filtering the water.
- **Permanent hardness** It occurs due to dissolved chlorides and sulphates of calcium and magnesium. This type of hardness cannot be removed by simple methods like boiling or filtration, so it is called **permanent hardness**.

Advantages of Soft Water

- Soft water is used for drinking purpose.
- Soft water is free from dissolved salts and possess pleasant taste.

Advantages of Hard Water

- Calcium and magnesium salts present in hard water are essential for the **growth of our bones and teeth**.
- Hard water checks the poisoning of water by lead pipes, i.e. **checks the lead poisoning**.
- Salts present in hard water make it tasty and therefore, it used in preparation of beverages and wines.

Disadvantages of Hard Water

- The hard water cannot be used for washing clothes because it contains Ca^{2+} and Mg^{2+} ions, which react with soap to form scum or precipitate of Ca/Mg stearate.
- Hard water is also harmful for boiler as the salts present in hard water gets deposited in the form of scale and thus, reduces the efficiency of the boilers.
- It is also harmful for industries like dying, printing, textiles, sugar, etc., as plenty of water is needed by them.

Removal of Hardness

The process of removal of hardness from water is called **softening of water**. Methods used for removal of hardness are as follows:

- **Boiling** Temporary hardness of water can be removed by boiling. These precipitates can be removed by filtration or decantation.

$$Mg(HCO_3)_2(aq) \xrightarrow{\Delta} \underset{\text{(Insoluble)}}{MgCO_3\downarrow} + CO_2\uparrow + H_2O$$

$$Ca(HCO_3)_2(aq) \xrightarrow{\Delta} \underset{\text{(Insoluble)}}{CaCO_3\downarrow} + H_2O + CO_2\uparrow$$

- **Treatment with washing soda** Permanent hardness of water can be removed by adding washing soda. Washing soda reacts with soluble salts in hard water to form insoluble carbonates that can be filtered off.

$$MCl_2 + Na_2CO_3 \longrightarrow MCO_3\downarrow + 2NaCl$$

$$MSO_4 + Na_2CO_3 \longrightarrow MCO_3\downarrow + Na_2SO_4$$ (where, M = Ca and Mg)

- **By addition of lime (Clark's process)** Lime is first mixed with water in a tank and then fed into another tank containing the hard water. Revolving paddles thoroughly mix the two solutions. Then calcium and magnesium carbonate settle down.

$$Ca(HCO_3)_2 + Ca(OH)_2 \longrightarrow 2CaCO_3\downarrow + 2H_2O$$

$$Mg(HCO_3)_2 + Ca(OH)_2 \longrightarrow MgCO_3\downarrow + CaCO_3\downarrow + 2H_2O$$

EXAM ORIENTED QUESTIONS

TYPE - 1   01 Mark

Multiple Choice Questions

Q.1 Water act as a universal solvent because
(a) it boils at hundred degrees celsius
(b) it has a high heat capacity
(c) it has high latent heat
(d) it is polar and has a high dielectric constant.

Ans. (d) It is polar and has a high dielectric constant.

Q.2 Alloys are example of
(a) solid solution (b) isotope
(c) isobars (d) isotones

Ans. (a) solid solution.

Q.3 The solution in which the amount of solute contained in a solution is less than the saturation level is called
(a) unsaturated solution (b) concentrated solution
(c) dilute solution (d) saturated solution

Ans. (a) The solution in which the amount of solute contained in a solution is less than the saturation level is called **unsaturated solution**.

Q.4 Consider the following statement regarding true solution.
I. It is homogeneous.
II. The particles of solute do not settle down even after long time.
III. The size of particle of solute is 10^{-10} m.
Choose the correct option.
(a) Only II (b) II and III
(c) I and III (d) All of these

Ans. (d) All of these

Q.5 A solution contains 50 g of common salt in 450 g of water. The concentration of the solution is
(a) 50% (b) 10%
(c) 20% (d) 5%

Ans. (b) 10%

w_2 (salt) = 50 g, w_1 (Water) = 450 g

$w_{solution} = w_1 + w_2 = 450 + 50 = 500$ g

$$\text{Concentration of solution} = \frac{w_2 \times 100}{w_{solution}} = \frac{50 \times 100}{500} = 10\%$$

Q.6 Maximum amount of a solid solute that can be dissolved in a specified amount of a given liquid solvent does not depend upon .....
(a) temperature (b) nature of solute
(c) pressure (d) nature of solvent

Ans. (c) This is because solids and liquids are nearly incompressible and are not significantly affected by change in **pressure**.

Q.7 The factors affecting solubility of a solid in a liquid is/are
I. Nature of solute II. Nature of solvent
III. Temperature IV. Pressure
Choose the correct option.
(a) Only III (b) Only IV
(c) I, II and III (d) All of these

Ans. (c) I, II and III

Q.8 Which of the following is the correctly represented solubility curve of $Na_2SO_4 \cdot 10H_2O$ (Glauber's salt)?

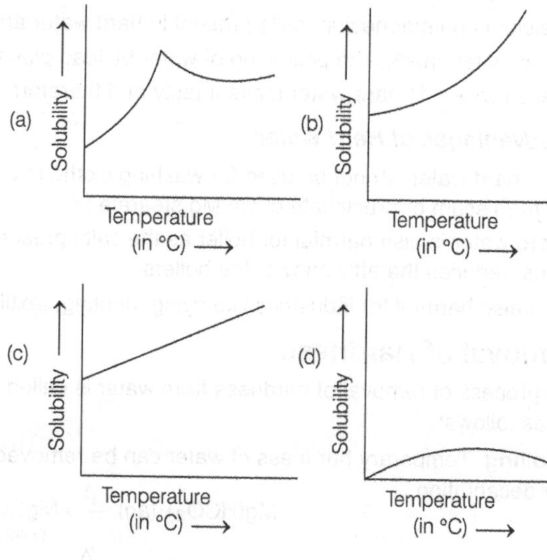

Ans. (a) $Na_2SO_4 \cdot 10H_2O$ (Glauber's salt) shows anomalous solubility behaviour. Its solubility first increase, and then decrease, with rise in temperature.

Q.9 Which of the following salt contain water of crystallisation?
(a) Potash alum (b) Blue vitriol
(c) Epsom salt (d) All of these

Ans. (d) Potash alum : $K_2SO_4 \cdot Al_2(SO_4)_3 \cdot 24H_2O$
Blue vitriol : $CuSO_4 \cdot 5H_2O$
Epsom salt: $MgSO_4 \cdot 7H_2O$

Q.10 What is the chemical name of white vitriol?

(a) Copper (II) sulphate pentahydrate
(b) Iron sulphate heptahydrate
(c) Cobalt sulphate heptahydrate
(d) Zinc sulphate heptahydrate

Ans. (d) Zinc sulphate heptahydrate

Q.11 A salt '*X*' commonly known as blue vitriol is heated in a test tube as shown in the figure below. The salt '*X*' turn into a white powdered solid on heating.

Which of the following could salt '*X*' be?

(a) $FeSO_4 \cdot 7H_2O$ (b) $CuSO_4 \cdot 5H_2O$
(c) $ZnSO_4 \cdot 7H_2O$ (d) $CaSO_4 \cdot 2H_2O$

Ans. (b) $CuSO_4 \cdot 5H_2O$

Q.12 Epsom salt is an example of

(a) hygroscopic substances (b) deliquescent substances
(c) anhydrous substances (d) efflorescent substances

Ans. (d) efflorescent substances

Q.13 The condition of efflorescence is

(a) vapour pressure of hydrated crystal = atmospheric vapour pressure
(b) vapour pressure of hydrated crystal ≠ atmospheric vapour pressure
(c) vapour pressure of hydrated crystal = atmospheric vapour pressure
(d) vapour pressure of hydrated crystal > atmospheric vapour pressure

Ans. (d) vapour pressure of hydrated crystal > atmospheric vapour pressure

Q.14 Which of the following is a dehydrating agent?

(a) P_2O_5 (b) CaO (c) $CaCl_2$ (d) Conc. H_2SO_4

Ans. (d) Conc. H_2SO_4

Q.15 Hardness of water is due to

(a) chloride of calcium (b) bicarbonate of magnesium
(c) sulphate of aluminium (d) Both (a) and (b)

Ans. (d) Both (a) and (b)

Q.16 Temporary hardness of water is due to the presence of

(a) calcium and magnesium chlorides
(b) calcium and magnesium sulphates
(c) calcium and magnesium phosphate
(d) calcium and magnesium hydrogen carbonates

Ans. (d) Calcium and mgnesium hydrogen carbonates.

Q.17 The list shows three process to remove hardness of water.

(i) Boiling
(ii) Treatment with washing soda
(iii) By addition of lime and soda-ash

Which method is used to remove the permanent hardness of water?

(a) (i) and (ii) only
(b) (i) and (iii) only
(b) (i), (ii) and (iii)
(d) (ii) and (iii) only

Ans. (d) (ii) and (iii) only

Q.18 The following equation represents a method to remove permanent hardness.

$$CaSO_4 + Na_2CO_3 \longrightarrow X + Y$$

What are the *X* and *Y* in the above reaction?

(a) $X = CaCO_3; Y = H_2SO_4$
(b) $X = H_2SO_4, Y = CaCl_2$
(c) $X = CaCO_3; Y = Na_2SO_4$
(d) $X = CaCl_2; Y = NaCl$

Ans. (c) $X = CaCO_3$; $Y = Na_2SO_4$

TYPE - 2 01 Mark

Assertion-Reason Questions

Directions (Q. Nos. 1-5) In the following questions statement are given Assertion and Reason.

(a) Both (A) and (R) are true and (R) is the correct explanation of (A).
(b) Both (A) and (R) are true but (R) is not the correct explanation of (A).
(c) (A) is true but (R) is false.
(d) (A) is false but (R) is true.

Q.1 Assertion (A) Water is called a universal solvent.

Reason (R) Water can dissolve a large variety of substances due to its polarity.

Ans. (a) Both (A) and (R) are true and (R) is the correct explanation of (A).
Polar nature of water allows it to dissolve many ionic and polar substances, making it a universal solvent.

Q.2 Assertion (A) A saturated solution cannot dissolve more solute at a given temperature.

Reason (R) The rate of dissolution equals the rate of crystallisation in a saturated solution.

Ans. (a) Both (A) and (R) are true, and (R) is the correct explanation of (A).

Q.3 **Assertion** (A) Hard water does not form lather easily with soap.

Reason (R) Hard water contains calcium and magnesium ions which react with soap to form scum.

Ans. (a) Both (A) and (R) are true and (R) is the correct explanation of (A).

Q.4 **Assertion** (A) Distilled water is an example of hard water.

Reason (R) Hard water contains dissolved salts of calcium and magnesium, whereas distilled water is free from any impurity.

Ans. (d) (A) is false, but (R) is true. Distilled water is an example of soft water, as it is free from any impurities.

Q.5 **Assertion** (A) Temporary hard water can be softened by boiling.

Reason (R) Boiling precipitates calcium and magnesium bicarbonates as insoluble carbonates.

Ans. (a) Both (A) and (R) are true and (R) is the correct explanation of (A).

Boiling converts bicarbonates of calcium and magnesium into insoluble carbonates, which can be filtered out, making the water soft.

TYPE - 3 01 Mark

Fill in the Blanks

Q.1 The component present in large amount in solution is known as ...... (solvent, solute).

Ans. solvent

Q.2 Air is an example of ...... solution. (liquid, gaseous)

Ans. gaseous

Q.3 If the solvent is a liquid other than water, the solution is known as ...... solution. (aqueous, non-aqueous).

Ans. non-aqueous

Q.4 A solution of iodine in alcohol is known as .... (tincture of iodine, amalgam)

Ans. tincture of iodine

Q.5 The mass of solid solute present in 100 g of solution is called .... (mass percent, solubility)

Ans. mass percent

Q.6 The amount of solute that dissolves in 100 g of solvent to form a saturated solution at a particular temperature is called .... (solubility, density)

Ans. solubility

Q.7 Anhydrous substance lack their .... (water of crystallisation, sulphate ion)

Ans. water of crystallisation

Q.8 Higher the temperature of the air, the .... is the efflorescence. (higher, lower)

Ans. higher

Q.9 ...... agent is used for removing water molecule of crystallisation from hydrated copper sulphate (Desiccating, Dehydrating).

Ans. Dehydrating

Q.10 Concentrated .... removes water of crystallisation molecules from blue vitriol (sulphuric acid, hydrochloric acid).

Ans. sulphuric acid

Q.11 ...... can be used to remove permanent hardness of water. (Na_2CO_3, NaOH)

Ans. Na_2CO_3

TYPE - 4 01 Mark

Correct the Incorrect Statement

Q.1 The freezing point of water increases with an increase in pressure.

Ans. The freezing point of water **decreases** with an increase in pressure.

Q.2 A solution in which more of the solute can be dissolved at a given temperature is called as saturated solution.

Ans. A solution in which more of the solute can be dissolved at a given temperature is called as **unsaturated** solution.

Q.3 Sodium nitrate show decrease in the solubility with rise in temperature.

Ans. Sodium nitrate show **increase** in their solubility with rise in temperature.

Q.4 An increase in pressure on the surface of water decreases the solubility of a gas in water.

Ans. An increase in pressure on the surface of water **increases** the solubility of a gas in water.

Q.5 Dehydrating agents are substances that can readily absorb moisture from other substances without chemically reacting with them.

Ans. **Drying agents** are substances that can readily absorb moisture from other substances without chemically reacting with them.

Q.6 Water free from soluble salts of calcium and magnesium is referred as hard water.

Ans. Water free from soluble salts of calcium and magnesium is referred as **soft** water.

TYPE - 5 01 × 05 = 05 Marks

Match the Columns

Q.1 Match the following columns.

Column I	Column II
A. Hydrated salt	1. Mist and fog
B. Solid state	2. Anhydrous calcium chloride
C. Liquid state	3. Ice, frost
D. Gaseous state	4. Well water, sea water
E. Drying agent	5. $CuSO_4 \cdot 5H_2O$

Ans. A → (5), B → (3), C → (4), D → (1), E → (2).

Q.2 Match the following columns.

Column I (Common name)		Column II (Formula)
A. Epsom salt	1.	$Na_2SO_4 \cdot 10H_2O$
B. Potash alum	2.	$Na_2CO_3 \cdot 10H_2O$
C. Glauber's salt	3.	$CuSO_4 \cdot 5H_2O$
D. Blue vitriol	4.	$K_2SO_4 \cdot Al_2(SO_4)_3 \cdot 24H_2O$
E. Washing soda	5.	$MgSO_4 \cdot 7H_2O$

Ans. A → (5), B → (4), C → (1), D → (3), E → (2).

TYPE - 6 01 Mark

Identify the Following

Q.1 What is the temperature at which water has a maximum density of 1g/cc?

Ans. 4°C.

Q.2 What is the property called which reduces force of attraction between the existing ions?

Ans. High dielectric constant.

Q.3 What is the size of the particle of solution?

Ans. 10^{-10} m.

Q.4 Name a solution in which both solute and solvent are solid?

Ans. Solid solution.

Q.5 Name two crystalline salts that does not contain water molecule of crystallisation.

Ans. Sodium chloride, ammonium chloride.

Q.6 Name the gas released when potassium nitrate is heated.

Ans. Oxygen

$$2KNO_3 \xrightarrow{\Delta} 2KNO_2 + O_2 \uparrow$$

Q.7 Give the chemical formula of soap.

Ans. Chemical formula for soap is $C_{17}H_{35}COO^-Na^+/K^+$.

Q.8 Name the type of hardness that can be removed simply by boiling.

Ans. Temporary hardness.

Q.9 The slimy precipitate of insoluble calcium and magnesium is usually given the name of?

Ans. Soap-curd or scum.

Q.10 Name the chemical used to remove temporary hardness in Clark's process.

Ans. Slaked lime or calcium hydroxide.

TYPE - 7 02 Marks

Short Answer Type I Questions

Q.1 (i) Rivers and lakes do not freeze easily. Explain.

(ii) Give a suitable reason for the following assertion. Water is an excellent liquid to be used as cooling agent.

Ans. (i) This is because of high specific heat capacity and latent heat of solidification due to which solidificaiton gives out large amount of heat before it freezes. **(1)**

(ii) Water has got a high value of specific heat capacity, i.e. it takes large amount of heat to get heated up. Therefore, it is commonly used as a cooling agent or coolant in motor car radiator or desert cooler etc. **(1)**

Q.2 Explain why

(i) Ice float on water.

(ii) The solute cannot be separated from a solution by filtration method.

Ans. (i) Ice floats on water because ice has lower density than water. **(1)**

(ii) The solute cannot be separated from a solution by filtration because solute particles are very small, 10^{-10} m in size and so, they pass through the pores of filter paper. **(1)**

Q.3 Complete the following table with *x*, *y* and *w*.

Types of solution	Example
Liquid in liquid	*x*
y	Sugar solution
Liquid in gas	*z*
w	Alloys

Ans. x = Alcohol, y = Solid in liquid, z = Soda water and w = Solid in solid. **(½ × 4 = 2)**

Q.4 Define dilute and concentrated solution with example.

Ans. The solution in which amount of solute is very less as compared to the amount of solvent is called dilute solution. e.g. dil. H_2SO_4. **(1)**

The solution in which amount of solute is relatively more as compared to the amount of solvent is called concentrated solution. e.g. conc. H_2SO_4. **(1)**

Q.5 **(i) Explain the effect of cooling on a saturated solution.**

(ii) Explain the effect of heat on a saturated solution.

Ans. (i) When a saturated solution is cooled, the solubility of the solute is lowered. Therefore, a part of the dissolved solute separates out in the form of crystals. The remaining solution is still saturated, but at lower temperature. **(1)**

(ii) When a saturated solution is heated, more solute can be dissolved in it at high temperature. That is the saturated solution is converted into unsaturated solution on heating. **(1)**

Q.6 Explain why:

(i) A solution is always clear and transparent.

(ii) In carbonated cold drinks gas rapidly bubbles out on opening the bottle.

Ans. (i) In a true solution, the particle size is around 10^{-10} m and occupies the intermolecular space. The particles are so small that they cannot be seen by naked eye. **(1)**

(ii) At high pressure, the solubility of gas is more. As the bottle is opened, pressure decreases which results in the decrease of solubility of carbon dioxide, hence the gas bubbles out. **(1)**

Q.7 **(i) A super saturated solution is *meta* stable. What do we mean by this?**

(ii) A solution is 20% mass by mass, what do we mean by this?

Ans. (i) It means that on slight disturbance like shaking, stirring, scratching the wall of the container, or adding a solute crystal to the solution, the additional amount of solute precipitates out thereby, resulting in the formation of saturated solution again. **(1)**

(ii) It means 20 g of solute is dissolved in 100 gram of solution. **(1)**

Q.8 Give a scientific term for the following.

(i) A line graph that plot changes in solubility of a solute in a solvent against changing temperature.

(ii) Substances that has more than negligible, but less than high solubility.

Ans. (i) Solubility curve (ii) Sparingly soluble **(1 × 2 = 2)**

Q.9 What is the effect of temperature on the solubility of the following compounds in water?

(i) $CaSO_4$

(ii) KNO_3

Ans. (i) The solubility of $CaSO_4$ in water **first increase then decreases** with the increase in temperature. **(1)**

(ii) The solubility of KNO_3 in water **increases** with the increase in temperature. **(1)**

Q.10 Write the effect of increasing temperature on the solubility of the gas in a liquid. Explain.

Ans. The solubility of gases in liquids **decreases** with increasing temperature. **(1)**

On heating a gas in water solution, the kinetic energy of the gas molecules increases and this overcomes the force holding them in solution, so the gas molecules leaves the solution. **(1)**

Q.11 A sample of hydrated magnesium sulphate, $MgSO_4 \cdot xH_2O$, is heated and the water of crystallisation is removed, leaving behind anhydrous $MgSO_4$. If 10 g of the hydrated salt loses water upon heating and leaves behind 5.4 g of anhydrous $MgSO_4$ then calculate the percentage of water of crystallisation.

Ans. Weight of water lost = 10g − 5.4g = 4.6 g

Percentage of water of crystallisation

$$= \frac{\text{Weight of water lost}}{\text{Weight of hydrated salt}} \times 100 = \frac{4.6}{10} \times 100 = 46\%$$ **(2)**

Q.12 Explain efflorescence. Why efflorescence increase with increase in temperature?

Ans. A phenomenon where a compound loses its water of crystallisation on exposure to dry air is called efflorescence. **(1)**

The higher the temperature of the air, the higher is the efflorescence. This is because at higher temperature, dry air can absorb more water, which evaporates from substances and leaving salts behind. **(1)**

Q.13 Name a substance in which there will be

(i) increase in mass

(ii) decrease in mass when they are exposed to the atmosphere

Ans. (i) **Concentrated sulphuric acid** (concentrated sulphuric acid is a drying agent, so it absorbs moisture from the atmosphere.). Also **table salt** (consist of impurities of magnesium chloride and calcium chloride, which are deliquescent in nature and absorb moisture from the atmosphere). **(1)**

(ii) **Sodium carbonate crystals** (sodium carbonate crystals are efflorescent in nature. Therefore, they lose water molecules of crystallisation when exposed to dry air). **(1)**

Q.14 Choose from the following substances given in box to answer the questions below.

$Na_2CO_3 \cdot 10H_2O$, NaOH, KOH, CaO, $MgCO_3$.

Each substance can be used once, more than once or not at all.

(i) The subtance(s) which shows deliquescence nature.

(ii) The subtance(s) which shows hygroscopic nature.

Ans. (i) NaOH, KOH **(1)**

(ii) CaO **(1)**

Q.15 Write two differences between drying and dehydrating agent.

Ans.	Drying agent	Dehydrating agent
(i)	They remove moisture from other substances.	They remove chemically combined elements of water in the ratio of 2 : 1 (hydrogen : oxygen) from a compound.
(ii)	They represent physical change as compositions do not change during drying of substances.	They represent chemical change as new substances are formed.
	e.g. Phosphorus pentoxide (P_2O_5), fused calcium chloride ($CaCl_2$)	e.g. Conc. sulphuric acid (H_2SO_4), alumina (Al_2O_3). **(2)**

Q.16 (i) What is the cause of hardness of water?

(ii) Why detergents are better cleansing agent than soaps?

Ans. (i) The cause of hardness of water is the presence of bicarbonates, sulphate and chlorides of calcium and magnesium. **(1)**

(ii) Soaps do not form lather with hard water but detergent can form lather with hard water. Therefore, detergents are better cleansing agent than soaps. **(1)**

Q.17 Explain cleansing action of soap.

Ans. Cleansing action of soap When a soap is dissolved in water, the molecules gather as clusters called **micelles**. Their tails dissolve in dirt and oil and the heads remain in H_2O.

The negatively charged heads present in water prevent the small globules from coming together and form aggregates. When water is stirred, oil and dirt tend to lift off from the dirty surface and dissociate into fragments.

Thus, oil and dirt are removed from the clothes when they are rinsed with water. **(2)**

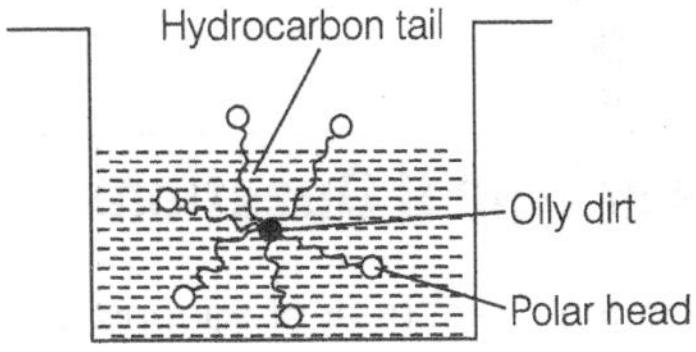

A micelle

Q.18 (i) Give a method to remove temporary hardness of water. Give with reaction involved.

(ii) Give reason for the following statement.

"Hard water is harmful for boiler".

Ans. (i) Temporary hardness of water can be removed by boiling. The precipitate formed can be removed by filtration or decantation.

The reaction is as follows

$$Ca(HCO_3)_2(aq) \xrightarrow{\Delta} \underset{\text{(Insoluble)}}{CaCO_3\downarrow} + H_2O + CO_2\uparrow \quad \textbf{(1)}$$

(ii) In the process of boiling to remove the hardness of water, the boiler efficiency is reduced because the salts present in hard water get deposited in the form of scale and form a thick layer inside the boiler. **(1)**

Q.19 The diagram represents method to remove hardness of water.

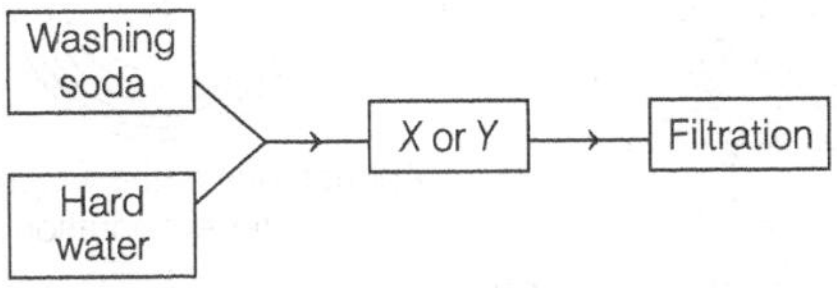

(i) Write the chemical formula of washing soda.

(ii) Identify insoluble salt obtained, (X) or (Y) in the process.

Ans. (i) Na_2CO_3 is the chemical formula of washing soda. **(1)**

(ii) The insoluble salts obtained in the process can be $CaCO_3$ or $MgCO_3$. **(1)**

Q.20 Washing soda is generally used to remove which type of hardness of water. Explain with reactions involved.

Ans. Permanent hardness of water can be removed by adding washing soda. In this treatment of hard water with washing soda, the soluble salt in hard water reacts with washing soda to form insoluble carbonates that can be filtered out. **(1)**

$$MCl_2 + \underset{\text{(Washing soda)}}{Na_2CO_3} \longrightarrow MCO_3\downarrow + 2NaCl$$

(where, M = Ca and Mg) **(1)**

Q.21 State any two disadvantages of using hard water.

Ans. Two disadvantages of using hard water

(i) Hard water is not suitable for producing steam.

(ii) Hard water is also unfit for washing and drinking purposes. **(1 × 2 = 2)**

TYPE - 8 — 03 Marks

Short Answer Type II Questions

Q.1 (i) What is the latent heat of vaporisation of water?

(ii) Write the importance of air dissolved in water?

(iii) What happens to the freezing point of water when dissolved impurities are present in it?

Ans. (i) The energy required to change water into its vapour at its boiling point without any change in temperature is called **latent heat of vapourisation of water**. **(1)**

(ii) Carbon dioxide and oxygen are the two gases of air which dissolves in water by diffusion. Oxygen is dissolved in water is taken by fishes to breathe. **(1)**

(iii) The freezing point of water **decreases** due to the presence of dissolved impurities in it. **(1)**

Q.2 Observe the experiment given below and answer the following questions.

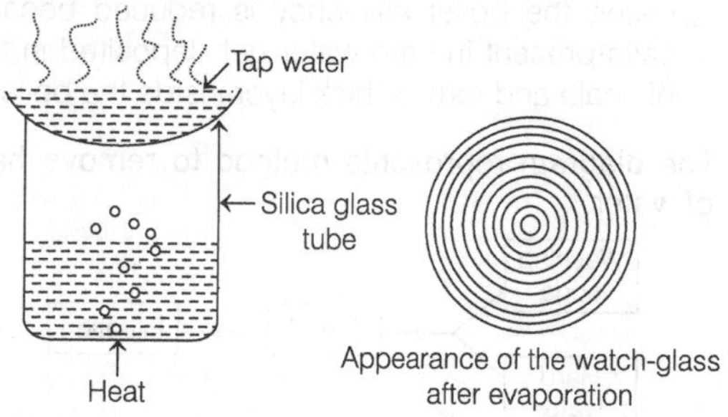

(i) State the aim of the experiment shown in the figure.

(ii) What is the main observation of this experiment.

(iii) Do we observe the same observation when the experiment is conducted with distilled water. Why?

Ans. (i) The aim of the experiment is to show that ordinary tap water contains dissolved solids. **(1)**

(ii) The main observation of this experiment is that a number of concentric rings of solid matter are seen on the watch glass. **(1)**

(iii) No, because distilled water does not contain dissolved solids (salts). So, concentric rings are not formed in this case. **(1)**

Q.3 Choose from the following terms to answer the questions below:

Dilute solution, Saturated solution, Binary solution True solution, Unsaturated solution.

(i) The solution in which amount of solute is very less as compared to the amount of the solvent.

(ii) A solution in which no more amount of solute can be dissolved at a given temperature.

(iii) A solution which is made up of two components.

Ans. (i) Dilute solution (ii) Saturated solution

(iii) Binary solution **(1 × 3 = 3)**

Q.4 What is saturated solution and how will you prepare a saturated solution?

Ans. A solution that cannot dissolve any more solute at a given temperature is called a saturated solution. **(1)**

Preparation of a saturated solution Take 100 g of distilled water in a beaker. Add 2 spoon of solute and stir with a glass rod till is dissolves. Add one more spoon of solute and stir it. It too will dissolve. A stage will come when no more of solute will dissolve at that temperature. The solution is then said to be saturated. **(2)**

Q.5 Give three characteristics of a true solution.

Ans. Characteristics of a true solution are:

(i) It is a homogeneous mixture.

(ii) The solute particles are very small, about 10^{-10} m.

(iii) Solute particles cannot be separated from the solution by the process of filtration. **(1 × 3 = 3)**

Q.6 40 g of sugar is dissolved in 3.45 kg of water. Calculate the concentration of solution.

Ans. Mass of solute = 40 g,

Mass of solvent = 3.45 kg = 3450 g

Mass of solution = Mass of solute + Mass of solvent

= 40 g + 3450 g = 3490 g

$$\text{Mass \%} = \frac{\text{Mass of solute} \times 100}{\text{Mass of solution}} = \frac{40 \times 100}{3490}$$

= 1.146% solution **(3)**

Q.7 3 litre of alcohol is present in 10 litre of aqueous solution of alcohol. Calculate the volume percent of the solution.

Ans. Volume of solute = 3L

Volume of solution = 10 L

$$\text{Volume percent} = \frac{\text{Volume of solute} \times 100}{\text{Volume of solution}}$$

$$= \frac{3}{10} \times 100 = 30\%$$ **(3)**

Q.8 From the curve given below answer the following questions.

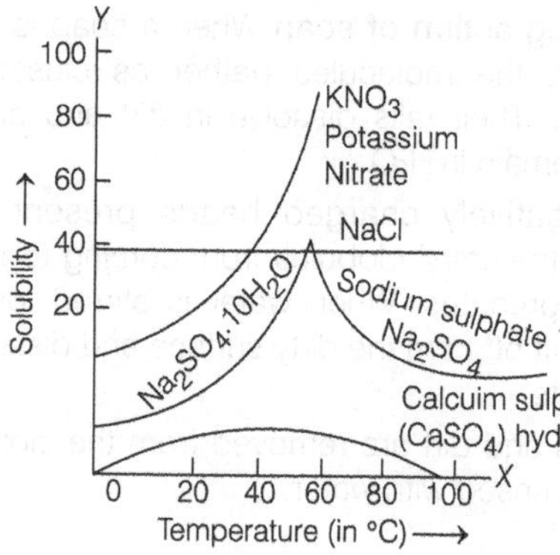

(i) What is the curve showing the changes in solubility of a solute in a solvent with changes in temperature referred as?

(ii) Name any one substance from the given curve which show increase in solubility with increase in temperature.

(iii) Choose a salt whose solubility first increases, and then decreases, with rise in temperature.

Ans. (i) Solubility curve. **(1)**

(ii) KNO_3 (Potassium nitrate) **(1)**

(iii) $Na_2SO_4 \cdot 10H_2O$ (Glauber's salt) **(1)**

Q.9 (i) What are hydrated substances? Give example.

(ii) What will you observe when hydrated copper sulphate, blue colour salt is heated?

(i) A substance that contains water molecules of crystallisation in its structure is known as a **hydrated substance**. e.g. Washing soda crystals, blue vitriol etc. **(1)**

(ii) When blue crystals of hydrated copper sulphate are heated in a test tube, they turn into a white powder, which turns back into a blue solid when a few drops of water are added.

$$\underset{\text{Hydrated blue colour salt}}{CuSO_4 \cdot 5H_2O} \underset{\text{Cool}}{\overset{\text{Heat}}{\rightleftharpoons}} \underset{\text{Anhydrous white colour salt powder}}{CuSO_4} + 5H_2O$$ **(2)**

Q.10 $CuSO_4$ contains fixed amount of xH_2O, water molecules along with its salt and exists as $CuSO_4 \cdot xH_2O$ which is blue in colour. A substance (z) is added to remove the chemically combined water moelcules from it.

(i) Identify x and write the complete molecular formula of salt $CuSO_4 \cdot xH_2O$.

(ii) Identify z and state the nature of z.

(iii) Write the chemical equation when z is added to $CuSO_4 . xH_2O$.

Ans. (i) $x = 5$ and the molecular formula of salt is $CuSO_4 \cdot 5H_2O$ **(1)**

(ii) z = conc. H_2SO_4. It is a **dehydrating agent**. **(1)**

(ii) $\underset{\text{(Blue)}}{CuSO_4 \cdot 5H_2O} \xrightarrow{\text{Conc. } H_2SO_4} \underset{\text{(White)}}{CuSO_4} + 5H_2O$ **(1)**

Q.11 Give one example of each of the following.

(i) A crystalline salt

(ii) Hygroscopic substance

(iii) Deliquescent substance

Ans. (i) Blue vitriol

(ii) Quick lime (calcium oxide)

(iii) Sodium hydroxide **(1 × 3 = 3)**

Q.12.

Common Name	Chemical Name	Property shown (Efflorescence/ Deliquescence	Formula
Washing soda	Sodium carbonate decahydrate	*A*	$Na_2CO_3 \cdot 10H_2O$
Glauber's salt	*B*	Efflorescence	*C*

By studying the table given below identify *A*, *B* and *C*.

Ans. *A* : Efflorescence

B : Sodium sulphate decahydrate

C : $Na_2SO_4 \cdot 10H_2O$ **(1 × 3 = 3)**

Q.13 Write three methods by which anhydrous substance is obtained.

Ans. Anhydrous substances can be obtained from hydrated substances by removing their water of crystallisation. It can be done through:

(a) direct heating

(b) by using a dehydrating agent like conc. H_2SO_4.

(c) Heating in dry air or hot air or under vacuum. **(3)**

Q.14 The following flowchart shows the process of softening of hard water. Complete the flow chart and answer the questions given below.

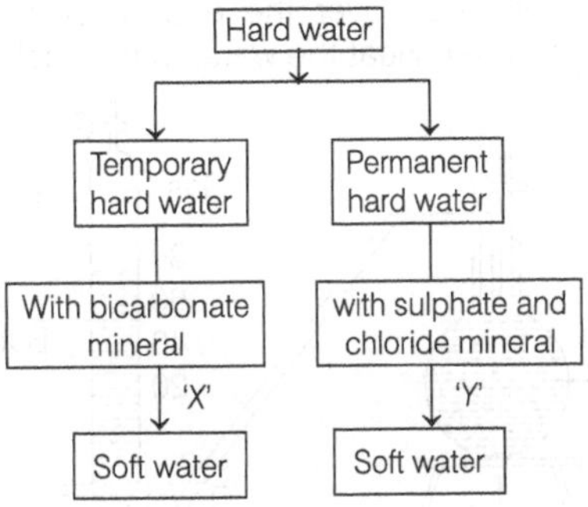

(i) Identify the process '*X*' and '*Y*' of removal of hardness of water.

(ii) (a) Write the chemical equation involved in process '*X*'.

(b) In the process '*Y*', write the balanced chemical equation used to remove hardness of sulphate mineral.

Ans. (i) The process '*X*' is **by heating** and '*Y*' is **by treating with chemical**, i.e. **washing soda**. **(1)**

(ii) (a) $M(HCO_3)_2 \longrightarrow MCO_3 \downarrow + H_2O + CO_2 \uparrow$

(where, M = Ca and Mg)

(b) $MSO_4 + \underset{\text{(Soda -Ash)}}{Na_2CO_3} \longrightarrow MCO_3 \downarrow + Na_2SO_4$ **(1)**

(where, M = Ca and Mg) **(1)**

Q.15 Answer the following.

(i) What are desiccating agents? Give any three examples.

(ii) Why hard water is not fit for industrial use ?

Ans. (i) Drying agents are also called desiccating agents. These substances can readily absorb moisture from other substances without chemically reacting with them. e.g. conc. H_2SO_4, P_2O_5, silica gel. **(2)**

(ii) Hard water is not fit for industrial use as calcium carbonate is deposited at the bottom of boilers and pipes as a result of boiling the hard water. These $CaCO_3$ deposits are bad conductors of heat.

As more hard water is boiled, more deposits are formed. Thus, it requires more time to boil the water and could lead to a dangerous boiler blasts. **(1)**

TYPE - 9 04/05 Marks

Long Answer Type Questions

Q.1 How will you show that tap water contains dissolved gases (air)?

Ans. Fill a round-bottom flask completely with tap water. A graduated tube or burrette completely filled with water is inverted over the end of delivery tube in a trough of water. Heat the water in the flask.

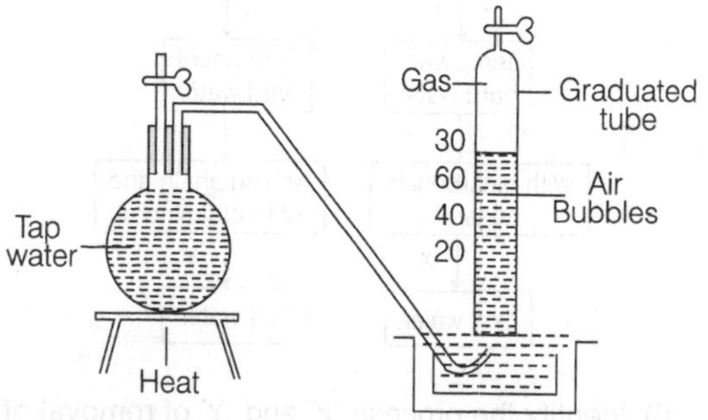

(2)

Gas bubbles are seen escaping from the water. They are collected in the graduated tube by downward displacement of water. The water vapour present in the gases condenses on coming in contact with cold water in tube. **(1)**

Conclusion The remaining gases come from the air dissolved in water, and they escape on heating. Read the volume of the gas thus collected.

The volume of the gas (air) collected in the graduated tube shows the presence of dissolved gases in tap water. **(1)**

Q.2 Give a suitable reason for the following assertion.

(i) Rainwater does not leave behind concentric rings when boiled.

(ii) Air dissolved in water contains higher proportion of oxygen.

(iii) Ice at 0°C is a better cooling agent than water at 0°C.

(iv) Steam at 100 degree celsius burns more severely than water at 100 degree celsius.

(v) Distilled water is kept in a bottle for a long time. It leaves itching on the surface of the glass.

Ans. (i) Rain water is pure form of water. It is free from dissolved salts. Therefore, it does not leave behind concentric rings when boiled.

(ii) Solubility of oxygen in water is more than solubility of nitrogen in water. Therefore, air dissolved in water contains more proportion of oxygen.

(iii) Ice at 0°C takes in more heat to melt first, which is equal to the latent heat of fusion. Therefore, ice is a better cooling agent, than water at 0°C.

(iv) Steam at 100°C burns more severely because steam gives out more heat equal to the latent heat of vaporisation of water.

(v) Water is a universal solvent, when kept in a bottle for long it dissolves even glass. Therefore, it leaves itching on the surface of glass. **(1×5=5)**

Q.3 Write the name of one substance whose solubility

(i) increases slightly with rise of temperature.

(ii) decreases with rise of temperature.

(iii) increases gradually with rise of temperature.

(iv) increases rapidly with rise of temperature.

(v) first increase, and then decrease, with rise in temperature.

Ans. (i) **Sodium chloride** (NaCl) Solubility increases slightly with rise of temperature. **(1)**

(ii) **Calcium sulphate** ($CaSO_4$) Solubility decreases with rise of temperature. **(1)**

(iii) **Potassium chloride** (KCl) Solubility increases gradually with rise of temperature. **(1)**

(iv) **Potassium nitrate** (KNO_3) Solubility increases rapidly with rise of temperature. **(1)**

(v) **Glauber's salt** ($Na_2SO_4 \cdot 10H_2O$) Solubility first increase and then decrease, with rise in temperature. **(1)**

Q.4 Draw the solubility curve for hydrated calcium sulphate, potassium nitrate, sodium chloride, and glauber's salt.

Ans. Solubility curve for hydrate calcium sulphate, potassium nitrate and sodium chloride is

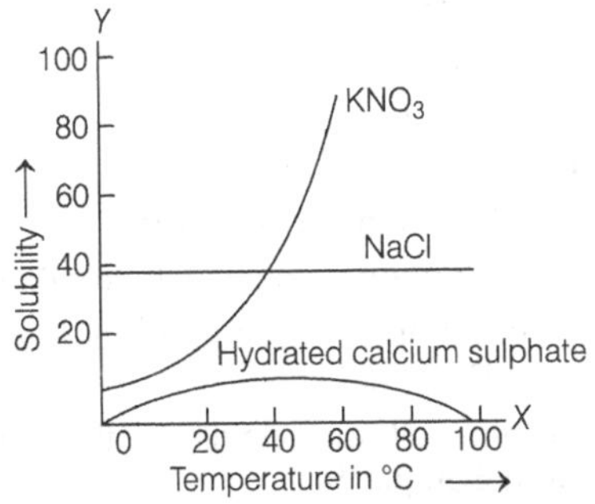

Solubility curve for (Glauber's salt) $Na_2SO_4.10H_2O$ $\left(2\frac{1}{2}\right)$

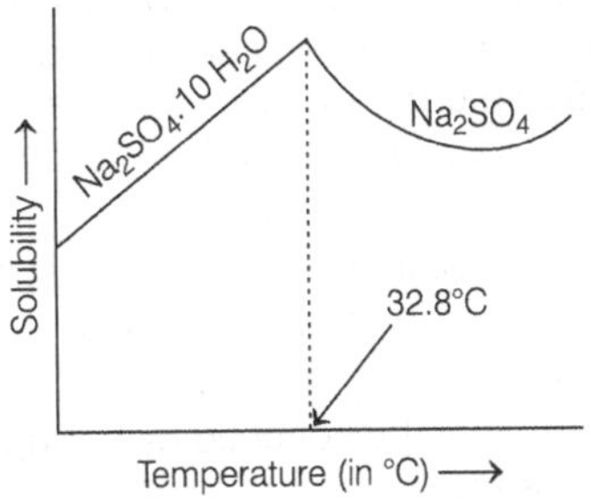

$\left(2\frac{1}{2}\right)$

Q.5 What is water of crystallisation? Among the following, choose the salt containing water of crystallisation. Epsom salt, Blue vitriol, Slaked lime, Ceric sulphate, Potash alum, White vitriol potassium permanganate.

Ans. The fixed amount of water that is associated with hydrated crystals and are an integral part of the crystal is said to be **water of crystallisation**.

The salts containing water of crystallisation are

Epsom salt - $MgSO_4 \cdot 7H_2O$

Potash alum - $K_2SO_4 \cdot Al_2(SO_4)_3 \cdot 24H_2O$

White vitriol - $ZnSO_4 \cdot 7H_2O$

Blue vitriol - $CuSO_4 \cdot 5H_2O$ **(5)**

Q.6 Give us suitable term for each of the following.

(i) A compound loses its water molecule of crystallisation on exposure to dry air.

(ii) A substance absorbs moisture from the atmosphere, but does not form a solution.

(iii) A substance which contains water molecule of crystallisation.

(iv) A solution where solvent is a liquid other than water.

(v) When a substance absorbs moisture on exposure to moist air and dissolves in the absorbed water and turn into a solution.

Ans. (i) Efflorescence (ii) Hygroscopic
(iii) Hydrated salt (iv) Non-aqueous solution
(v) Deliquescence **$(1 \times 5 = 5)$**

Q.7 What do you observe when?

(i) Glauber's salt is kept in the atmosphere.

(ii) Washing soda crystals are kept in the atmosphere.

(iii) Concentrated sulphuric acid bottle is kept open in the atmosphere for a few days.

(iv) Ferric chloride crystals are left in the atmosphere.

(v) Sodium hydroxide is left in the atmosphere.

Ans. (i) Glauber's salt becomes a powdery anhydrous substance, and there is also a decrease in mass.

(ii) Washing soda crystal turns into a white powdery substance and also there is a decrease in its mass.

(iii) There is an increase in volume of concentrated sulphuric acid, and also, its temperature increases (as it absorbs moisture from the atmosphere and gets diluted).

(iv) It turns into a solution(because ferric chloride is deliquescent).

(v) Sodium hydroxide turns into a solution (it is deliquescent). **$(1 \times 5 = 5)$**

Q.8 Among the following salts, write which shows increases in weight, decrease in weight or remain same when exposed to atmosphere.

(i) Epsom salt (ii) Soda ash
(iii) Magnesium chloride (iv) Conc. sulphuric acid
(v) Sodium hydroxide (vi) Washing soda
(vii) Glauber's salt (viii) Common salt
(ix) Gypsum (x) White vitriol

Ans. (i) Decreases (ii) Remain same
(iii) Increases (iv) Increases
(v) Increases (vi) Decreases
(vii) Decreases (viii) Increases
(ix) Remain same (x) Remain same **$(\frac{1}{2} \times 10 = 5)$**

Q.9

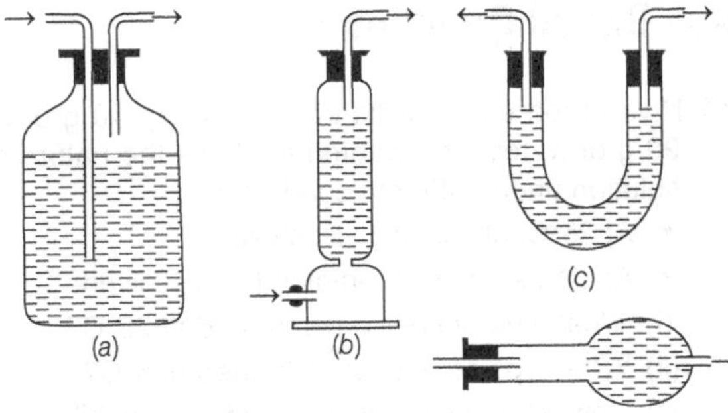

(i) What are the apparatus '*b*' and '*d*' known as?

(ii) What is the apparatus shown in '*a*' called?

(iii) Name the chemical filled in apparatus '*a*' to dry an acidic gas.

(iv) Which chemical is filled in apparatus '*d*'?

(v) Why is quick lime suitable to dry ammonia?

Ans. (i) *b* = drying tower and *d* = drying bulb

(ii) Drying bottle

(iii) Concentrated sulphuric acid

(iv) Anhydrous calcium chloride

(v) Quick lime is basic in nature, so it does not react with basic ammonia gas. **(1×5 = 5)**

Q.10 Explain the following with suitable reason.

(i) The level of conc. H_2SO_4 in the jar increases when exposed to atmosphere for few hours.

(ii) Common salt becomes wet during rainy season.

(iii) Ferric chloride is stored in airtight bottles.

(iv) Washing soda loses its weight when exposed to atmosphere.

(v) Permanent hard water is treated with slaked lime.

Ans. (i) Conc. sulphuric acid (H_2SO_4) is **hygroscopic** in nature. Hence, when exposed to atmosphere it absorbs moisture and the level of sulphuric acid in the jar increases.

(ii) Common salt (NaCl) contains the impurities of magnesium chloride which is deliquescent in nature. Thus, common salt becomes wet during rainy season. Sodium chloride is not deliquescent in nature.

(iii) Ferric chloride is highly deliquescent in nature and forms saturated solution. Hence, it should be stored in airtight bottles.

(iv) Washing soda is an efflorescent salt and it loses its water molecules of crystallisation, so there is a decrease in its weight.

(v) When permanent hard water is treated with (slaked lime) $Ca(OH)_2$ then it gives calcium carbonate ($CaCO_3$) and magnesium carbonate ($MgCO_3$). Thus, this removes hardness. **(1 × 5 = 5)**

TYPE - 10 — 03 Marks

Case Based Questions

Q.1 Riya prepared a solution by dissolving 10 g of salt in 90 g of water. She wanted to check the nature of the solution under different conditions:

- At 25°C, all the salt dissolved.
- At 5°C, some salt remained undissolved.

(i) What type of solution is formed at 25°C?

(ii) What type of solution is formed at 5°C?

(iii) How does temperature affect the solubility of most solutes in water?

Ans. (i) At 25°C, an **unsaturated solution** is formed because all the solute dissolves at room temperature.

(ii) At 5°C, an unsaturated solution turns into a **saturated solution** with undissolved solute.

(iii) The solubility of most solutes in water **increases** with temperature, meaning more solute dissolves at higher temperatures. **(1 × 3 = 3)**

Q.2 Ravi conducted an experiment by taking two water samples:

1. Sample *A* : Rainwater
2. Sample *B* : Water from a well.

He added soap to both samples and observed the following:

- Sample *A* formed lather easily.
- Sample *B* formed a scum instead of lather.

(i) Why did Sample *A* form lather easily while Sample *B* formed scum?

(ii) Name one salt responsible for the hardness of water in Sample *B*.

(iii) Suggest a method to soften hard water.

Ans. (i) **Sample *A*** formed lather easily because rainwater is **soft water**, which lacks calcium and magnesium salts. **Sample *B*** formed scum because it is **hard water** containing dissolved calcium and magnesium salts.

(ii) Hardness in water is due to the presence of bicarbonates, chlorides or sulphates of calcium or magnesium.

(iii) Hard water can be softened by boiling or by adding washing soda. **(1 × 3 = 3)**

Q.3 A student was testing a water sample and he found that the water sample does not lather with soap. He then boiled and added lime to this water sample separately. After this, he noticed that water was lathering with soap.

(i) Which type of hardness of water is present in the water sample?

(ii) Name the process in which hardness of water is removed by adding lime. Give its reaction.

(iii) What happens when washing soda is added to hard water containing permanent hardness?

Ans. (i) **Temporary hardness of water** is present in the water sample.

(ii) **Clark's process** is used to remove hardness of water by adding lime.

$$Ca(HCO_3)_2 + Ca(OH)_2 \longrightarrow 2CaCO_3\downarrow + 2H_2O$$

$$Mg(HCO_3)_2 + Ca(OH)_2 \longrightarrow MgCO_3\downarrow + CaCO_3\downarrow + 2H_2O$$

(iii) Washing soda reacts with soluble salts in hard water containing permanent hardness to form insoluble carbonates that can be filtered off.

$$MCl_2 + Na_2CO_3 \longrightarrow MCO_3\downarrow + 2NaCl$$

$$MSO_4 + Na_2CO_3 \longrightarrow MCO_3\downarrow + Na_2SO_4.$$

(M = Ca and Mg) **(1 × 3 = 3)**

04

ATOMIC STRUCTURE AND CHEMICAL BONDING

Atom

- An atom is the smallest particle of an element that exhibit all the properties of that element. Atom may or may not exist independently but takes part in a chemical reaction.
- An element is a pure substance which is made up of only one type of atoms.

Constituents of an Atom

An atom consist of three fundamental particles; electron, proton and neutron.

Basic Properties of Electrons, Protons and Neutrons

Name	Symbol	Absolute charge/C	Relative charge	Mass/kg	Mass/u	Approx. mass/u	Position	Discoverer
Electron	e or $_{-1}e^0$	-1.6022×10^{-19}C	−1	9.10939×10^{-31}	0.00054	0	Outside the nucleus	J.J. Thomson
Proton	p or $_1p^1$	$+1.6022\times 10^{-19}$C	+1	1.67262×10^{-27}	1.00727	1	Inside the nucleus	E. Goldstein
Neutron	n or $_0n^1$	0	0	1.67493×10^{-27}	1.00867	1	Inside the nucleus	J. Chadwick

Atomic Number and Mass Number

Atomic Number

- It is defined as the number of protons present in the nucleus of an atom.
- All the atoms of the same element have the same number of protons in their nuclei and hence, they have the same atomic number.
- It is denoted by Z and written as a subscript to the left of the symbol.

  ∴ Atomic number = Number of protons

  e.g. atomic number of hydrogen is 1 ($Z = 1$) as there is only one proton present in the nucleus of its atom. Similarly, for carbon, $Z = 6$ as there are 6 protons present in the nucleus of its atom.
- As number of protons and number of electrons in a neutral atom is equal, so atomic number is also equal to number of electrons in the atom.

Mass Number

- It is defined as the sum of number of protons and neutrons present in the nucleus of an atom. Protons and neutrons together are called as **nucleons**. Mass number is denoted by A.

  ∴ Mass number (A) = Number of protons + Number of neutrons.

  e.g. Carbon has 6 protons and 6 neutrons, thus, its mass number is $6 + 6 = 12$ u.
- Number of neutrons = Mass number (A) − Atomic number (Z) (∵ Atomic number = Number of protons)

- Mass number is written as a superscript to the left of the symbol. In the notation for an atom, the atomic number, mass number and symbol of the element are to be written as

Mass number
Symbol of element or $^{A}_{Z}X$
Atomic number

e.g. Nitrogen is written as $^{14}_{7}N$.

Distribution of Electrons in Different Orbits (Shells)

The distribution of electrons into different orbits (shells) of an atom was suggested by **Bohr** and **Bury**. For writing the number of electrons in different energy levels or shells, some rules are followed. These are as follows

- The **maximum number of electrons** present in a shell is given by the formula $\mathbf{2n^2}$, where, n is the orbit number or energy level, 1, 2, 3, ...

  Therefore, the maximum number of electrons in different shells are as follows

  – First orbit or ***K*-shell** $= 2 \times (1)^2 = 2$

  – Second orbit or ***L*-shell** $= 2 \times (2)^2 = 8$

  – Third orbit or ***M*-shell** $= 2 \times (3)^2 = 18$

  – Fourth orbit or ***N*-shell** $= 2 \times (4)^2 = 32$ and so on.

- The maximum number of electrons that can be accommodated in the outermost orbit is 8 (except helium which has only one shell and can accommodate only two electrons).
- Electrons are not accommodated in a given shell, unless the inner shells are filled (i.e. the **shells are filled in a step-wise manner**).

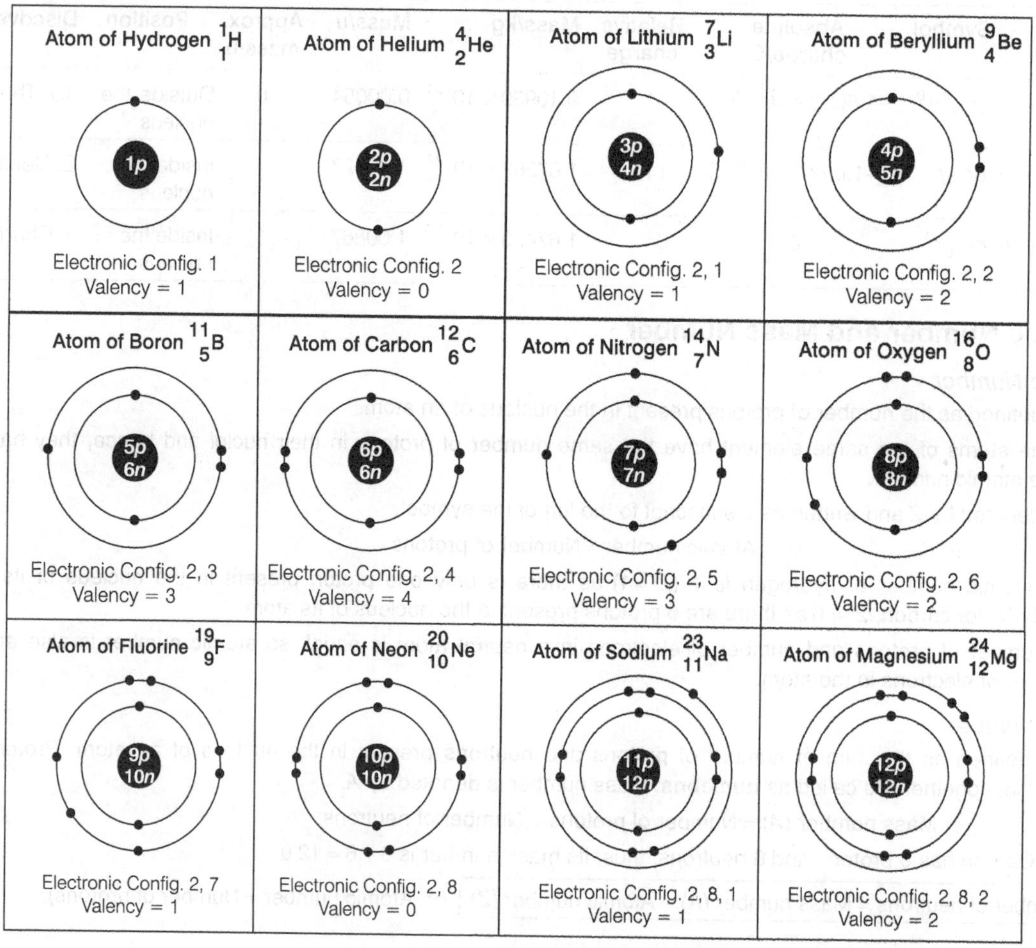

Atom of Aluminium $^{27}_{13}Al$

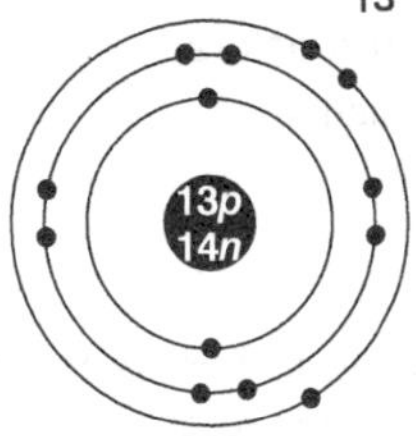

Electronic Config. 2, 8, 3
Valency =3

Atom of Silicon $^{28}_{14}Si$

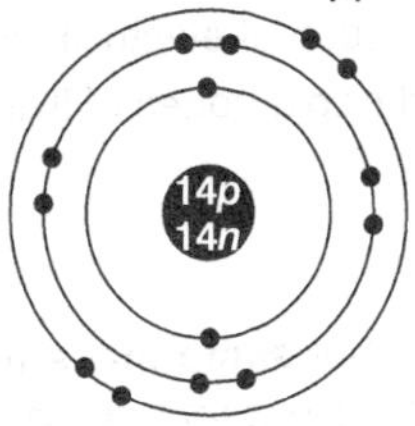

Electronic Config. 2, 8, 4
Valency =4

Atom of Phosphorus $^{31}_{15}P$

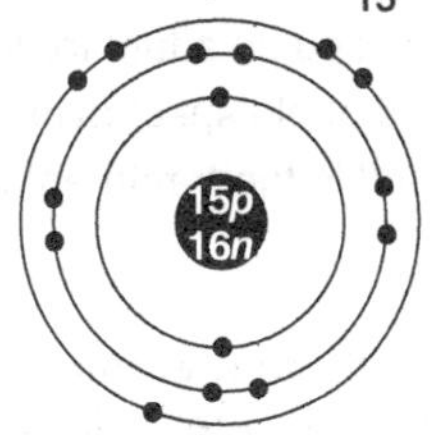

Electronic Config. 2, 8, 5
Valency = 3

Atom of Sulphur $^{32}_{16}S$

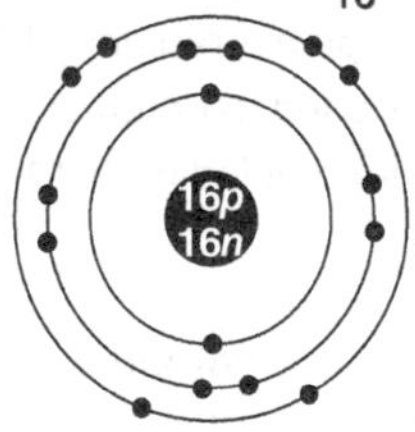

Electronic Config. 2, 8, 6
Valency = 2

Atom of Chlorine $^{35}_{17}Cl$

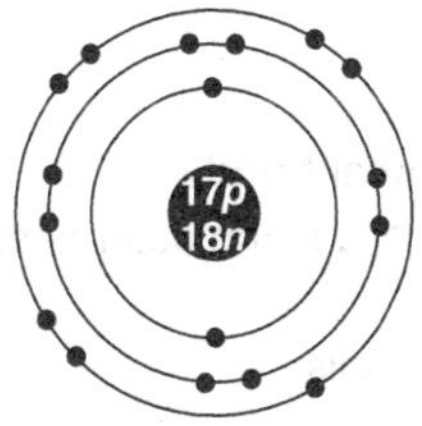

Electronic Config. 2, 8, 7
Valency = 1

Atom of Argon $^{40}_{18}Ar$

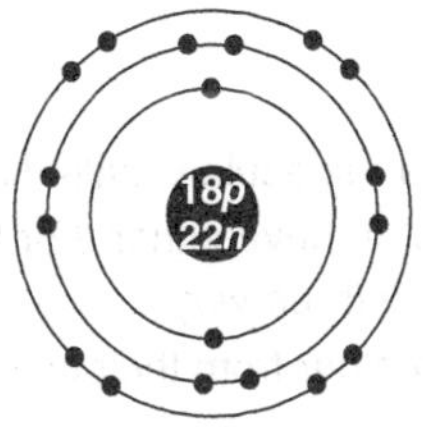

Electronic Config. 2, 8, 8
Valency = 0

Atom of Potassium $^{39}_{19}K$

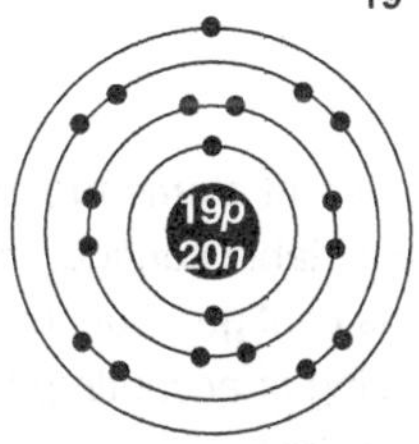

Electronic Config. 2, 8, 8, 1
Valency = 1

Atom of Calcium $^{40}_{20}Ca$

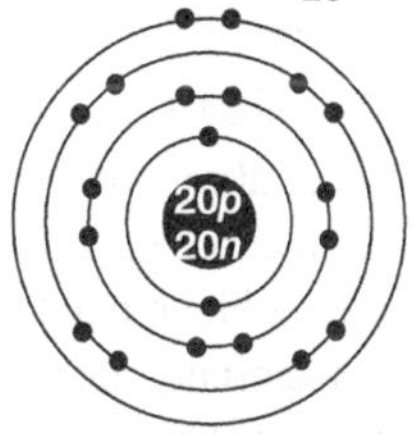

Electronic Config. 2, 8, 8, 2
Valency = 2

Reason for Chemical Reactivity of an Atom

- Atoms of all noble gases (except helium) have **eight electrons** in their outermost (valence) shell and this arrangement is known as **octet**.
- The chemical reactivity of an atom depends upon the number of electrons in its valence shell.
- Chemically active atoms have incomplete octet. These elements tend to combine with one another to attain stable electronic configuration of the nearest noble gas, i.e. 8 electrons. This is known as **octet rule**.

Isotopes

Isotopes are defined as the atoms of the **same element**, having the **same atomic number** but **different mass numbers**. In other words, it can be said that isotopes have same number of protons but they differ in the number of neutrons.

(i) **Hydrogen** It has three isotopes all having atomic number equal to one but mass numbers as 1, 2 and 3.

Isotopes	Atomic number	Mass number	No. of electrons	No. of protons	No. of neutrons
Protium $^{1}_{1}H$	1	1	1	1	0
Deuterium $^{2}_{1}H$ or $^{2}_{1}D$	1	2	1	1	1
Tritium $^{3}_{1}H$ or $^{3}_{1}T$	1	3	1	1	2

(ii) **Carbon** It has three isotopes as listed below.

Isotopes	Atomic number	Mass number	No. of electrons	No. of protons	No. of neutrons
C-12 or $^{12}_{6}C$	6	12	6	6	6
C-13 or $^{13}_{6}C$	6	13	6	6	7
C-14 or $^{14}_{6}C$	6	14	6	6	8

(iii) **Chlorine** It has many isotopes found in traces. Two major isotopes of it are listed below.

Isotopes	Atomic number	Mass number	No. of electrons	No. of protons	No. of neutrons
Cl-35 or $^{35}_{17}Cl$	17	35	17	17	18
Cl-37 or $^{37}_{17}Cl$	17	37	17	17	20

- An isotope of cobalt (Co-60) is used in radiotherapy for treating cancer and other diseases.
- An isotope of uranium (U-235) is used as a fuel for the production of electricity in nuclear reactors.
- C-14 is used to determine the age of old specimens of wood or old bones of living organisms.
- An isotope of iodine (I-131) is used in the treatment of goitre.

Isobars

Atoms of **different elements** with **different atomic numbers** but **same mass number** are known as **isobars**. In other words, isobars are the atoms of different elements that have *same number of nucleons* (protons + neutrons) but they differ in the number of protons.

e.g. $^{40}_{18}Ar$ and $^{40}_{20}Ca$ are isobars.

Since, isobars have different atomic number as well as different electronic configuration. Thus, they also have both different physical and chemical properties.

Chemical Bond

- The force of attraction that hold different atoms together in a molecule is called a **chemical bond.**
- Atoms form chemical bond to attain stable configuration, i.e. to have either 2 or 8 electrons in the outermost shell.
- Atoms can achieve stable electrons configuration in following three ways
  (i) by transferring electrons (donating or accepting) to each other from their outermost shells.
  (ii) by mutual sharing the pair of electrons.
  (iii) by donating a pair of electrons from one atom to another for sharing.

Types of Chemical Bonds

On the basis of transfer or share of electrons between atoms, there are three types of bond.

- **Electrovalent bond** Formed by transfer of electrons from one atom to another.
- **Covalent bond** Formed by mutual sharing of one or more pair of electrons between two or more atoms.
- **Coordinate or dative bond** Formed by donating a pair of electrons for sharing from one atom to another.

Electrovalent or Ionic Bond

- These bonds are formed by the complete transfer of electron(s) from one atom to another. Here, metal or electropositive element loses electrons and non-metal or electronegative element atom gains those electrons. The compounds formed by ionic bonds are called **ionic compounds.**
- Electrovalent bond is called **ionic bond** because it involves formation of ions.
- These bonds are easily formed between a metallic atom and a non-metallic atom.
- Metallic atom easily loses electron(s) to form **cations (+ ve ion)** and is called an **electropositive element**. Non-metallic atom easily gains electron(s) to form **anions (–ve ion)** and is called an **electronegative element**. Thus, ionic bond is formed by ions, i.e. **cations** and **anions**.

Atomic Orbit Structure of Some Electrovalent Compounds

1. Sodium Chloride (NaCl)

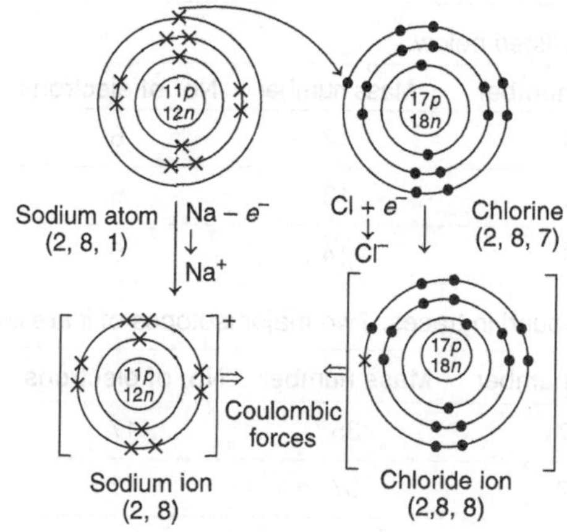

2. **Magnesium Chloride** ($MgCl_2$)

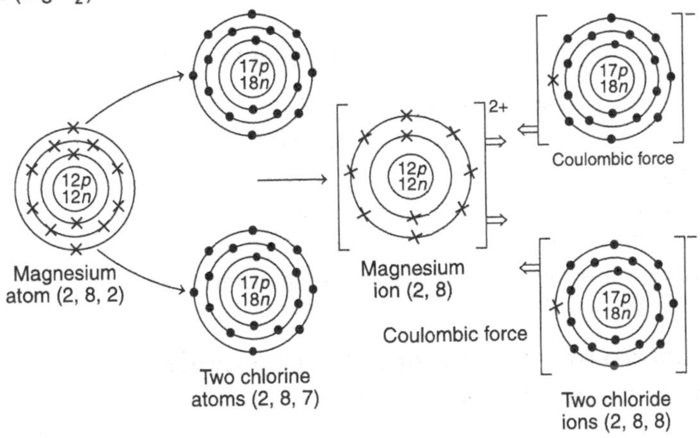

3. **Calcium Oxide** (CaO)

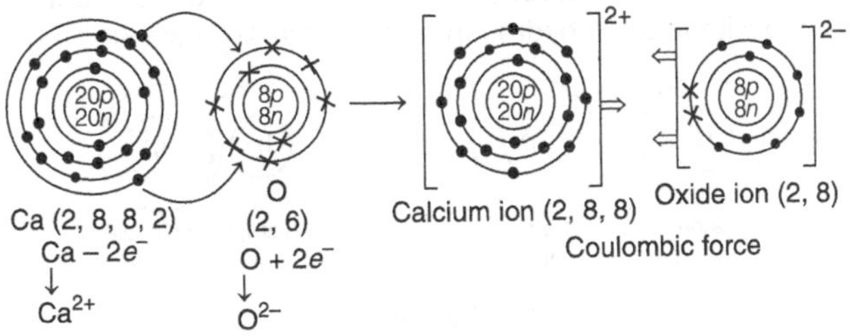

Oxidation and Reduction on the Basis of Loss or Gain of Electrons

- Loss of electrons is called **oxidation** while gain of electrons is called **reduction**.
- The elements that loses electrons and get oxidised are called as **reducing agents**.
- The elements that gains electrons and get reduced are called as **oxidising agents**.

Covalent Bond or Molecular Bond

- The bond formed by the mutual sharing of electrons between two or more atoms is called the **covalent bond**.
- This bond is generally formed between two electronegative, i.e. non-metallic elements.
- The compounds formed by covalent bonds are called **covalent compounds**.

Types of Covalent Bonds

1. On the Basis of Sharing of Electrons

(i) **Single covalent bond** It is formed by the sharing of one pair of electrons between two atoms. It is represented by a single line (—). e.g

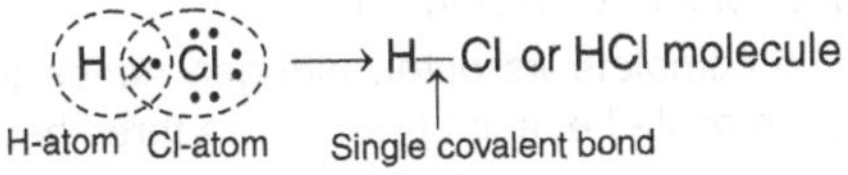

(ii) **Double covalent bond** It is formed by the sharing of two pair of electrons between two atoms. It is represented by a double line (=). e.g.

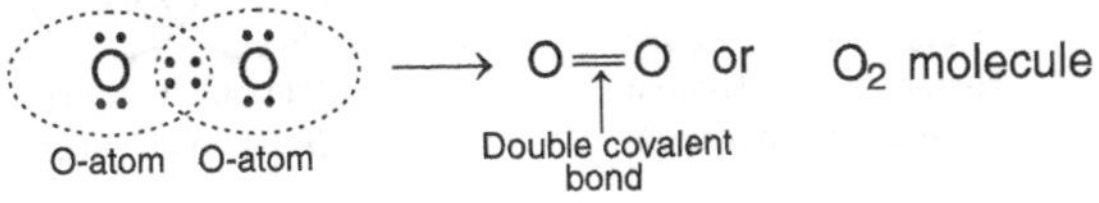

(iii) **Triple covalent bond** It is formed by the sharing of three pair of electrons between two atoms. It is represented by a triple line (≡). e.g.

N-atom N-atom ⟶ N≡N or N_2 molecule

↑ Triple covalent bond

2. On the Basis of Polarity

(i) **Polar Covalent Bond** It is formed when the combining elements have significant difference in their electronegativity. e.g. water, ammonia, etc

(ii) **Non-polar Covalent Bond** It is formed when the combining elements have no or very less difference in their electronegativity. e.g. Cl_2, N_2, CH_4, CCl_4 etc.

Atomic Orbital Structure of Some Covalent Compounds

The structures of some covalent compounds shown below.

1. Hydrogen Molecule (H_2, Non-polar Covalent Compound)

A hydrogen atom has one electron in its outermost shell. It needs one more electron to complete its duplet. Thus, hydrogen atom shares its electron with another hydrogen atom to form H_2 molecule. e.g.

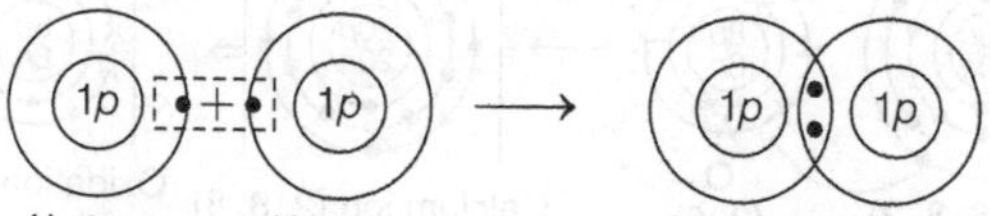

H-atom H-atom (Before combination) Hydrogen molecule (After combination)

H—H or H_2 molecule

↑ Single covalent bond

2. Oxygen Molecule (O_2, Non-polar Covalent Compound)

Electronic configuration of O is 2, 6. To complete its octet, oxygen needs two electrons. Hence, each O-atoms share two electrons to form O_2 molecule. e.g.

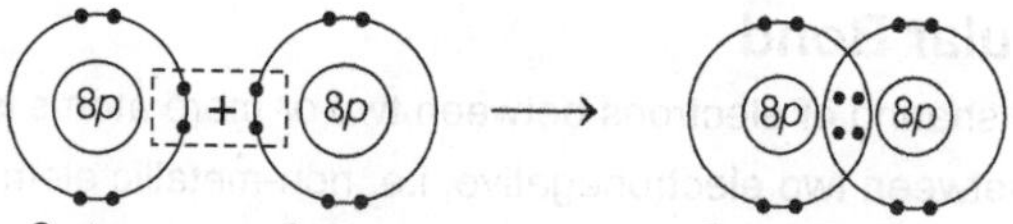

O-atom O-atom (Before combination) Oxygen molecule (After combination)

O=O or O_2 molecule

↑ Double covalent bond

3. Nitrogen Molecule (N_2, Non-polar Covalent Compound)

Electronic configuration of N is 2, 5. To complete its octet, nitrogen needs three electrons. Hence, two N-atoms share three pair of electrons to form N_2 molecule i.e. each N atom has three bond pairs of electrons.

e.g.

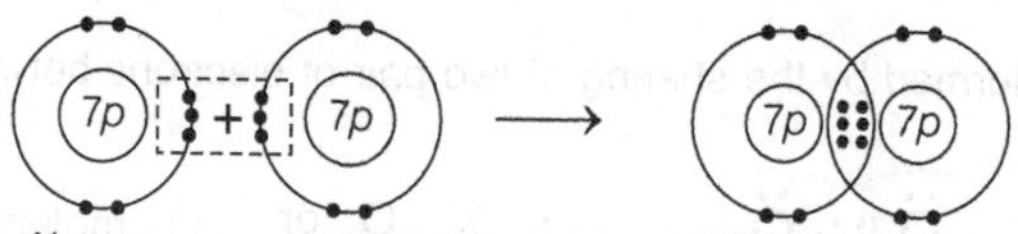

N-atom N-atom (Before combination) Nitrogen molecule (After combination)

N≡N or N_2 molecule

↑ Triple covalent bond

4. Ammonia Molecule *(NH_3, Polar Compound)*

Electronic configuration of N is 2, 5 and that of H is 1. Nitrogen needs three electrons to complete its octet while hydrogen needs one electron to complete its duplet. Number of covalent bonds involved in $NH_3 = 3$

e.g.

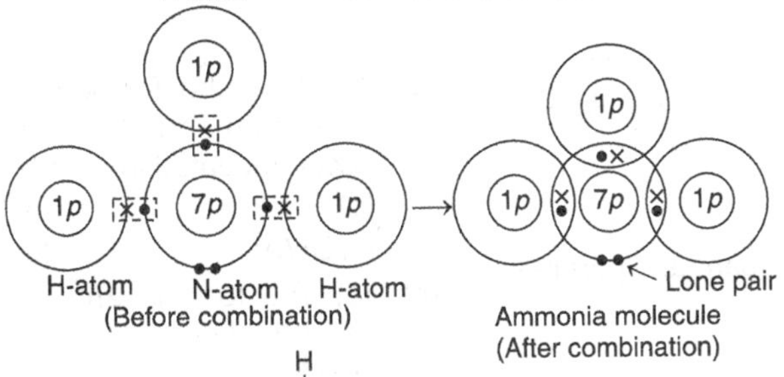

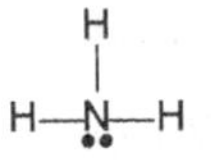

or $\ddot{N}H_3$ molecule

3-single covalent bonds

5. Carbon Tetrachloride Molecule *(CCl_4) (Non-polar Covalent Compound) [liquid]*

Electronic configuration of C = 2, 4 and Cl = 2, 8, 7. Carbon needs 4 electrons while Cl requires one more electron to attain the stable electronic configuration of nearest noble gas by completing their octet.

e.g.

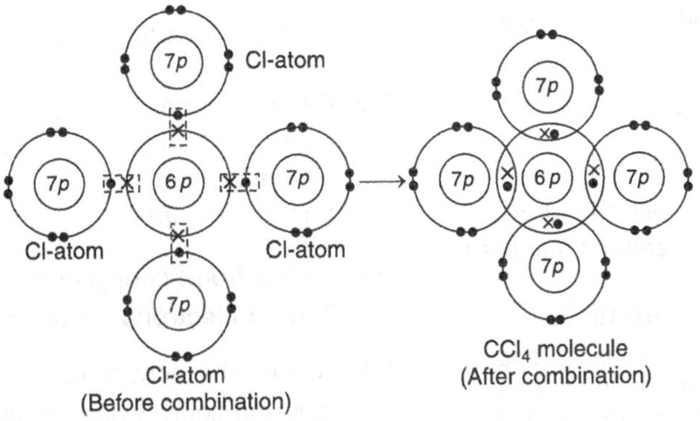

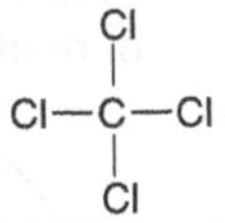

or CCl_4 molecule

4-single covalent bonds

EXAM ORIENTED QUESTIONS

TYPE - 1   01 Mark

Multiple Choice Questions

Q.1 Name of the smallest particle which can take part in a chemical reaction independently is
(a) atom (b) proton
(c) neutron (d) electron

Ans. (a) atom

Q.2 The constituent particle of an element showing almost all the properties of element is
(a) electron (b) proton (c) atom (d) molecule

Ans. (c) atom

Q.3 A pure substance, constituted of only one type of particles is called a/an
(a) atom (b) element
(c) compound (d) None of these

Ans. (b) Element

Q.4 An element X forms a positive ion with the electronic structure 2,8,8. What is the proton (atomic) number of X?
(a) 16 (b) 17 (c) 18 (d) 19

Ans. (d) As the element X forms a positive ion, it must be belonging to group 1, 2 or 3 in the periodic table. In this case option (d), **atomic number** 19, (2, 8, 8, 1) belongs to group one.

Q.5 The diagram represents an atom of an element, X.

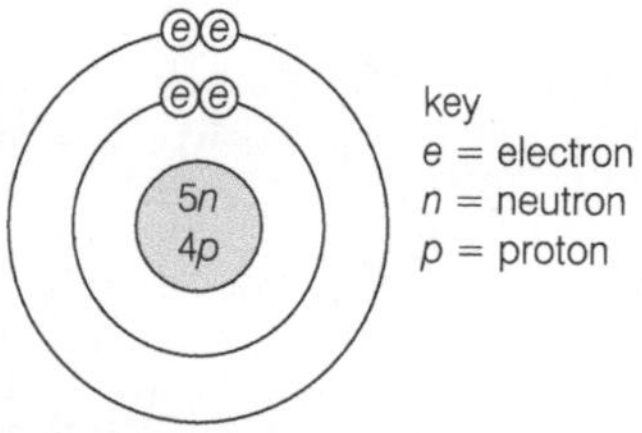

Which symbol represents this atom?
(a) $^{9}_{4}X$ (b) $^{9}_{5}X$
(c) $^{4}_{9}X$ (d) $^{5}_{9}X$

Ans. (a) Let the symbolic representation of element be $^{A}_{Z}X$.
Atomic number (Z) = number of protons (p) = 4
Mass number (A) = number of neutrons (n) + number of protons (p) = 5 + 4 = 9
$\therefore$ Symbol = $^{9}_{4}X$

Q.6 Which of the following formula is used to find the maximum number of electrons that can be accommodated in an orbit?
(a) $2n+2$ (b) $2(n+2)$
(c) $2n/n^2$ (d) $2n^2$

Ans. (d) The formula $\mathbf{2n^2}$ is used to find the maximum number of electrons in an orbit, where n is the number of orbit.

Q.7 Which one of the following is a correct electronic configuration of magnesium (Mg)?
(a) 2, 8 (b) 8, 2, 1
(c) 2, 1, 8 (d) 2, 8, 2

Ans. (d) 2, 8, 2
Since atomic number of Mg = 12
So, Electronic configuration = $\begin{matrix} K & L & M \\ 2 & 8 & 2 \end{matrix}$

Q.8 If the electronic configuration of X = 2, 8, 7, then the number of electrons in the M shell of an atom of element X is
(a) 2 (b) 8 (c) 7 (d) 0

Ans. (c) Electronic configuration of X: $\begin{matrix} K & L & M \\ 2 & 8 & 7 \end{matrix}$
Thus, **7 electrons** are present in 'M' shell.

Q.9 Identify the schematic atomic structure of Mg^{2+} ion from the figure where, n and p represent the number of neutrons and protons respectively.

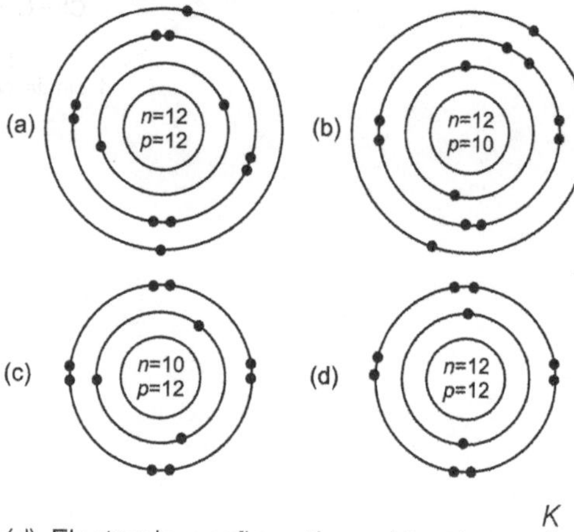

Ans. (d) Electronic configuration $_{12}$Mg atom = $\begin{matrix} K & L & M \\ 2 & 8 & 2 \end{matrix}$ and that of Mg^{2+} ion = 2, 8
i.e. In K-shell = 2 electron
In L-shell = 8 electrons

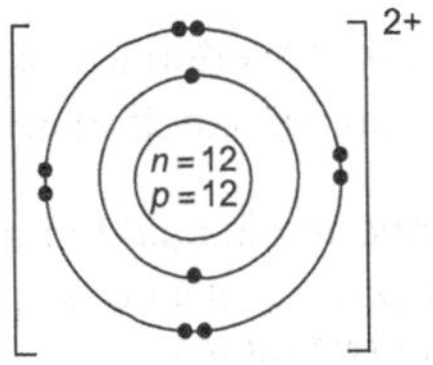

Number of protons in Mg atom = 2 + 8 + 2 = 12

Number of neutrons in Mg atom = 24 − 12 = 12

[as mass number of Mg atom = 24 and number of neutrons = mass number − number of protons]

Therefore, option (d) is the correct answer.

Q.10

Atoms	Mass number	Atomic number
A	40	20
B	7	3
C	14	7
D	16	8

Which of these atom contain 7 protons?

(a) *A* (b) *B* (c) *C* (d) *D*

Ans. (c) Proton count is equal to the atomic number of an element. Hence, **atom *C*** contains 7 protons.

Q.11 Number of valence electrons in Cl^- ion are

(a) 16 (b) 8 (c) 17 (d) 18

Ans. (b) 8 (Electronic configuration of Cl^- = 2, 8, 8).

Q.12 The picture shows the arrangement of electrons in the shells of different atoms. **(Competency Based Que.)**

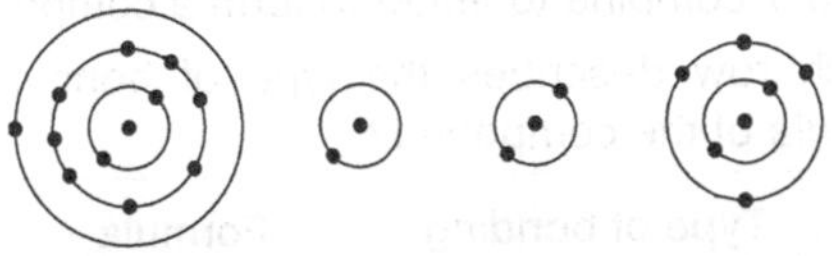

Atom 1 Atom 2 Atom 3 Atom 4

Which two atoms have the same valency?

(a) Atom 1 and atom 2 (b) Atom 2 and atom 3

(c) Atom 3 and atom 4 (d) Atom 4 and atom 1

Ans. (a) Valency of **atom 1 and atom 2** is same, i.e. **1**.

Q.13 The valency of fluorine atom is

(a) 1 (b) 2 (c) 3 (d) 0

Ans. (a) 1 (Electronic configuration of 2, 7).

Q.14 To atomic number of some elements is shown

Element	Atomic number
Beryllium (Be)	4
Oxygen (O)	8
Silicon (Si)	14
Chlorine (Cl)	17

Which elements have a valency of 2?

(a) Be and Si (b) Si and Cl

(c) Be and O (d) Cl and O

Ans. (c) Among the given elements, **Be and O** have a valency of 2. The electronic configuration of these elements are:

Be = 2, 2 O = 2, 6

Si = 2, 8, 4 Cl = 2, 8, 7

Q.15 Which statement about the isotopes of bromine is correct?

They are atoms with the same number of

(a) electrons and a different number of protons.

(b) neutrons and the same number of electrons.

(c) protons and the same chemical properties.

(d) protons and the same physical properties.

Ans. (c) Isotopes are atoms of same element which have **same number of protons** but different number of neutrons and they have **same chemical properties** but different physical properties.

Q.16 Which of the following is not an isotope of hydrogen?

(a) ${}^{1}_{1}H$ (b) ${}^{2}_{1}H$

(c) ${}^{3}_{1}H$ (d) ${}^{4}_{1}H$

Ans. (d) ${}^{4}_{1}H$

Q.17 Which isotope of hydrogen is used in making heavy water?

(a) Protium (b) Deuterium

(c) Tritium (d) Both (b) and (c)

Ans. (b) Deuterium

Q.18 Which radioactive element is used in the treatment of cancer?

(a) Iodine-131 (b) Uranium-234

(c) Plutonium-239 (d) Cobalt-60

Ans. (d) **Cobalt-60** is a radioactive element which is used in the treatment of cancer.

Q.19 Which isotopes is used in the nuclear power plants to generate electricity?

(a) Uranium-235 (b) Iodine-131

(c) Cobalt-60 (d) Uranium-238

Ans. (a) **Uranium-235** is used in the nuclear power plants to generate electricity.

Q.20 Which of the following atoms are isobars?

(a) ${}^{12}_{6}C$ and ${}^{14}_{6}C$ (b) ${}^{14}_{6}C$ and ${}^{40}_{18}Ar$

(c) ${}^{40}_{18}Ar$ and ${}^{40}_{20}Ca$ (d) ${}^{6}_{3}Li$ and ${}^{12}_{6}C$

Ans. (c) Atoms of different elements with different atomic numbers but same mass number are known as isobars. Thus, **${}^{40}_{18}Ar$ and ${}^{40}_{20}Ca$** are isobars having mass number 40.

Q.21 Which of the following is the characteristic of an electrovalent compound?

(a) It is formed by sharing of electrons.
(b) It is formed between metals and non-metals.
(c) It is formed between two non-metals.
(d) It often exists as a liquid.

Ans. (b) Since, bonds formed between metals and non-metals are ionic or electrovalent bonds therefore, electrovalent compound is formed between metals and non-metals.

Q.22 Electrovalent compounds have high melting and boiling point because

(a) the molecules have strong force of attraction.
(b) the ions are held by strong electrostatic force of attraction.
(c) the molecules easily conduct electricity.
(d) the molecules dissolve in water.

Ans. (b) The ions are held by strong electrostatic force of attraction.

Q.23 Which of the following is not a common feature of ionic bonding?

(a) Metal atoms always lose outermost shell electrons to form positive ions.
(b) Non-metals with one exception of hydrogen always gain electron to become negative ions.
(c) In both the cases, the ion formed have a more stable electronic arrangement.
(d) There is a weak force of attraction between the oppositely charged ions.

Ans. (d) Electrovalent compounds have a very **strong electrostatic force of attraction** between their ions.

Q.24 Ionic compound are generally

(a) hard solids (b) soft solids or liquids
(c) gases (d) liquid with low boiling points

Ans. (a) **Hard solids** (because of strong electrostatic force of attraction between the oppositely charged ions).

Q.25 When a metal ion gets converted to a metal atom

(a) it loses electron and get oxidised
(b) it gains electron and get reduced
(c) gain electron and get oxidised
(d) lose electron and get oxidised

Ans. (b) It **gains electron** and get **reduced**. Metal ion is a cation, when a cation gains electron, it becomes a neutral atom and gets reduced.

Q.26 Which of the following is an example of reduction reaction?

(a) Chloride ion converted to chlorine atom.
(b) Chlorine atom converted to chloride ion.
(c) Sodium atom converted to sodium ion.
(d) Aluminium atom converted to aluminium ion.

Ans. (b) Chlorine atom converted to chloride ion.

$Cl + 1e^- \longrightarrow Cl^-$ (Gain of electron is reduction)

Q.27 A covalent compound is said to be polar when

(a) the shared pair of electrons are at equal distance between the two atoms.
(b) the shared pair of electrons are not at equal distance between the two atoms.
(c) the shared pair of electrons are contributed by one of the two combining atoms.
(d) there is no sharing of electron, but transfer of electrons.

Ans. (b) The shared pair of electrons are not at equal distance between the two atoms. Polar covalent bonds are formed where there is considerably high difference in electronegativity between two non-metals so that the shared pair of electron is slightly shifted towards the stronger non-metal (i.e. towards more electronegative non-metal).

Q.28 The electronic structures of two atoms *X* and *Y* are

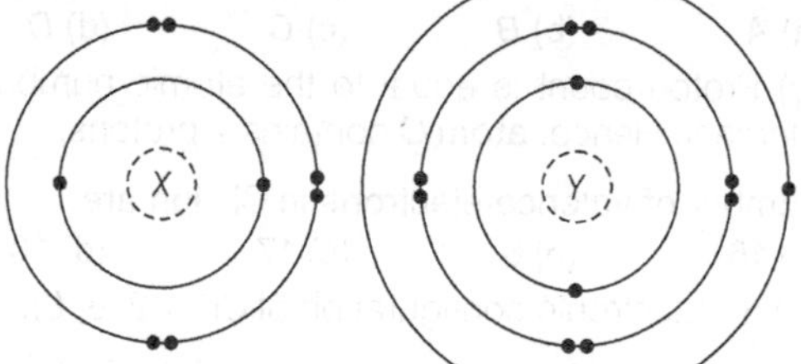

X and *Y* combine together to form a compound.

Which row describes the type of bonding and the formula of the compound?

	Type of bonding	Formula
(a)	Covalent	Y_2X
(b)	Covalent	YX_2
(c)	Ionic	Y_2X
(d)	Ionic	YX_2

Ans. (c) ***X* is a non-metal and *Y* is a metal**. Therefore, the bond formed would be **ionic**. Each atom of *X* requires 2 donated electrons from *Y* to achieve the stable octet structure. However, each atom of *Y* can only donate 1 electron. Therefore, the formula is Y_2X.

Q.29 Which of the following is an example of a polar covalent molecule?

(a) Methane
(b) Ammonia
(c) Carbon tetrachloride
(d) Sodium chloride

Ans. (b) Ammonia

Q.30 Four shared pair of electrons are present in
(a) ammonia
(b) water
(c) carbon tetrachloride
(d) all ionic compounds

Ans. (c) Carbon tetrachloride

Q.31 In the formation of carbon tetrachloride molecule, the nearest noble gas configuration, attained by carbon and chlorine respectively are
(a) argon and neon
(b) helium and neon
(c) neon and argon
(d) helium and argon

Ans. (c) Neon and argon

TYPE - 2 01 Mark

Assertion-Reason Questions

Directions (Q. Nos. 1-7) In the following questions statement are given Assertion and Reason.
(a) Both (A) and (R) are true and (R) is the correct explanation of (A).
(b) Both (A) and (R) are true but (R) is not the correct explanation of (A).
(c) (A) is true but (R) is false.
(d) (A) is false but (R) is true.

Q.1 Assertion (A) The maximum number of electrons in the second energy level (shell) of an atom is 8.

Reason (R) The number of electrons in any energy level is given by the formula $2n^2$, where n is the energy level number.

Ans. (a) Both (A) and (R) are correct and (R) is the correct explanation of (A). The formula for the maximum number of electrons in the nth shell is $2n^2$. For the second shell ($n = 2$), the maximum is $2 \times 2^2 = 8$ electrons.

Q.2 Assertion (A) Atoms of all elements, other than inert gases, combine to complete their octet.

Reason (R) Inert gases have complete outermost shell, whereas other elements have incomplete valence shell and tends to attain stable electronic configuration.

Ans. (a) Both (A) and (R) true and (R) is the correct explanation of (A).

Q.3 Assertion (A) The chlorine atom with mass number 35 undergoes same reaction as the chlorine atom with mass number 37.

Reason (B) Both chlorine 35 and chlorine 37 have same atomic number, so same electronic configuration and same valence electrons.

Ans. (a) Both (A) and (R) are true and (R) is the correct explanation of (A).

Q.4 Assertion (A) The atoms of different elements having same mass number but different atomic number are known as isobars.

Reason (R) The sum of protons and neutrons, in the isobars is always different.

Ans. (c) (A) is true but (R) is false.
As mass number is equal to the sum of number of protons and number of neutrons and mass number remains same in case of isobars.

Q.5 Assertion (A) Ionic compounds do not conduct electricity in the solid state.

Reason (R) In the solid state, the ions are held by very strong coulombic or electrostatic force of attraction.

Ans. (a) Both (A) and (R) are true and (R) is the correct explanation of (A). In the solid state, ions in ionic compounds are immobile because they are held together by strong coulombic force, so the ions are not free to move.

Q.6 Assertion (A) Electrovalent compounds are stable.

Reason (R) Electrostatic force of attraction between the oppositely charged ions is very less.

Ans. (c) (A) is true but (R) is false. Electrostatic compounds are stable as the ions of the compounds are held together by very strong electrostatic force of attraction.

Q.7 Assertion (A) In the shell diagram of ammonia (NH_3), nitrogen (N) forms three single covalent bonds with three hydrogen (H) atoms.

Reason (R) Nitrogen has five valence electrons, and it needs three more electrons to complete its octet, which it shares with three hydrogen atoms.

Ans. (a) Both (A) and (R) are true and the (R) is the correct explanation of (A). In ammonia (NH_3), nitrogen shares one electron with each of three hydrogen atoms to form three single covalent bonds. This satisfies nitrogen's need for three electrons to complete its octet.

TYPE - 3 01 Mark

Fill in the Blanks

Q.1 .... are the imaginary paths where electrons revolve around the nucleus of the atom. (Orbits, Nucleus)

Ans. Orbits

Q.2 ...... is an element with atomic number three. (Lithium, Helium)

Ans. Lithium

Q.3 The size of an atom is decided by the number of .... (electrons, protons)

Ans. electrons

Q.4 Mass number of an element is the total number of .... (electrons, protons) and neutrons present in its nucleus

Ans. protons

Q.5 First energy level can have maximum of .... electrons. (2, 4)

Ans. 2

Q.6 Maximum number of electrons occupied by *L*-shell is .... (8, 9)

Ans. 8

Q.7 Electronic configuration of neon atom is .... [(2, 8), (2, 8, 1)]

Ans. (2, 8)

Q.8 The outermost shell of an atom is called its .... (valence, incomplete) shell.

Ans. valence

Q.9 An element having atomic number 13 has valency equal to .... (3, 5)

Ans. 3

Q.10 Isotope of .... is used to determine the age of old specimens of wood. (carbon, chlorine)

Ans. carbon

Q.11 A ....element whose atom readily accepts electron(s) to form negatively charged ion, is called an electronegative element. (metallic, non-metallic).

Ans. non-metallic

Q.12 .... molecule is an example of formation of triple covalent bond between N atoms. (Ammonia, Nitrogen).

Ans. Nitrogen.

TYPE - 4 01 Mark

Correct the Incorrect Statement

Q.1 Electronic configuration refers to the distribution of electrons in same shells.

Ans. Electronic configuration refers to the distribution of electrons in **different** shells.

Q.2 The outermost shell of an atom is called its sub shell.

Ans. The outermost shell of an atom is called its **valence** shell.

Q.3 Atoms of different elements that have the same mass number but different atomic number are called isotopes.

Ans. Atoms of different elements that have the same mass number but different atomic number are called **isobars**.

Q.4 Bonds formed between metals and non-metals are coordinate or electrovalent bonds.

Ans. Bonds formed between metals and non-metals are **ionic** or electrovalent bonds.

Q.5 The double covalent bond is formed by sharing four pairs of electrons between the combining atoms.

Ans. The double covalent bond is formed by sharing **two** pairs of electrons between the combining atoms.

TYPE - 5 $01 \times 05 = 05$ Marks

Match the Columns

Q.1 Match the following columns.

Column A (Element)	Column B (Valency)
A. Magnesium	1. 4
B. Silicon	2. 2
C. Aluminium	3. 0
D. Argon	4. 1
E. Fluorine	5. 3

Ans. A → (2), B → (1), C → (5), D → (3), E→ (4).

Q.2 Match the following columns.

Column A	Column B
A. Ionic Bond	1. Sharing of electrons between atoms.
B. Covalent Bond	2. Arrangement of 8 electrons.
C. Isotope	3. A bond formed between a metal and a non-metal.
D. Electronic Configuration	4. Arrangement of electrons in shells around the nucleus.
E. Octet	5. Atoms with the same number of protons but different neutrons.

Ans. A → (3), B → (1), C → (5), D → (4), E→ (2).

TYPE - 6 01 Mark

Identify the Following

Q.1 What is the absolute charge on neutron?

Ans. 0 (zero)

Q.2 What is the magnitude of charge that an electron carries?

Ans. -1.602×10^{-19} coulombs

Q.3 Give the complete symbol isotope of carbon with 6 protons and 8 neutrons.

Ans. ${}^{14}_{6}C$

Q.4 Name the electrons present in the outermost shell of an atom

Ans. Valence electrons

Q.5 What do you call the force of attraction between two atoms that bind them together as a unit?

Ans. Chemical bond

Q.6 State the term for "The number of electrons that an atom of an element loses or gain to perform an electrovalent bond".

Ans. Electrovalency

Q.7 What is the bond formed by share pair of electrons, each bonding atom contributing one electron to the pair.

Ans. Covalent bond

Q.8 State the term for the number of electrons taking part in the formation of shared pairs of electron.

Ans. Covalency

Q.9 What is the type of covalent bond formed between two atoms, where the sharing of electron is at equal distance from the combining atoms.

Ans. Non-polar covalent bond

Q.10 Name two compounds that are covalent when taken in pure, but produce ions when dissolved in water.

Ans. Ammonia and HCl

TYPE - 7 — 02 Marks

Short Answer Type I Questions

Q.1 Write the mass number of neon and argon from the data given below.

Element	Number of protons	Number of neutrons
Neon	10	10
Argon	18	22

Ans. Mass number = Number of protons + Number of neutrons

For neon, mass number $= 10 + 10 = 20$ **(1)**

For argon, mass number $= 18 + 22 = 40$ **(1)**

Q.2 The atom of an element is made up of 4 protons, 5 neutrons and 4 electrons. What are its atomic number and mass number?

Ans. Atomic number or number of protons or number of electrons = 4 **(1)**

Mass number = Number of protons + Number of neutrons

$= 4 + 5 = 9$ **(1)**

Q.3 An ion M^{3-} contains 10 electrons and 7 neutrons. What is the atomic number and mass number of the element M? Name the element.

Ans. The number of protons in M^{3-} ion $= 10 - 3 = 7$

∴ The atomic number is 7.

Mass number = Number of protons + Number of neutrons

$= 7 + 7 = 14$ **(1)**

∴ The element is nitrogen. **(1)**

Q.4 An atom of an element has three electrons in the M shell. What is the (i) atomic number (ii) number of protons in this element?

Ans. Number of electrons in the M shell = 3

So, the number of electrons in the K and L shells will be = 2, 8.

(i) Hence, atomic number $= 2 + 8 + 3 = 13$ **(1)**

(ii) We know that, atomic number = number of protons.
Thus, number of protons = 13 **(1)**

Q.5 (i) Which element which does not contain neutron?

(ii) If an atom contains one electron and one proton, will it carry any charge or not?

Ans. (i) **Hydrogen** does not contain a neutron. **(1)**

(ii) If an atom contains one electron and one proton, it will be **neutral** in charge. **(1)**

Q.6 (i) What is the difference between Na and Na^+ in terms of number of electrons?

(ii) Consider the following few energy levels in an atom.

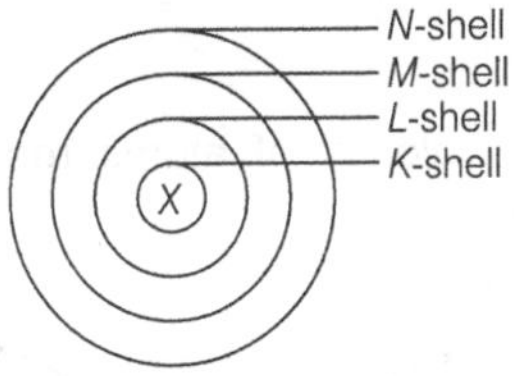

What does X represent in the atomic model?

Ans. (i) The number of electrons in Na and Na^+ are different.
It can be calculated as:

Number of electrons in Na = 11

Number of electrons in $Na^+ = 11 - 1 = 10$

[∵ In case of positive ion, number of electrons = Number of protons − Total positive charge] **(1)**

(ii) In atomic model, atom consists of positively charged nucleus around which electrons revolve in discrete orbits. Thus, X represent **nucleus**. **(1)**

Q.7 **(i) Write the name of any element whose atom has same number of sub-atomic particles. Draw the atomic structure of the atom.**

(ii) Draw atomic structure of an atom with same number of electrons in *L* and *M*-shells.

Ans. (i) Name of element: **Oxygen** ($^{16}_{8}O$)

Number of electrons = 8

Number of protons = 8

Number of neutrons = 16 – 8 = 8

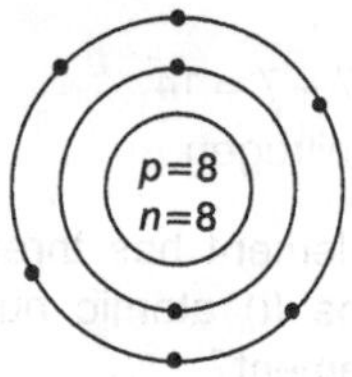

(ii) **(1)**

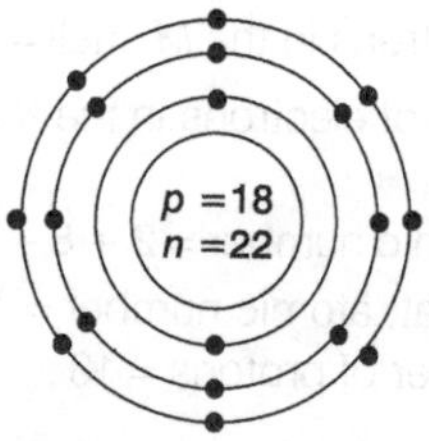

Number of electrons in *L*-shell = 8

Number of electrons in *M*-shell = 8

So, element is **argon**.

Atomic number (18) = 2 8 8 (*K L M*) **(1)**

Q.8 **Write the electronic configuration of the following:**

(i) $^{40}_{20}Ca$ (ii) $^{32}_{16}S$

Ans. (i)

K	L	M	N
2	8	8	2

(1)

(ii)

K	L	M
2	8	6

(1)

Q.9 **Find out the valency of atoms represented by the following figures.**

(i)

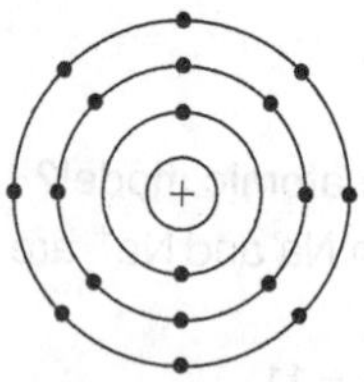

(ii)

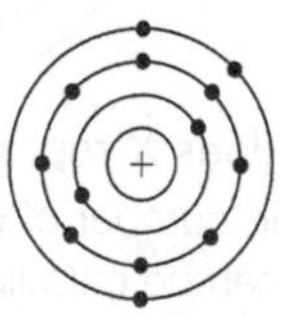

Ans. (i) Valency = 0 [∵ number of valence electrons = 8] **(1)**

(ii) Valency = 3 [∵ number of valence electrons =3] **(1)**

Q.10 **Elements *A, B, C* and *E* have atomic numbers 4, 9, 13 and 20 respectively.**

(i) Write their electronic distribution.

(ii) Determine their valency.

Ans. (i) The electronic distribution of elements *A, B, C* and *E* are given below:

	K	*L*	*M*	*N*
A (4)	2	2		
B (9)	2	7		
C (13)	2	8	3	
E (20)	2	8	8	2

(1)

(ii) As valency of an element depends on the valence shell electrons thus, for the given elements valencies are *A* = 2; *B* = (8 – 7) = 1; *C* = 3 ; *E* = 2. **(1)**

Q.11 **The atom of an element has 9 protons, 9 electrons and 10 neutrons.**

(i) What is the atomic number of the element?

(ii) Predict the valency of the element.

Ans. (i) Atomic number of elements is 9, because we know that atomic number = no. of protons or electrons. **(1)**

(ii) As its atomic number = 9

So its electronic configuration = 2, 7

It has 7 valence electrons, so the element will need 1 electron to complete its octet therefore, its valency = 1. **(1)**

Q.12 **Which of the two would be chemically more reactive: element *A* with atomic number 18 or element *D* with atomic number 16 and why?**

Ans. Electronic configuration of $_{18}A$ = 2, 8, 8

It would be chemically inert due to its complete octet.

Electronic configuration of $_{16}D$ = 2, 8, 6

To complete its octet, it will gain 2 electrons, therefore it will be more reactive. **(2)**

Q.13 **(i) What is an octet rule?**

(ii) Make a schematic atomic structure of magnesium. [Given number of protons of magnesium = 12]

Ans. (i) Tendency to have eight electrons in the outermost shell to attain stability. **(1)**

(ii) Atomic number of magnesium = 12

Atomic structure of Mg

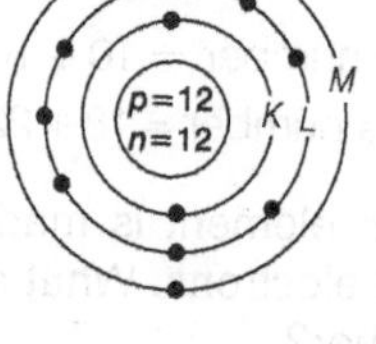

Distribution of electrons in $_{12}Mg$ = 2 8 2 (*K L M*) **(1)**

Q.14 Two elements are represented as $_{17}X^{35}$ and $_{12}Y^{24}$.

(i) How many electrons element X needs to complete its outermost shell?

(ii) What is the number of neutrons present in atom of element 'Y'?

Ans. (i) As there are 7 electrons in M-shell of its atom, which is the outermost shell (2, 8, 7).

Hence, it needs **one electron** to complete this shell. **(1)**

(ii) Element Y has mass number 24 and atomic number 12.

Number of neutrons = 24 − 12 = 12 **(1)**

Q.15 The element germanium has five naturally occurring isotopes.

An isotope of germanium is represented by the symbol shown.

$^{76}_{32}Ge$

(i) What is the meaning of the term isotopes?

(ii) Deduce the number of neutrons in one atom of this isotope of germanium.

Ans. (i) **Isotopes** are defined as atoms of the same element with equal number of protons but different numbers of neutrons. **(1)**

(ii) No. of neutrons = 76 − 32 = 44 **(1)**

Q.16 The diagram shows the atomic structure of an atom of element X.

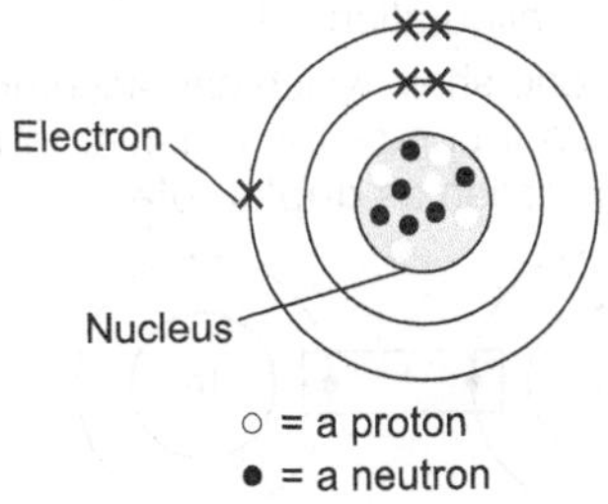

(i) Carbon-12 has the symbol $^{12}_{6}C$.

Write the symbol for an atom of element X.

(ii) Draw a shell diagram to show the atomic structure of another isotope of element X.

Ans. (i) $^{11}_{5}B$ **(1)**

(ii)

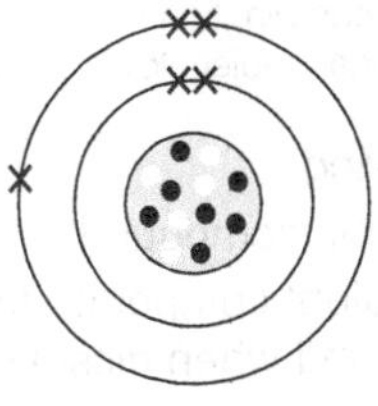

(1)

Q.17 Study the data given below and answer the questions which follow

Particle	Electrons	Protons	Neutrons
A	2	3	4
B	10	9	8
C	8	8	8
D	8	8	10

(i) Write the mass number and atomic number of particles *A, B, C, D*.

(ii) Which particles represent a pair of isotopes? Explain.

Ans. (i)

Particle	Atomic number	Mass number
A	3	3 + 4 = 7
B	9	9 + 8 = 17
C	8	8 + 8 = 16
D	8	8 + 10 = 18

(1)

(ii) **Particles *C* and *D*** represent a pair of isotopes as they have same number of protons, i.e. same atomic number but different mass number. **(1)**

Q.18 (i) Identify the pair of isotopes from the following

$^{16}_{8}X$, $^{16}_{7}X$, $^{17}_{8}X$

(ii) Write one application of isotopes in the field of medical treatment.

Ans. (i) $^{16}_{8}X$ and $^{17}_{8}X$ are isotopes as they have same atomic number, but different mass number. **(1)**

(ii) An isotope of iodine (I-131) is used in the treatment of goitre. **(1)**

Q.19 Explain fractional atomic mass. What is the fractional mass of chlorine?

Ans. The weighted average of all the naturally occurring isotopes of that element is called its **fractional atomic mass.** **(1)**

Chlorine contains 75% of $^{35}_{17}Cl$ and 25% $^{37}_{17}Cl$, i.e., these isotopes are in the ratio of 3 : 1 respectively.

Thus, average atomic mass of chlorine is calculated as $\frac{35 \times 3 + 37 \times 1}{4} = 35.5$

Therefore, atomic mass of chlorine atom is 35.5 u. **(1)**

Q.20 (i) Name the charged particles which attract one another to form ionic compounds.

(ii) In the formation of electrovalent compounds; electrons are transferred from one element to another. How are electrons involved in the formation of a covalent compounds?

Ans. (i) Cation and anion (ions) **(1)**

(ii) By mutual sharing of electrons. **(1)**

Q.21 Why ionic compounds have high boiling and melting point?

Ans. Since ionic compounds are made up of cations and anions, these oppositely charged ions are held together in a solid lattice by the strong electrostatic forces of attraction, due to this ionic compounds have high melting and boiling points. **(2)**

Q.22 Metal *M* forms a chloride with the formula *M*Cl, which is a solid with high melting point. What type of bond can seen in *M*Cl. Write the formula of the compound when *M* combines with sulphur and nitrogen.

Ans. The bond formed between a metal and a non-metal is ionic bond. Thus, the bond formed between metal *M* and chlorine is **ionic bond**. Valency of *M* is 1.

When metal *M* combines with sulphur – M_2S.

When metal *M* combines with nitrogen – M_3N **(2)**

Q.23 Ca (At. no. = 20) and oxygen (At. no. = 8) form a compound. Explain the formation of the compound on the basis of oxidation, reduction, reducing agent and oxdising agent.

Ans. Ca (20): 2, 8, 8, 2 (metal)

O (8): 2, 6 (non-metal)

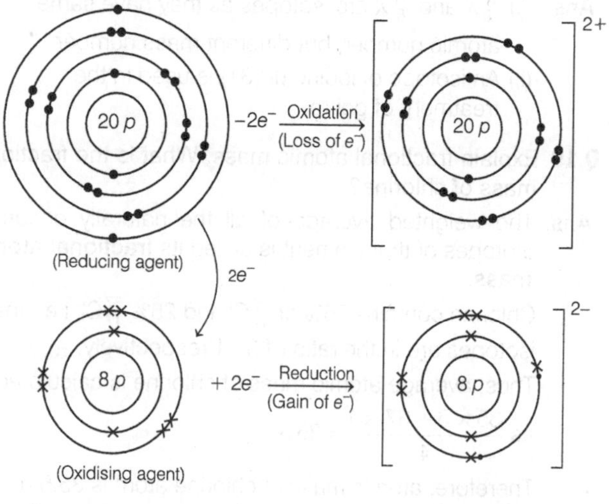

Remember that loss of electron is oxidation and element that gets oxidised is a reducing agent. Gain of electron is reduction and element that gets reduced act as an oxidising agent. **(2)**

Q.24 Element *X* has electronic configuration 2, 8, 1. Without identifying *X*,

(i) predict the sign and charge on a simple ion of *X*.

(ii) Write if *X* will be an oxidising agent or reducing agent. Why?

Ans. (i) +ve sign, i.e. X^+. **(1)**

(ii) Reducing agent, because it can easily donate its valence electron, and reduce the other element. **(1)**

Q.25 Explain, redox reaction in terms of loss and gain of electrons.

Ans. A reaction in which oxidation and reduction takes place simultaneously is known as a **redox reaction**. Oxidation involves loss of electron, whereas reduction involves gain of electron.

Let us consider formation of sodium chloride molecule. Sodium atom loses electron and form sodium cation. This is oxidation.

$$Na - 1e^- \longrightarrow Na^+$$

Chlorine atom, gains electron, and gets converted to chloride anion. This is reduction.

$$Cl + 1e^- \longrightarrow Cl^-$$

Sodium ion and chloride ion attract each other by strong electrostatic force of attraction and form NaCl molecule. **(2)**

Q.26 Explain duplet rule for the formation of hydrogen.

Ans. H (At. no. = 1)

K

Electronic configuration = 1

It has only one shell, which can accommodate only two electrons, so it completes it duplet to becomes stable and thus, is called as **duplet rule**.

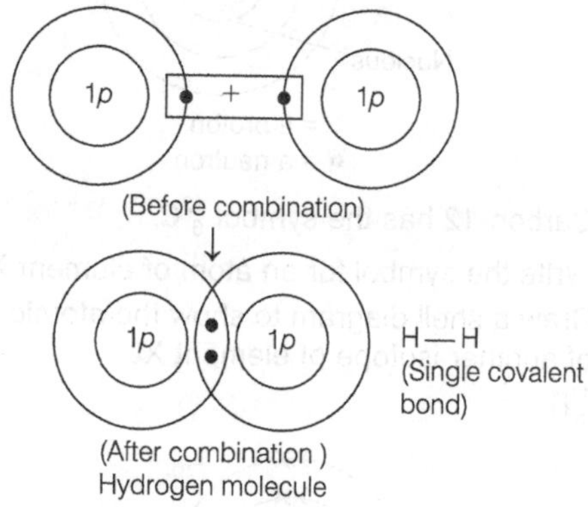

(2)

Q.27 Name the following.

(i) The most ionic compound

(ii) A polar covalent compound that behaves as an ionic compound when dissolved in water.

Ans. (i) CsF. (Cs (caesium) has the maximum tendency to lose an electron while fluorine has the maximum tendency to gain an electron). **(1)**

(ii) HCl **(1)**

TYPE - 8

03 Marks

Short Answer Type II Questions

Q.1 Complete the following table.

Symbol of element	Atomic number	Mass number	No. of neutrons	No. electrons
C	6	12	–	6
Al	–	27	–	13

Ans.

Symbol of element	Atomic number	Mass number	No. of neutrons	No. electrons
C	6	12	6	6
Al	13	27	14	13

(1 × 3 = 3)

Q.2 The electronic configuration of some elements is given below.

$X = 2, 8, 5$

$Y = 2, 8, 8, 2$

$Z = 2, 8, 1$

Identify X, Y and Z

Ans. Atomic number of $X = 2 + 8 + 5 = 15$

So, X = **Phosphorus (P)** **(1)**

Atomic number of $Y = 2 + 8 + 8 + 2 = 20$

So, Y = **Calcium (Ca)** **(1)**

Atomic number of $Z = 2 + 8 + 1 = 11$

So, Z = **Sodium (Na)** **(1)**

Q.3 A element X(2, 8, 1) and Y(2, 8, 7) were studied by a student.

(i) Out of X and Y, the element that is metal. ....

(ii) Number of electrons in element X . ...

(iii) The atomic number of element Y ......

Ans. (i) X (ii) 11 (iii) 17 **(1 × 3 = 3)**

Q.4 State the number of protons and neutrons in the nucleus of sulphur. Give a simple diagram to show the arrangement of electrons in an atom of sulphur.

Ans. Atomic number = 16

Atomic mass = 32

Number of protons = 16 **(1)**

Number of electrons = 16

Number of neutrons = 32 – 16 = 16 **(1)**

Electronic configuration = 2, 8, 6

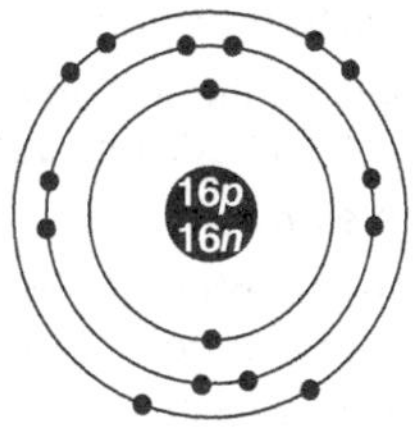

(1)

Q.5 Draw diagrams representing the atomic structures of the following.

(i) Chloride ion (ii) Carbon atom (iii) Oxide ion

Ans. (i) Chloride ion

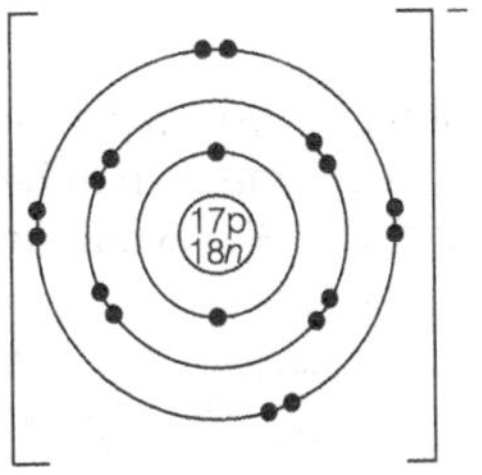

(1)

(ii) Carbon atom

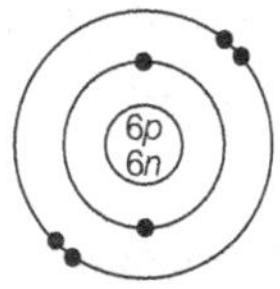

(1)

(iii) Oxide ion

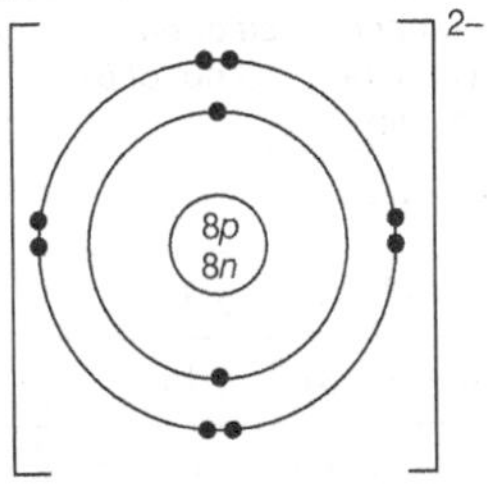

(1)

Q.6 (i) What are inert elements?

(ii) Why do inert elements exist as monoatoms in molecules?

(iii) What are valence electrons?

Ans. (i) Elements whose outermost orbital is completely filled are known as **inert elements**. **(1)**

(ii) Inert elements exist as monoatoms because they have their complete octet or duplets which makes them stable. **(1)**

(iii) Electrons present in the outermost shell are known as **valence electrons**. **(1)**

Q.7 Name or state the following.

(i) An element having valency zero.

(ii) Metal with valency two.

(iii) The shell closest to the nucleus of an atom.

Ans. (i) Helium (ii) Magnesium (iii) K shell **(1 × 3 = 3)**

Q.8 Answer the following questions.

(i) The electronic configuration of an element is 2(*K*), 8(*L*), 2(*M*). Predict its valency.

(ii) Name of the element.

(iii) Determine the number of protons and neutrons in the element. (mass no. = 24)

Ans. (i) *M*-shell has 2 electrons therefore, its valency is 2.

(ii) The element has atomic number $= 2 + 8 + 2 = 12$

$\therefore$ The element is **magnesium** (Mg).

(iii) Number of protons = Number of electrons = 12

Number of neutrons $= A - Z = 24 - 12 = 12$

(as mass number of magnesium is 24. **(1 × 3 = 3)**

Q.9 What information do you get from the figure about the atomic number, mass number and valency of atoms *X*, *Y* and *Z*? Give your answer in a tabular form.

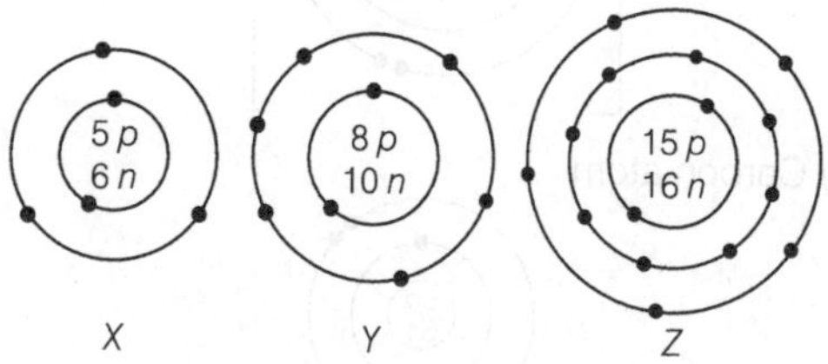

X *Y* *Z*

Ans. The tabular form is as below

Element	Atomic number (= no. of *p*)	Mass number {= no. of (*p* + *n*)}	Number of electrons (= no. of *p*)	Electronic configuration	Valency
X	5	5 + 6 = 11	5	2, 3	3
Y	8	8 + 10 = 18	8	2, 6	2
Z	15	15 + 16 = 31	15	2, 8, 5	3, 5

(1 × 3 = 3)

Q.10 Elements *X*, *Y* and *Z* have atomic numbers 6, 9 and 12 respectively. Which one:

(i) forms an anion

(ii) forms a cation

(iii) has four electrons in its valence shell?

Ans. It is given that the atomic number of *X*, *Y* and *Z* are 6, 9 and 12 respectively

So, electronic configuration of *X*, *Y* and *Z* are

$X = K \quad L$
$\quad\;\; 2 \quad 4$

$Y = K \quad L$
$\quad\;\; 2 \quad 7$

$Z = K \quad L \quad M$
$\quad\;\; 2 \quad 8 \quad 2$

Hence

(i) *Y* forms anion. **(1)**

(ii) *Z* forms cation. **(1)**

(iii) *X* has 4 valence electrons. **(1)**

Q.11 Answer the following questions.

(i) What is the number of electrons in Cl^- ion? (Cl = 17)

(ii) What is the electronic configuration of sodium? (Na = 11)

(iii) Which isotope of uranium is used in nuclear fuel?

Ans. (i) Cl^- ion, 17 + 1 (gained) = 18 electrons (because negative charge shows gain of electrons.) **(1)**

(ii) Atomic number of sodium = 11

K L M

Electronic configuration = 2 8 1 **(1)**

(iii) Uranium-235 isotope. **(1)**

Q.12 The diagram shows the **nuclei** of five different atoms.

key

○ Neutron

● Proton

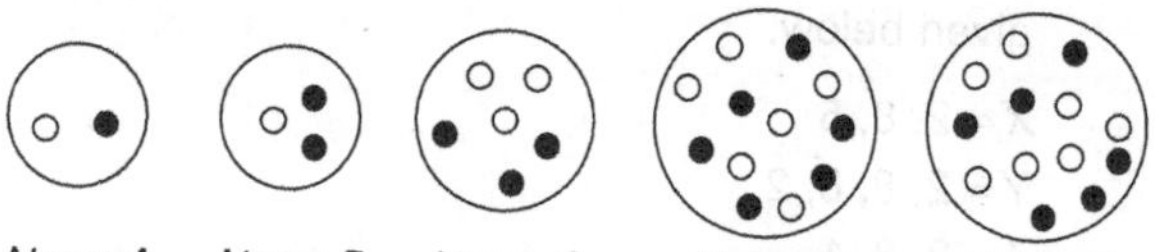

Atoms *A* Atoms *B* Atoms *C* Atoms *D* Atoms *E*

(i) Which atom has an atomic number of 3?

(ii) Which atom has a mass number of 6?

(iii) Which two atoms are isotopes of the same element?

Ans. (i) Atom *C*.

(ii) Atom *C*.

(iii) Atom *D* and Atom *E* (have same no. of *p*). **(1 × 3 = 3)**

Q.13 (i) Identify which of the following pairs are isotopes and which are isobars? Give reasons for your choice.

$$^{58}A_{26},\ ^{58}B_{28},\ ^{79}X_{35},\ ^{80}Y_{35}$$

(ii) Do isobars also have identical chemical properties like isotopes? State reason.

Ans. (i) ***A* and *B* are isobars** as they are atoms of different elements having the same mass number.

***X* and *Y* are isotopes** as they are atoms of same element having same atomic number but different mass numbers. **(2)**

(ii) **No**, isobars do not have identical chemical properties because they have different atomic numbers as well as different electronic configurations. **(1)**

Q.14 Elements from A to F have the distribution of electrons, protons and neutrons in the following way.

Atom/Ion	Number of electrons	Number of protons	Number of neutrons
A	4	3	4
B	10	11	12
C	17	17	18
D	17	17	20
E	18	18	22
F	19	19	21

From the table, find

(i) a pair of ions.

(ii) a pair of isobars.

(iii) a pair of isotopes.

Ans. (i) ***A* and *B***, because number of electrons and protons are different for these elements. **(1)**

(ii) ***E* and *F***, because these have same mass number (number of protons + number of neutrons) but different atomic number. **(1)**

(iii) ***C* and *D***, because these have same atomic number (number of protons) but different mass number. **(1)**

Q.15 The atomic species X and Y have different number of protons but the same number of nucleons. While atoms A and B have the same number of protons but different number of nucleons.

(i) Which of them are

(a) isotopes

(b) isobars

(ii) Give one example of each.

Ans. (i) (a) ***A* and *B* are isotopes**, as they have same atomic number but different mass number.

(b) ***X* and *Y* are isobars**, as they have same mass number but different atomic number. **(2)**

(ii) Example of isotopes : $^{35}_{17}Cl$ and $^{37}_{17}Cl$

Example of Isobars : $^{40}_{18}Ar$ and $^{40}_{20}Ca$ **(1)**

Q.16 Draw an appropriate orbit structure and show bond formation between sodium and chlorine, and state the type of bond present in it.

Ans. Electronic configuration of sodium (Na)= 2, 8, 1 (metal)

Electronic configuration of chlorine (Cl) = 2, 8, 7 (non-metal)

So, the bond formed between them is **electrovalent**.

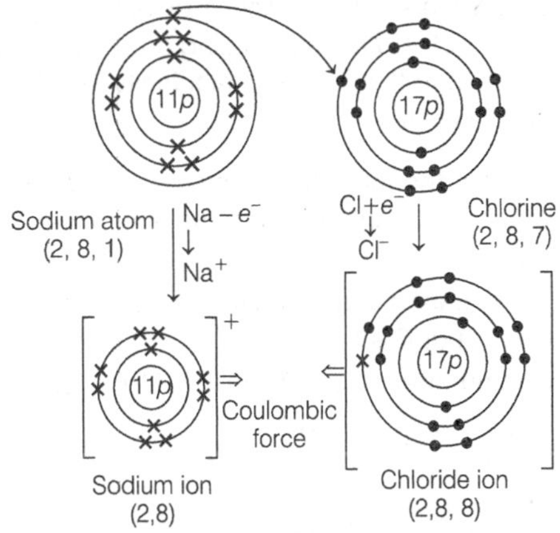

The above two oppositely charged ions are held together by **electrovalent bond or ionic bond.** **(3)**

Q.17 The structure of sodium chloride and chlorine are shown below.

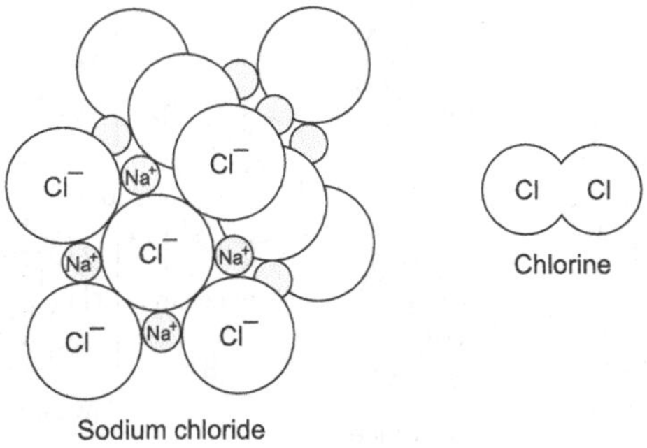

(i) The melting point of sodium chloride is 801°C.

The melting point of chlorine is −101°C.

Explain, in terms of structure and bonding, the difference between the melting points of these two substances.

(ii) Explain why molten sodium chloride conducts electricity but solid sodium chloride does not.

(iii) State some important properties of electrovalent compounds.

Ans. (i) Sodium chloride is an ionic compound with strong electrostatic forces of attraction between the oppositely charged ions. Chlorine has a simple covalent structure, with weak van der Waal's forces of attraction between molecules. Hence the melting point of sodium chloride is much higher than that for chlorine. **(1)**

(ii) In solid NaCl, the ions are not free to move as they are held by strong electrostatic force of attraction, whereas in molten form, ions are free to move. **(1)**

(iii) Electrovalent compounds are hard, brittle, crystalline solids consisting of ions. They are non-volatile, with high boiling and high melting points and they conduct electricity in fused or in aqueous state. **(1)**

Q.18 (i) Explain the formation of calcium oxide and magnesium chloride with the help of orbit diagram.

(ii) Give reason why formula of calcium oxide is not Ca_2O_2 but CaO.

(Atomic number : Ca = 20, O = 8, Mg = 12, Cl = 17)

Ans. (i) $\underset{\text{(2, 8, 2) atom}}{Mg} - 2e^- \longrightarrow \underset{\text{(2, 8) cation}}{Mg^{2+}}$

$\underset{\text{(2, 8, 7) 2Cl atoms}}{2Cl} + 2e^- \longrightarrow \underset{\text{(2, 8, 8) 2 chloride anions}}{2Cl^-}$

Orbit structure of formation of magnesium chloride ($MgCl_2$).

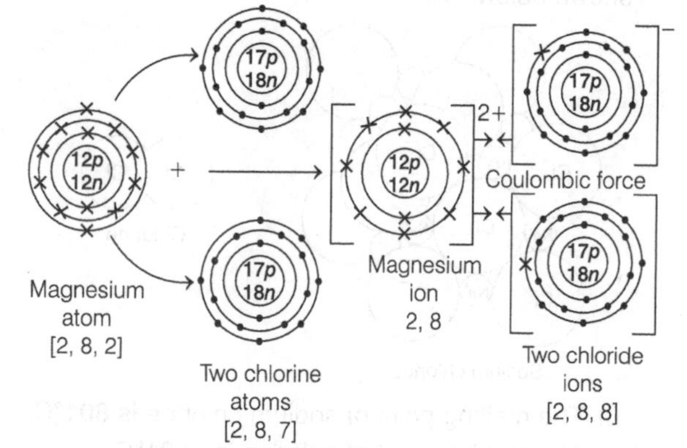

$\underset{\text{(2, 8, 8, 2) atoms}}{Ca} - 2e^- \longrightarrow \underset{\text{(2, 8, 8) cation}}{Ca^{2+}}$ and $\underset{\text{(2, 6) atom}}{O} + 2e^- \longrightarrow \underset{\text{(2, 8) anion}}{O^{2-}}$

Orbit structure of formation of calcium oxide (CaO).

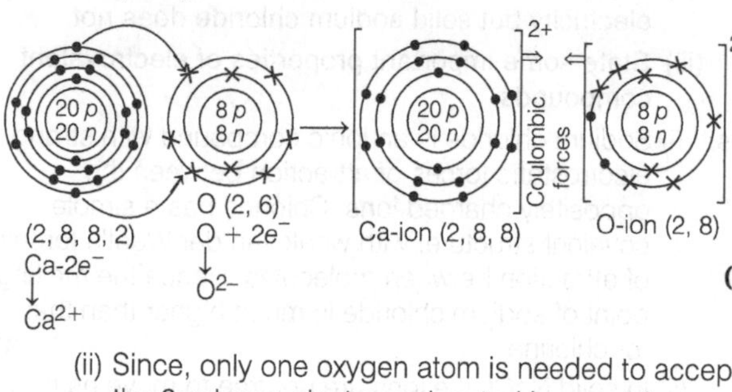

(2)

(ii) Since, only one oxygen atom is needed to accept the 2 valence electrons donated by a calcium atom thus, the formula of calcium oxide is CaO and not Ca_2O_2. **(1)**

TYPE - 9 — 04/05 Marks

Long Answer Type Questions

Q.1 Choose from the following particles given in the box to answer the questions below.

$^{8}_{4}Be$, $^{14}_{6}C$, $^{40}_{20}Ca$, $^{37}_{17}Cl^-$, $^{39}_{19}K^-$, $^{24}_{12}Mg^{2+}$, $^{20}_{10}Ne$, $^{17}_{8}O$, $^{16}_{8}O^{2-}$, $^{32}_{16}S^{2-}$, $^{28}_{17}Si^{4-}$

Each particle can be used once, more than once or not at all.

Which particle

(i) has only eight electrons

(ii) has only four electrons in its outer shell

(iii) has only eight neutrons

(iv) has only ten protons

Ans. (i) $^{17}_{8}O$ (ii) $^{14}_{6}C$ (iii) $^{16}_{8}O^{2-}$ (iv) $^{20}_{10}Ne$ **(1 × 4 = 4)**

Q.2 Complete the table given below by identifying *P*, *Q*, *R* and *S*.

Element	Symbol	No. of Protons	No. of Neutrons	No. of Electrons
Sodium	$^{23}_{11}Na$	11	*P*	11
Chlorine	$^{35}_{17}Cl$	*Q*	18	17
Uranium	R	92	146	92
S	$^{19}_{9}F$	9	10	9

Ans. *P* = 12, *Q* = 17, *R* = $^{238}_{92}U$, *S* = Fluorine **(1 × 4 = 4)**

Q.3 How are the electrons distributed in different orbits (shells)?

Ans. The electrons are distributed in different orbits in the following ways.

(i) The maximum number of electrons present in a shell is given by the formula $2n^2$, where *n* is the orbit number or energy level, 1, 2, 3...... .

Therefore, the maximum number of electrons in different shells are as follows

First orbit or *K*-shell = $2 \times 1^2 = 2$

Second orbit or *L*-shell = $2 \times 2^2 = 8$

Third orbit or *M*-shell = $2 \times 3^2 = 18$

Fourth orbit or *N*-shell = $2 \times 4^2 = 32$ and so on.

(ii) The maximum number of electrons that can be accommodated in the outermost orbit is 8.

(iii) The penultimate shell (i.e. the second last shell) cannot accommodate more than 18 electrons.
The anti-penultimate shell (i.e. the third last shell) can have a maximum of 32 electrons.

(iv) Electrons are not accommodated in a given shell, unless the inner shells are filled, i.e. the shells are filled in a stepwise manner. **$(1 \times 4 = 4)$**

Q.4 Match the atomic numbers 4, 8, 10, 15 and 19 with each of the following:
(i) Element which can form trivalent ion.
(ii) An element with 4 shells.
(iii) Element with 6 valence electrons.
(iv) Element which does not form an ion.

Ans. (i) Electronic configuration of an element with atomic number 15 is [2,8, 5], hence, it needs three electrons to complete its octet and forms a trivalent ion. **(1)**
(ii) Electronic configuration of an element with atomic number 19 is [2, 8, 8, 1], hence, it has *K, L, M, N* shells. **(1)**
(iii) Electronic configuration of an element with atomic number 8 is [2, 6], hence it has 6 electrons in the outermost shell called valence electrons. **(1)**
(iv) Electronic configuration of an element with atomic number 10 is [2, 8], so its octet is complete and it does not form ions. **(1)**

Q.5 A metal (mass number = 40) having same number of protons and neutrons, combines with two chlorine atoms. Identify the element with which the outer electronic configuration of this metal matches after it forms bond.

Ans. As, mass number = Number of protons + Number of neutrons

$\Rightarrow 40 = 2 \times$ number of protons
$\Rightarrow$ Number of protons = 20 **(1)**
Hence, the metal is **calcium (Ca)**. **(1)**
Since, it combines with 2 Cl-atoms ($\therefore$ total valency = 2)
Hence, it will acquire 2 positive charge, after losing 2 electrons. **(1)**

Electronic configuration of Ca^{2+} ion = $\overset{K}{2}\ \overset{L}{8}\ \overset{M}{8}$

This electronic configuration matches to that of **argon (Ar)**. **(1)**

Q.6 The electronic configurations of five atoms are shown.

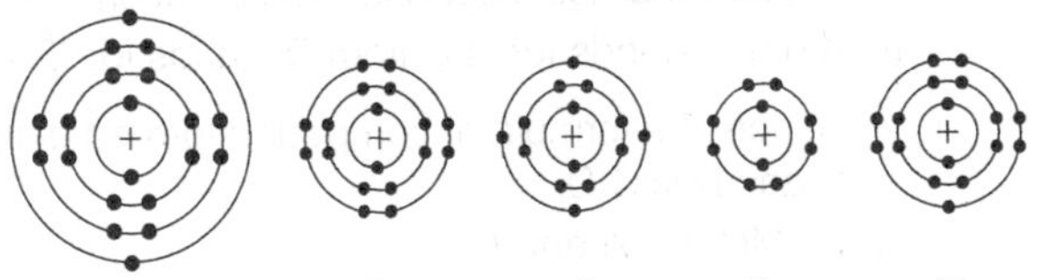

A *B* *C* *D* *E*

Which electronic configuration represents each of the following descriptions?
Each electronic configuration may be used once, more than once or not at all.
(i) A sulphur atom.
(ii) An atom with 14 proton.
(iii) An atom of a noble gas with three occupied electron shells.
(iv) An atom which will form a noble gas electronic configuration after losing two electrons.

Ans. (i) *E* (ii) *C* (iii) *B* (iv) *A* **$(1 \times 4 = 4)$**

Q.7 Write down the electronic configuration of first four elements in the periodic table, and also mention their outermost energy level.

Ans. (i) Hydrogen, atomic number = 1
Outermost shell is *K*.
Electronic configuration = 1
(ii) Helium, atomic number = 2
Outermost shell is *K*.
Electronic configuration = 2
(iii) Lithium, atomic number = 3
Outermost shell is *L*.
Electronic configuration = 2, 1
(iv) Beryllium, atomic number = 4
Outermost shell is *L*.
Electronic configuration = 2, 2 **$(1 \times 4 = 4)$**

Q.8 Explain the following:
(i) Mass of an atom is concentrated inside the nucleus of the atom.
(ii) Atoms combine by transfer and sharing of electron(s).
(iii) An element has atoms with different mass number.
(iv) Carbon-12 and carbon-14 both show similar chemical properties.

Ans. (i) Atom is made of primarily three sub-atomic particles namely electrons, protons and neutrons.
An electron has negligible mass, and protons and neutron lies inside the nucleus, hence, mass of an atom is majorly present in the nucleus. **(1)**
(ii) Elements tend to combine with one another to attain the stable electronic configuration of the nearest noble gas. This is achieved either by gaining electrons or losing electrons or sharing of electrons with other atoms of the same element or another element to form a chemical compound. **(1)**
(iii) Due to the presence of different number of neutrons in the nucleus. **(1)**
(iv) $^{12}_{6}C$ and $^{14}_{6}C$ have same atomic number so they have same electronic configuration. Thus, they have same valency and same chemical properties. **(1)**

Q.9 **Draw the shell diagram to show formation of**

(i) **polar covalent liquid.**

(ii) **non-polar covalent liquid.**

(iii) **a green house gas containing C.**

(iv) **a basic gas.**

Ans. (i) Polar covalent liquid = H_2O

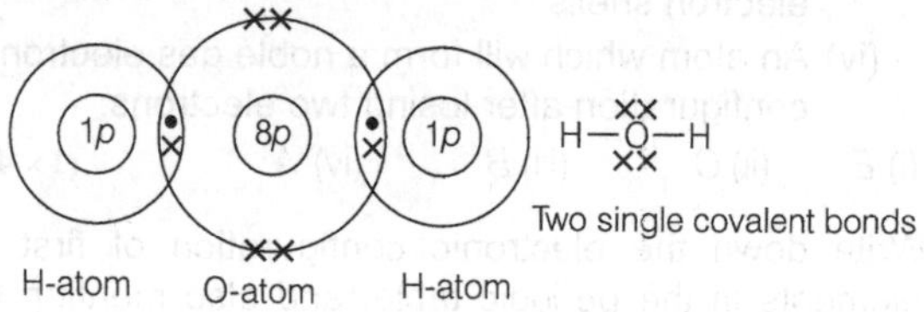

(ii) Non-polar covalent liquid = CCl_4

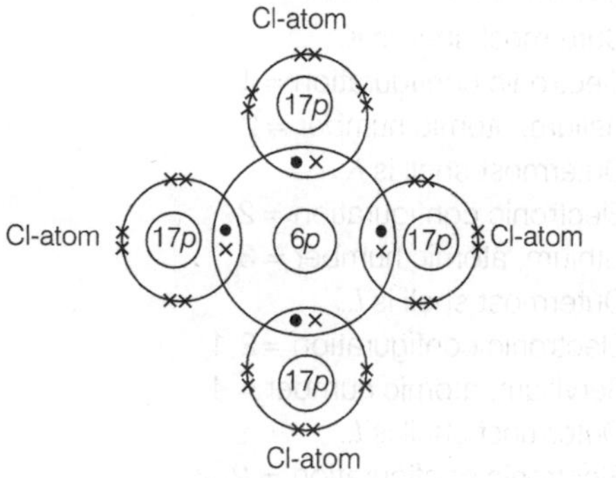

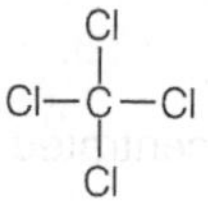

Four single covalent bonds

(iii) A green house gas containing carbon (C) is methane.

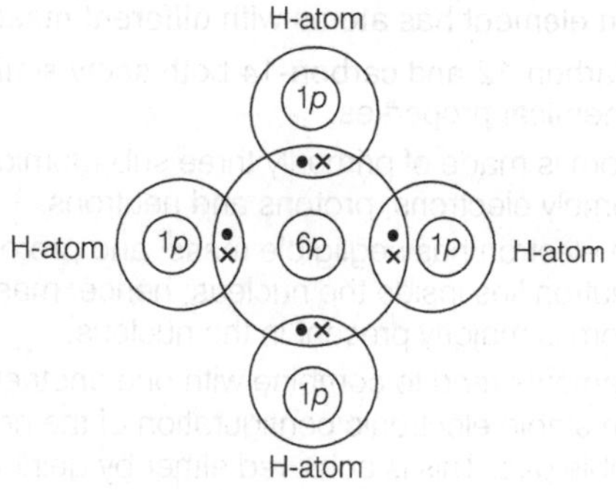

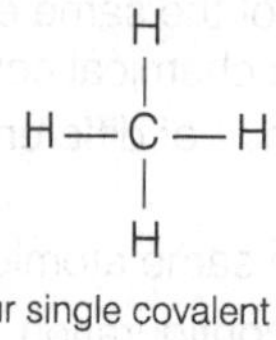

(Four single covalent bonds)

(iv) A basic gas is NH_3 (ammonia)

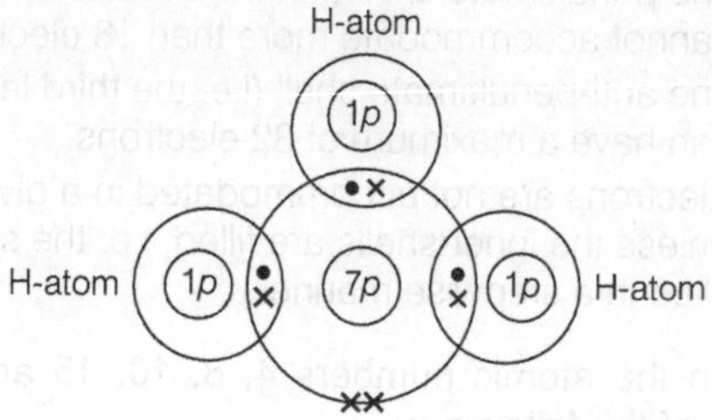

Three single covalent bond

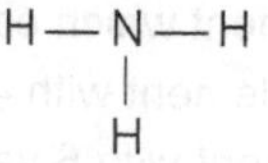

(1 × 4 = 4)

Q.10 **An atom of an element *Y* may be written as ^9_4Y.**

(i) **What does the figure 9 indicate?**

(ii) **What does the figure 4 indicate?**

(iii) **What is the number of protons in atom *Y*?**

(iv) **What is the number of neutrons in atom *Y*?**

(v) **How many electrons are there in the outermost shell of an atom of element *Y*?**

Ans. (i) Mass number (ii) Atomic number

(iii) 4 protons (iv) 5 Neutrons

(v) Electronic configuration, $\underset{2}{K}\ \underset{2}{L}$

So, number of electrons in outermost shell = 2

(1 × 5 = 5)

Q.11 **Five atoms are labelled *A* to *E*.**

Atoms	Mass No.	Atomic No.
A	40	20
B	19	9
C	7	3
D	16	8
E	14	7

(i) **Which one of these atoms**

(a) **contains 7 protons?**

(b) **has electronic configuration 2, 7?**

(ii) **Write down the formula of the compound formed between *C* and *D*.**

(iii) **Predict : (a) metals (b) non-metals.**

Ans. (i) (a) **Atom *E*** contains 7 protons.

(b) **Atom *B*** has electronic configuration 2, 7. **(2)**

(ii) Atom *C* stands for ^7_3Li, atom *D* stands for $^{16}_8O$.

Hence, the formula of compound formed between *C* and *D* is C_2D. **(1)**

(iii) (a) Metals : ***A* and *C***

(b) Non-metals : ***B*, *D* and *E***. **(2)**

Q.12 In the figure given below :

(i) (a) Name the shells denoted by *A, B* and *C*.

(b) Which shell has least energy?

(ii) (a) Name *X* represented in the figure.

(b) State the charge on it.

(iii) Total number of electrons that can be filled in shell *A*.

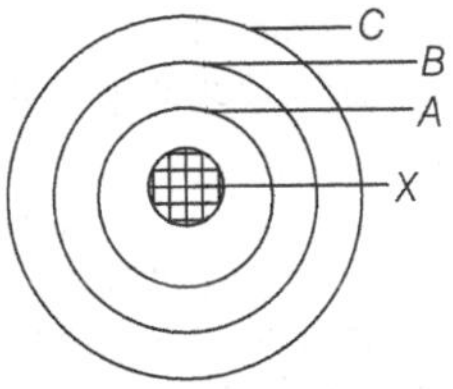

Ans. (i)(a) The shells denoted by

A = *K* shell

B = *L* shell

C = *M* shell

(b) The orbit closest to nucleus is ***K* shell** and it has least amount of energy. **(2)**

(ii) (a) 'X' is **nucleus**.

(b) It has **positive charge** on it. **(2)**

(iii) 2 electrons. **(1)**

Q.13 Give examples for each of the following.

(i) The element which has no neutron in its nucleus.

(ii) Element with 'Zero' valency.

(iii) Metal with valency 1.

(iv) Atoms of same element with same number of electrons and protons but with different number of neutrons.

(v) The shell closest to the nucleus of an atom.

Ans. (i) Hydrogen

(ii) Helium/Neon/Argon

(iii) Sodium/potassium

(iv) Protium/deuterium/tritium

(v) *K* shell **(1 × 5 = 5)**

Q.14 Match the atomic numbers 4, 6, 11,15 and 18 with each of the following:

(i) A solid non-metal of valency 3.

(ii) A gas having zero valency.

(iii) An element with 2 electrons in the valence shell.

(iv) A non-metal of valency 4.

(v) A metal with one electron in the third shell.

Ans. Atomic number

(i) 15 (ii) 18

(iii) 4 (iv) 6

(v) 11 **(1 × 5 = 5)**

Q.15 The atom of an element *A* has 6 electrons in its *M* shell.

(i) Write the electronic configuration of element *A*.

(ii) What is the atomic number of element *A* ?

(iii) Is it a metal or a non-metal ?

(iv) What type of ion will be formed by an atom of element *A* ? Write the symbol of the ion formed.

(v) What could element *A* be ?

Ans. (i) Electronic configuration of element *A*

$$\underset{2}{K}\ \underset{8}{L}\ \underset{6}{M}$$

(ii) Atomic number = 16

(iii) Non-metal

(iv) Anion i.e. A^{2-}

(v) Sulphur **(1 × 5 = 5)**

Q.16 In what respect do the three isotopes of hydrogen differ? Give their structures.

Ans. The three isotopes of hydrogen differ only in the number of neutrons.

Hydrogen has three isotopes. They are protium ${}^1_1H$, deuterium ${}^2_1D$ and tritium ${}^3_1T$. All the three have same atomic number 1, but different mass number that is 1, 2, 3 respectively. **(2)**

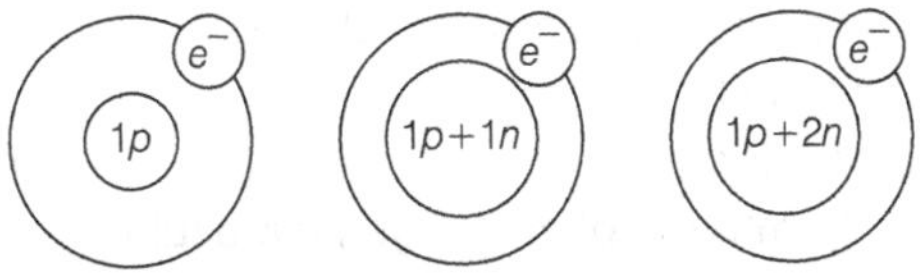

(3)

Q.17 (i) What is the average atomic mass of bromine if it has 49.7% ${}^{79}_{35}Br$ and 50.3% ${}^{81}_{35}Br$?

(ii) A sample of an element *A* contains two isotopes ${}^{16}_{8}A$ and ${}^{18}_{8}A$. If the average atomic mass of the element is 16.2 amu, calculate the percentage of the two isotopes in this sample.

Ans. (i) Average atomic mass of Br = [Atomic mass of ${}^{79}_{35}Br$ × percentage + Atomic mass of ${}^{81}_{35}Br$ × percentage]/100

$$= \frac{[79 \times 49.7 + 81 \times 50.3]}{100}$$

= 80.006 u

The correct answer = 80.006 u **(2)**

(ii) The mass of ${}^{16}_{8}X$ isotope is 16 u. Suppose its percentage in the sample is x%.

The mass of ${}^{18}_{8}X$ isotope is 18 u. Its percentage in the sample will be (100 – *x*)%.

So, Average atomic mass of *A*

$$= \frac{\%_1 \times m_1 + \%_2 \times m_2}{100}$$

$$16.2 = \frac{x \times 16 + 18(100 - x)}{100}$$

or $16.2 = \frac{16x + 1800 - 18x}{100}$

or $16.2 \times 100 = 1800 - 2x$

or $2x = 1800 - 1620$

or $2x = 180$

and $x = \frac{180}{2}$

or $x = 90$

Thus, the percentage of isotope ${}^{16}_{8}X$ in the sample is 90%. The percentage of the other isotope ${}^{18}_{8}X$ in the sample will be

100 − 90 = 10%. **(3)**

Q.18 In the formation of oxygen molecule state the following:

(i) Electronic configuration of nearest inert gas attained.

(ii) How many electrons are shared/transferred in bond formation?

(iii) Which type of bonds these compounds form?

(iv) Draw their orbital diagrams.

Ans. In the formation of oxygen molecule:

(i) Neon (10): 2, 8

(ii) Two pairs of electrons are shared.

(iii) Covalent bond.

(iv) Orbital Diagram: **(1 × 4 = 4)**

Formation of an oxygen molecule

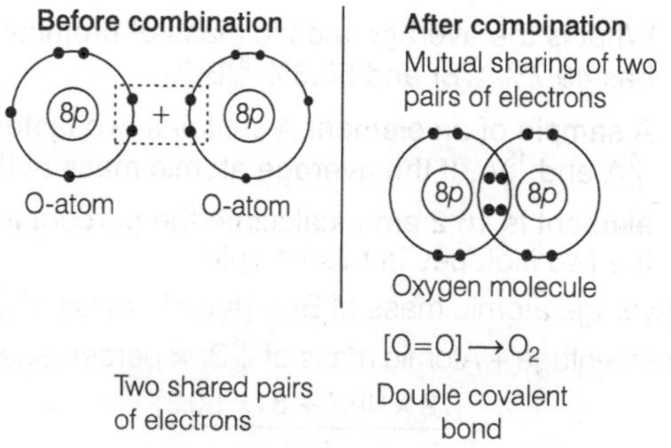

(1)

Q.19 State the type of bonding in the following molecules.

(i) Water

(ii) Magnesium oxide

(iii) Hydrogen chloride

(iv) Sodium chloride

(v) Ammonia

Ans. (i) Polar covalent bond

(ii) Electrovalent bond

(iii) Polar covalent bond

(iv) Electrovalent bond

(v) Polar covalent bond **(1 × 5 = 5)**

Q.20 Give a suitable reason for the following assertion:

(i) Shells are called energy levels.

(ii) Metals act as good reducing agents.

(iii) Isotopes have same chemical properties, but different physical properties.

(iv) Formation of an electrovalent bond is an example of a redox reaction.

(v) Sodium chloride is an electrovalent compound while hydrogen chloride is a covalent compound but both conduct electricity in their aqueous solutions.

Ans. (i) Shells are called energy levels because they are associated with a fixed amount of energy.

(ii) Because metals have a tendency to lose electrons and get oxidised, therefore, they reduce the other element and act as reducing agent.

(iii) Isotopes have same atomic number, therefore, similar electronic configuration and same valency due to same valence electrons. They have same chemical properties. But isotopes have different number of neutrons and different mass numbers due to which their physical properties are different.

(iv) Electrovalent bond formation involves oxidation of a metal atom to form cation and reduction of a non-metal to form anion. Therefore, it is an example of a redox reaction.

(v) Sodium chloride is an electrovalent compound, so it has free ions in aqueous solution due to which it conducts electricity. Hydrogen chloride is a polar covalent compound, when added to water, it forms hydrogen ions and chloride ions which are free to conduct electricity. **(1 × 5 = 5)**

TYPE - 10   03 Marks

Case Based Questions

Q.1 Sanjay and Priya were studying two different elements, Carbon (C) and Neon (Ne), in their chemistry class. Sanjay learnt that carbon has an atomic number of 6 and a mass number of 12, while neon has an atomic number of 10 and a mass number of 20.

(i) What is the difference between the atomic number and the mass number of an element?

(ii) How many protons, neutrons and electrons are there in a carbon atom?

(iii) How many protons, neutrons, and electrons are there in a neon atom?

Ans. (i) The atomic number of an element represents the number of protons in the nucleus of an atom. It also determines the element's identity and its position in the periodic table.

The mass number is the sum of the protons and neutrons in an atom's nucleus. It represents the approximate mass of an atom.

(ii) For Carbon (C):

Protons = Atomic number = 6

Since Carbon is neutral,

the number of electrons = number of protons = 6

Neutrons = Mass number – Atomic number

$= 12 - 6 = 6$

Therefore, **carbon has 6 protons, 6 neutrons and 6 electrons**.

(iii) For Neon (Ne):

Protons = Atomic number = 10

Since Neon is neutral,

the number of electrons = number of protons = 10

Neutrons = Mass number – Atomic number

$= 20 - 10 = 10$

Therefore, **neon has 10 protons, 10 neutrons and 10 electrons**. **(1 × 3 = 3)**

Q.2 Ram and Krish are both conducting an experiment in their chemistry lab. Ram is studying magnesium (Mg), which is an alkaline earth metal, and Krish is studying oxygen (O), a non-metal. They are trying to understand how these two elements form compounds by chemical bonding.

Ram knows that magnesium has the atomic number 12 and has the electronic configuration 2, 8, 2. Krish, on the other hand, knows that oxygen has the atomic number 8 and the electronic configuration 2, 6. Both are curious about how these elements form stable compounds.

(i) Which element will lose electrons to achieve a stable electronic configuration?

(ii) What type of bond is formed between magnesium and oxygen when they react?

(iii) What will be the formula of the compound formed between magnesium and oxygen?

Ans. (i) **Magnesium (Mg)** will lose electrons to achieve a stable electronic configuration.

Magnesium has 2 electrons in its outermost shell (configuration: 2, 8, 2). To achieve the stable configuration of the nearest noble gas, neon (2, 8), magnesium loses 2 electrons.

This results in the formation of a Mg^{2+} ion.

(ii) An **ionic bond** is formed between magnesium (Mg) and oxygen (O). Magnesium (Mg) loses 2 electrons to form a Mg^{2+} ion, and oxygen (O) gains 2 electrons to form an O^{2-} ion.

The oppositely charged ions (Mg^{2+} and O^{2-}) are strongly attracted to each other by electrostatic forces, resulting in the formation of an ionic bond.

(iii) The formula of the compound formed between magnesium and oxygen is **MgO**.

Magnesium forms a Mg^{2+} ion, and oxygen forms an O^{2-} ion. Since both ions have the same charge magnitude (2+ and 2–), one ion of magnesium will combine with one ion of oxygen to form the neutral compound magnesium oxide (MgO). **(1 × 3 = 3)**

Q.3 In a chemistry class, the students were studying different elements and their atomic structures. Saanvi learned about isotopes when she came across two forms of Hydrogen (H): Hydrogen-1 (Protium) and Hydrogen-2 (Deuterium).

Aryan, meanwhile, studied isobars. He had learnt that calcium-40 (Ca-40) and argon-40 (Ar-40) are examples of isobars.

(i) What are isotopes? Give one example other than given in the case.

(ii) Define isobars. Give one example other than given in the case.

(iii) Why is the concept of isotopes important in understanding atomic mass?

Ans. (i) Isotopes are atoms of the same element that have the same number of protons but a different number of neutrons, resulting in different mass numbers.

Example: Carbon-12 and Carbon-14 are isotopes of carbon.

(ii) Isobars are atoms of different elements that have the same mass number but different atomic numbers (different numbers of protons).

e.g. ${}^{54}_{24}Cr$ and ${}^{54}_{26}Fe$ are isobars.

(iii) The concept of isotopes is important in understanding atomic mass because the atomic mass of an element is a weighted average of the masses of its isotopes, considering their relative abundances. Different isotopes of the same element contribute to the overall atomic mass. **(1 × 3 = 3)**

THE PERIODIC TABLE

There are 118 elements known at present, out of which 98 are naturally occurring. To study the properties of all these elements separately, the elements having similar properties are grouped together.

Dobereiner's Triads (1817)

- He classified elements with similar chemical properties in the increasing order of atomic mass into groups of three elements each called **triads**.
- When elements in the triads were arranged in increasing order of atomic mass, the atomic mass of the middle element was approximately equal to the arithmetic mean (average) of the atomic masses of the other two elements of that triad.

e.g.										
Elements	**Li**	**Na**	**K**	**Cl**	**Br**	**I**	**Ca**	**Sr**	**Ba**
Atomic mass	7	23	39	35.5	80	127	40	88	137
Average atomic mass of first and third elements	$\frac{7+39}{2}=23$			$\frac{35.5+127}{2}=81.25$			$\frac{40+137}{2}=88.5$		

Limitation

- Dobereiner could not arrange all the known elements in the form of triads.
- The law did not fully apply even within the same family. e.g. Halogen family-Fluorine (19), Chlorine (35.5) and Bromine (80), the atomic mass of chlorine was much lower than the arithmetic mean of 19 and 80.

Newlands' Law of Octaves (1866)

John Newlands arranged the known elements in the order of increasing atomic masses and found that every eighth element had properties similar to that of the first element, just as the eight note of a musical octave is the same as its first note.

Newlands' Octaves

sa (do)	**re** (re)	**ga** (me)	**ma** (fa)	**pa** (so)	**dha** (la)	**nee** (ti)
H	Li	Be	B	C	N	O
F	Na	Mg	Al	Si	P	S
Cl	K	Ca	Cr	Ti	Mn	Fe
Co and Ni	Cu	Zn	Y	In	As	Se
Br	Rb	Sr	Ce and La	Zr	–	–

Limitations

- This law was applicable only upto calcium.
- This classification did not work with heavier elements.
- In order to fit elements into his table. Newlands' adjusted two elements in the same slot and also put some unlike elements under the same column.

  e.g. Cobalt and nickel are in the same slot and these are placed in the same column as fluorine, chlorine and bromine which have very different properties than these elements.

Mendeleev's Periodic Table

- He arranged 63 elements (known at that time) in the increasing order of their **atomic masses** and found that the elements with similar properties occur at regular intervals.
- **Mendeleev's periodic law** states that "physical and chemical properties of elements are a periodic function of their atomic masses".

Essential Features of Mendeleev's Periodic Table

- This table contains 8 **vertical columns**, called **groups** and 6 **horizontal rows**, called **periods**.
- All the groups were divided in two sub groups *A* and *B*, except the group VIII.
- All the elements of a sub group or group show similar properties and same valency.
- Period 4, 5, 6 are divided into two series, first series and second series.
- In a period, on moving from left to right across the horizontal row, the metallic character decreases.

Merits of Mendeleev's Periodic Table

(i) **Simplified study of elements** Elements in the same group had similar properties, making it easier to predict the behaviour of other elements in the group.

(ii) **Prediction of undiscovered elements** Mendeleev left blank spaces for elements yet to be discovered and accurately predicted their properties (e.g. scandium, gallium, germanium).

(iii) **Corrected atomic masses** He corrected atomic masses of certain elements, like gold and platinum, and placed them strictly according to their properties.

Defects in Mendeleev's Periodic Table

(i) **Position of hydrogen** The position of hydrogen was uncertain, as it could be placed in both Group I (like alkali metals) and Group VII (like halogens).

(ii) **No fixed position for isotopes** Isotopes of an element, having different atomic masses but similar chemical properties, could not be placed in separate slots.

(iii) **Anomalous atomic mass order** Some elements were placed out of the order of their atomic masses to fit into group with similar properties (e.g. iodine was placed after tellurium, cobalt was placed before nickel).

(iv) **Grouping of chemically dissimilar element** Elements such as copper and silver bear no resemblance to alkali metals, but they have been placed together in the first group.

(v) **Separation of chemically similar elements** Elements that are chemically similar, such as gold and platinum have been placed in separate groups.

(vi) **Electron arrangement** It does not explain the electron arrangement of elements.

Basis of Mendeleev's Periodic Table

- Atomic mass
- Chemical properties of oxides and hydrides of various elements.

Modern Periodic Law

- Modern periodic law states that "physical and chemical properties of the elements are a periodic function of their atomic number".
- When the elements were arranged in the increasing order of their **atomic number**, the obtained table was called **modern periodic table**.
- This table has 18 vertical columns, known as **groups** and 7 horizontal rows, known as **periods**.

Features of Groups

- These groups are named as I to VIII. Out of these group I to VII are further divisible into sub groups A and B. At the end, a separate zero (0) group is also present.
- Elements of group III B to II B are called as **transition elements**.
- Elements of group zero are called **inert gases** or **noble gases** due to their stable electronic configuration.
- The elements present in a group have the same number of valence electrons.
- The elements present in a group have the same valency.
- The number of shells increases as we go down the group.

- The physical properties of the elements such as melting point, boiling point and density in a group vary gradually.
- The elements present in a group have identical chemical properties.

Features of Periods

- Elements of a period contain the same number of shells.
- The number of valence shell electrons increases by one unit as the atomic number increases by one unit on moving from left to right in a period. Therefore, the atoms of different elements with same number of shells are placed in the same period.
- As the number of valence shell electrons changes, the chemical properties of the elements also change.
- **The 1st period** contains only two elements with atomic number 1 and 2. It is the **shortest period.**
- **The 2nd and 3rd periods** contain eight elements each. Elements with atomic number 3-10 are placed in 2nd period and 11-18 in 3rd period. These are **short periods.**
- **The 4th and 5th periods** contain eighteen elements each (i.e. from atomic number 19 to 36 in the fourth and from atomic number 37 to 54 in the fifth period). These are **long periods.**
- **The 6th period** contains 32 elements (from atomic number 55 to 86). It is the **longest period.**
- **The 7th period** contains 32 elements (from atomic number 87 to 118). It is also a **longest period.**
- **In group III B** (Group number 3) of the **sixth period**, there is a set of elements with atomic number 57 to 71. (La-Lu), beginning with lanthanum (La-57). These elements are called **lanthanides.**
- **In group III B** (Group number 3) of the **7th period**, there is a set of elements with atomic number 89 to 103 (Ac-Lr), beginning with actinium (Ac-89). These elements are called as **actinides** (radioactive elements).
- Lanthanides and actinides have similar properties as they belong to the same group, group III B. But they are shown at the bottom of periodic table because they are large in number and showing them in the main body of the table will distort the shape of it.

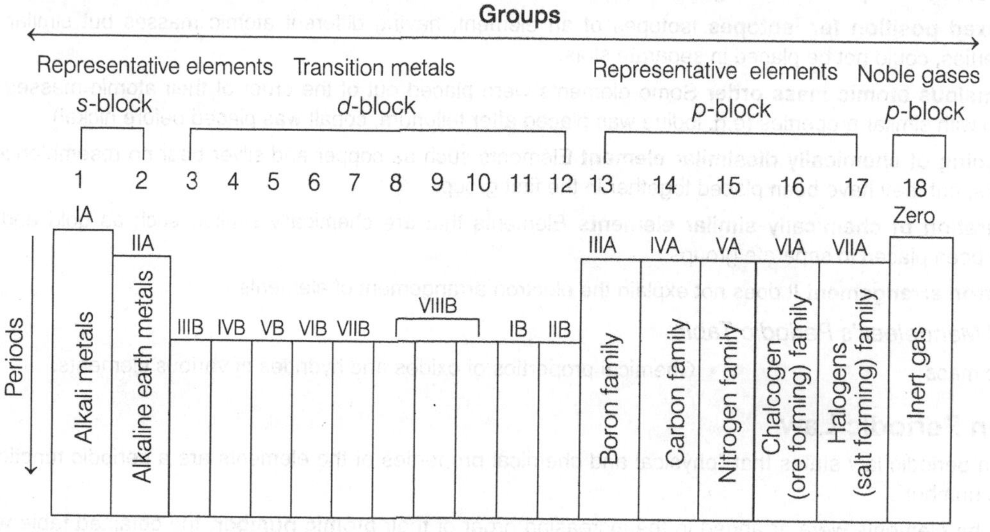

Modern Periodic Table

Types of Elements

- Representative elements
- Transition elements
- Inner transition elements
- Inert gases

Representative Elements

- Elements that have only their valence shell incomplete are called representative elements. *s*- and *p*-block elements (except for the inert gases) are representative elements.
- Representative elements include both metals as well as non-metals.
- For metals, the reactivity increases down the group.
- For non-metals, the reactivity decreases down the group.

Transition Elements or the d-block Elements

- Transition elements have last two shells incomplete, i.e. their valence shell and penultimate shells are incomplete.
- Elements of group 3 to 12 are transition elements.
- Transitional elements are metals with high melting and boiling points.
- They show variable valencies.
- They are good conductors of heat and electricity.
- They form coloured salts.

Inner Transition Elements or f-block Elements

- They have last three shells, incomplete and include lanthanoids and actinoids.
- They are heavy metals with high melting and boiling points.
- They show variable valencies.
- A few of them are radioactive.

Explanation of the Anomalies of Mendeleev's Classification of Elements

Different anomalies of Mendeleev's periodic table can be explained with the help of modern periodic table as:

- The fundamental basis for modern periodic table is atomic number, not atomic mass, hence it is more accurate.
- Since, the table is based on atomic number and isotopes have same atomic number and chemical properties, so they can be put at one place in the same group of the periodic table.
- In this periodic table, a unique position has been given to hydrogen. It is kept at the top left corner because of its unique characteristics.
- The position of cobalt and nickel is justified because atomic number of cobalt is less than atomic number of nickel.

Basis of Modern Periodic Table

- Electronic configuration
- Atomic number

Study of Some Specific Groups

The elements present in a group exhibit similar properties, as they have same number of valence electrons and same electronic configuration.

Alkali Metals (Group 1)

- The elements which belong to the group 1 (except H) of the periodic table are called as **alkali metals**. These are lithium (Li), sodium (Na), potassium (K), rubidium (Rb), caesium (Cs) and francium (Fr).
- They have one electron in their outermost orbit and show one valency. So, they are placed in group 1 of the periodic table.

General Characteristics of Alkali Metals

(i) **Electronic configuration** These have similar electronic configuration. e.g. $_{3}$Li–2, 1; $_{11}$Na–2, 8, 1; $_{19}$K–2, 8, 8, 1, etc.

(ii) **Occurrence** These are highly reactive elements and occur in the combined state only.

(iii) **Nature** Soft in nature (can be cut with a knife) and have low melting and boiling points.

(iv) They are generally soft and when freshly cut, they show typical **silvery white metallic lustre** but on exposure to the air, they turn dull black due to oxidation with atmospheric oxygen.

(v) They can easily form **unipositive ions.**

$$M - e^{-} \longrightarrow M^{+}$$

(vi) **Bonding** Alkali metals have one electron in the valence shell, i.e. their valency is 1, so they form ionic bond (except some salts of lithium) by loosing electrons.

(vii) They are strong **reducing agents** because they have a tendency to lose electron.

(viii) **Action of air** On exposure to moist air, they react rapidly with oxygen and form metal oxide. Hence, these metals (Na and K) are kept immersed in kerosene.

$$4M + O_2 \longrightarrow 2M_2O \qquad \text{(where, } M = \text{any alkali metal)}$$

The reactivity increases on moving down the group.

(ix) **Action of water** React violently with water to produce alkali and hydrogen gas.

$$2M + 2H_2O \longrightarrow \underset{\text{Alkali}}{2MOH} + H_2 \uparrow \quad \text{(where, } M = \text{any alkali metal)}$$

(x) **Action of acids** React violently with dil. HCl and dil. H_2SO_4 and produce H_2 gas.

$$2M + \underset{\text{Dil.}}{2HCl} \longrightarrow 2MCl + H_2 \uparrow, \quad 2M + \underset{\text{Dil.}}{H_2SO_4} \longrightarrow M_2SO_4 + H_2 \uparrow \text{ (where, } M = \text{any alkali metals)}$$

(xi) They **impart colour to the flame**, e.g. lithium (crimson red), sodium (golden yellow), potassium (pale violet).

(xii) Alkali metals are obtained by the **electrolysis of their molten salts**, e.g. Na metal can be easily obtained from NaCl salt.

Alkaline Earth Metals (Group 2 or IIA)

- The hydroxides of alkaline earth metals are alkaline in nature and their oxides occur in the earth's crust, that's why they are known as **alkaline earth metals.**
- The elements belonging to this group are beryllium (Be), magnesium (Mg), calcium (Ca), strontium (Sr), barium (Ba) and radium (Ra).

General Characteristics Alkaline Earth Metals

(i) **Electronic configuration** There possess similar electronic configuration. e.g. ${}_{4}Be$–2, 2; ${}_{12}Mg$–2, 8, 2; ${}_{20}Ca$–2, 8, 8, 2; etc

(ii) **Occurrence** They are reactive elements thus, occur in the combined state only.

(iii) **Nature** They are slightly harder than alkali metals. These can also be out with a sharp knife.

(iv) Melting and boiling points are comparatively low but higher than the alkali metals.

(v) They form **dipositive ion.**

$$M - 2e^- \longrightarrow M^{2+} \quad \text{(where, } M = \text{any alkaline earth metal)}$$

(vi) **Bonding** They possess two electrons in the valence shell hence form dipositive cations and shows ionic bonding (except beryllium).

(vii) They also act as **reducing agents** because they have a tendency to lose electron.

(viii) **Action of air** On exposure to moist air, they react slowly. Upon heating in the presence of air they form oxide.

e.g.

$$2M + O_2 \longrightarrow 2MO \quad \text{(where, } M = \text{any alkaline earth metals)}$$

Their reactivity increases on moving down the group.

(ix) **Action of water** They react with water to produce base and hydrogen gas.

$$\underset{\substack{\text{Alkaline}\\ \text{earth metal}}}{M} + 2H_2O \longrightarrow \underset{\text{Alkali}}{M(OH)_2} + H_2 \uparrow$$

(x) **Action of acids** They react with dil. HCl and dil. H_2SO_4, respectively to produce hydrogen gas.

$$\underset{\substack{\text{Alkaline}\\ \text{earth metal}}}{M} + 2HCl \longrightarrow MCl_2 + H_2 \uparrow, \quad \underset{\substack{\text{Alkaline}\\ \text{earth metal}}}{M} + H_2SO_4 \longrightarrow MSO_4 + H_2 \uparrow$$

(xi) Generally, all the alkaline earth metals **impart colour to the flame** (except beryllium and magnesium), e.g. Ca (Brick red), Sr (Crimson), Ba (Apple green), Ra (Crimson).

(xii) They are also obtained by the electrolysis of their molten salts.

e.g.

$$MgCl_2 \rightleftharpoons Mg^{2+} + 2Cl^-$$

Halogens (Group 17)

Fluorine (F), Chlorine (Cl), Bromine (Br), Iodine (I) and Astatine (At) belongs to group 17 and are collectively known as **halogens**, meaning salt forming.

General Characteristics of Halogens

(i) **Electronic configuration** These elements have similar electronic configuration. e.g. ${}_{9}F$–2, 7; ${}_{17}Cl$–2, 8, 7; ${}_{35}Br$–2, 8, 18, 7; etc.

(ii) **Occurrence** They are highly reactive non-metallic elements.

(iii) **Nature** Fluorine and chlorine are gases, bromine is liquid and iodine is solid.

(iv) **Colour** All these halogens are coloured. F_2 is yellow, Cl_2 is greenish yellow, Br_2 is reddish brown and I_2 is violet in colour.

(v) Halogens can react with most of elements in the periodic table. However, the order of reactivity of the group members decreases down the group as $F > Cl > Br > I$.

(vi) **Bonding** Halogens due to the presence of seven electrons in their valence shell, are highly reactive and form ionic compounds with highly electropositive metals. However, with weakly electropositive metals and non-metals, they form covalent bonds.

(vii) Most of the metals react with halogens to form metal halides as

$$2M + nX_2 \longrightarrow 2MX_n$$

(Here, M = metal, n = oxidation state of metal, X = F, Cl, Br or I)

Noble Gases (Group 18 or Zero Group)

- Helium (He), Neon (Ne), Argon (Ar), Krypton (Kr), Xenon (Xe) and Radon (Rn) belong to group 18. These are collectively known as **noble gases**. These are inert or less reactive in nature.
- Due to their inertness, these gases were discovered on the basis of study of their physical properties such as density.

General Characteristics of Noble Gases

(i) **Electronic configuration** These have similar electronic configuration. e.g. $_2$He–2; $_{10}$Ne–2, 8; $_{18}$Ar–2, 8, 8; etc.

(ii) **Occurrence** Due to inert nature of these gases, they always occur in free state.

(iii) **Nature** These are colourless, odourless and tasteless gases.

(iv) These are monoatomic gases and are sparingly soluble in water.

(v) They have **low melting and boiling points** due to weak dispersion forces. Helium has the lowest melting point of any known substance.

(vi) Helium is a *s*-block element but has been placed in group 18, at the top, as its chemical inertness is similar to the rest of the members of group 18.

(vii) Helium is used in filling balloons for meteorological observations as it is a non-flammable and light gas. Neon is used in discharge tubes. Neon bulbs are used in botanical gardens and in greenhouses.

(viii) Argon because of its inert nature is used to provide an inert atmosphere in high temperature metallurgical process.

Predicting the Position of an Element in the Periodic Table

Group

For group IA and IIA

Group number = Number of valence electrons

e.g. Na (11) = $\overset{K}{2}\ \overset{L}{8}\ \overset{M}{1}$

Valence electrons = 1, so group number = 1 or IA

e.g. Mg (12) = 2, 8, 2

Valence electrons = 2, so group number = IIA or 2

For group III A (13) to VIII (18 group)

Group number = 10 + no. of valence electron

e.g. N (7) = $\overset{K}{2}\ \overset{L}{5}$

Group number = 10 + 5 = 15 or VA

Period

Period number = Number of shells in the element.

e.g. Cl (17) = $\overset{K}{2}\overset{L}{8}\overset{M}{7}$

Number of shells = 3

Period number = III

EXAM ORIENTED QUESTIONS

TYPE - 1 — 01 Mark

Multiple Choice Questions

Q.1 Which of the following is the correct set of elements of Dobereiner's triads?

(a) Li Na K — 7 23 39
(b) Br Cl I — 80 35.5 127
(c) Fe Ni Co — 55.85 58.71 58.93
(d) Data is insufficient

Ans. (a) $\underset{7}{Li}$ $\underset{23}{Na}$ $\underset{39}{K}$

The mean of the atomic masses of Li and K

$$= \frac{7 + 39}{2} = \frac{46}{2} = 23$$

This is same as atomic mass of Na.

Q.2 Newland law of octaves seemed to be true for upto which element.

(a) Calcium (b) Argon (c) Potassium (d) Zinc

Ans. (a) The law of octaves was found to be applicable only upto **calcium (Ca)**. Newlands' theory was not applicable to elements of higher atomic masses. As the atomic mass increased, the elements with similar properties appeared much after the eighth element, i.e. heavier elements could not be accommodated into octaves.

Q.3 Which of the following is correct?

(a) Law of triads seemed to work only for large elements.
(b) John Newlands' (law of octaves) arranged the elements in the increasing order of their atomic weights.
(c) Dobereiner arranged elements by the help of triads method.
(d) Both (b) and (c)

Ans. (d) Both (b) and (c)

Q.4 Which of the following is incorrect explanation about Mendeleev's periodic table?

(a) Mendeleev arranged elements in horizontal rows only.
(b) Mendeleev strictly arranged elements with increasing atomic mass.
(c) Mendeleev's system of classifying elements was more elaborated
(d) Both (a) and (b)

Ans. (d) Both (a) and (b)

Statement (a) is incorrect because Mendeleev arranged elements both in horizontal rows (periods) and vertical columns (groups) in his periodic table.

Statement (b) is partially true, but there were exceptions. Mendeleev prioritised grouping elements with similar properties over strictly following atomic mass order (e.g., Co and Ni).

Statement (c) is correct because Mendeleev's periodic table was well organised and included predictions of undiscovered elements.

Q.5 Which of the following statement(s) about the modern periodic table is correct?

(a) The elements in the modern periodic table are arranged on the basis of their decreasing atomic number.
(b) The elements in the modern periodic table are arranged on the basis of their increasing atomic masses.
(c) Isotopes are placed in adjoining group(s) in the periodic table.
(d) The elements in the modern periodic table are arranged on the basis of their increasing atomic number.

Ans. (d) The elements in the modern periodic table are arranged on the basis of their **increasing atomic number**.

Q.6 The element with atomic number 16 is placed in the modern periodic table in

(a) 2nd period and VI A group
(b) 3rd period and IV A group
(c) 3rd period and VI A group
(d) 2nd period and IV A group

Ans. (c) 3rd period and VI A group.

Electronic configuration = 2, 8, 6
No. of shells = 3, so period no. = III
No. of valence = 6, so group no. = 10 + 6 = 16 or VI A.

Q.7 On the basis of electronic configuration, the position of $^{9}_{5}B$ in the periodic table is

(a) 2 and III A
(b) 3 and II A
(c) 4 and VI A
(d) 5 and VII A

Ans. (a) 2 and III A

Q.8 $_1H^2$ is an isotope of hydrogen. In the modem periodic table it will
(a) be placed before hydrogen
(b) be placed after hydrogen
(c) be placed at the same position as hydrogen
(d) not have any position in the periodic table

Ans. (c) $_1H^2$ (deuterium) is an isotope of hydrogen, which will be placed at the same position as hydrogen in the modern periodic table.

Q.9 The table contains four elements and their atomic numbers.

Element	*W*	*X*	*Y*	*Z*
Atomic number	7	14	15	18

Which two elements are in the same group of the Periodic Table?
(a) *W* and *X* (b) *X* and *Z*
(c) *X* and *Y* (d) *W* and *Y*

Ans. (d) *W* and *Y*.
$W = 2, 5$; $X = 2, 8, 4$; $Y = 2, 8, 5$; $Z = 2, 8, 8$
W* and *Y have same number of valence electrons, thus they belong to the same group.

Q.10 Which of the following statement is correct with respect to the elements Na, Mg, Al, Si, P, S, Cl and Ar ?
(a) Each element belongs to the same group.
(b) Valency of each element is the same.
(c) Each element belongs to the same period.
(d) They are all non-metals.

Ans. (c) Each element belongs to the same period.

Q.11 An element *X* forms an ion X^{2-}. Which group of the periodic table is this element found in?
(a) Group I (b) Group II
(c) Group V (d) Group VI

Ans. (d) Group VI (It is a non-metal with valency 2).

Q.12 Which of the elements *A*, *B*, *C*, *D* and *E* with atomic number 2, 3, 7, 10 and 30, respectively belong to the same period?
(a) *A*, *B*, *C*
(b) *B*, *C*, *D*
(c) *A*, *D*, *E*
(d) *B*, *D*, *E*

Ans. (b) *B*, *C*, *D* elements belong to 2nd period.
Because the elements ***B*, *C* and *D*** with atomic number 3, 7 and 10 have the **same valence shell** (*L*-shell).

Q.13 Two elements *M* and *N* belong to group 2 and 3, respectively in the same period. The formulae of their oxides are
(a) MO, N_2O_3 (b) M_3O_2, N_3O_2
(c) M_2O_3, N_3O_2 (d) M_3O_2, N_2O_3

Ans. (a) MO, N_2O_3

Oxide of element *M* belonging to group 2

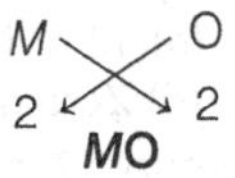

MO

Oxide of element *N* belonging to group 3,

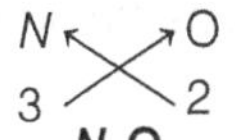

$\mathbf{N_2O_3}$

Q.14 Part of the periodic table is shown.

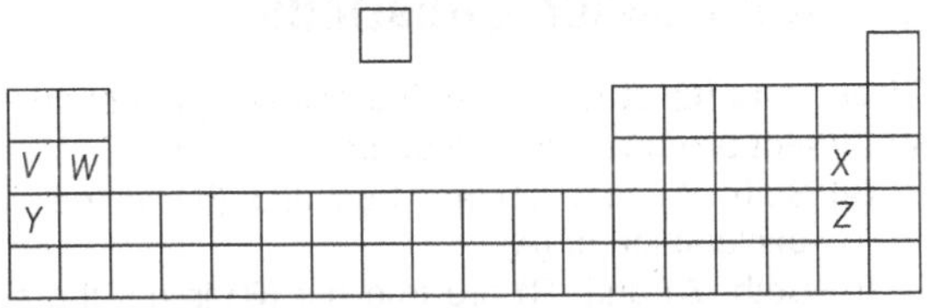

The letters are not the symbol of the elements.
Which statement is correct?
(a) *V* is more reactive than *Y*.
(b) *W* has more metallic character than *V*.
(c) *Y* is more reactive than *V*.
(d) *Z* is more reactive than *X*.

Ans. (c) The reactivity of group I elements (Alkali metals) increases down the group. So, ***Y* is more reactive than *V*.**

Q.15 Which row shows the properties of a group I metal?

	Density	Hardness
(a)	High	Hard
(b)	High	Soft
(c)	Low	Hard
(d)	Low	Soft

Ans. (d) Density-low, hardness-soft.

Q.16 Group 1 elements act as
(a) oxidising agent (b) reducing agent
(c) titrating agents (d) indicators

Ans. (b) Group I elements have one valence electron, so they readily lose electron and get oxidised to complete their outermost shell. Hence, they act as **reducing agent**.

Q.17 Which one among the following is an alkaline earth metal?
(a) Potassium (b) Calcium
(c) Lead (d) Copper

Ans. (b) Calcium

Q.18 A halogen found in period 3 and group 17 is
(a) chlorine (b) bromine
(c) fluorine (d) sulphur

Ans. (a) chlorine

Q.19 Strongest oxidising agents are the elements of group.
(a) IA (b) 13 or III A
(c) VII A (d) Zero group

Ans. (c) VIII A or 17. Group 17 elements have 7 valence electrons, so they readily gain one electron to complete their octet, thus act as strongest oxidising agents.

TYPE - 2 01 Mark

Assertion-Reason Questions

Directions (Q. Nos. 1-5) In the following questions statement are given Assertion and Reason.
(a) Both (A) and (R) are true and (R) is the correct explanation of (A).
(b) Both (A) and (R) are true but (R) is not the correct explanation of (A).
(c) (A) is true but (R) is false.
(d) (A) is false but (R) is true.

Q.1 **Assertion** (A) Mendeleev's periodic table was arranged based on increasing atomic masses.

Reason (R) Mendeleev grouped elements with similar chemical properties together in the same column.

Ans. (b) Both (A) and (R) are true but (R) is not the correct explanation of (A).

Mendeleev organised elements based on increasing atomic masses, while ensuring elements with similar properties were grouped together, making this table both systematic and predictive.

Q.2 **Assertion** (A) Mendeleev left gaps in his periodic table.

Reason (R) Mendeleev predicted the existence and properties of undiscovered elements.

Ans. (a) Both (A) and (R) are true and (R) is the correct explanation of (A).

Mendeleev left gaps in his periodic table for elements yet to be discovered, such as gallium and germanium, whose properties he successfully predicted.

Q.3 **Assertion** (A) Elements in the modern periodic table are arranged based on increasing atomic number.

Reason (R) Atomic number determines the number of protons in an atom, which affects the element's properties.

Ans. (b) Both (A) and (R) are true but (R) is not the correct explanation of (A).

In the modern periodic table, elements are arranged in increasing atomic number, which defines their chemical and physical properties accurately.

Q.4 **Assertion** (A) Elements in the same group of the periodic table have different numbers of valence electrons.

Reason (R) Elements in a group have the same number of shells.

Ans. (d) (A) is false but (R) is true.

Elements in the same group have the same number of valence electrons but different numbers of shells, which increases as we go down the group.

Q.5 **Assertion** (A) The reactivity of alkali metals increases as we move down the group.

Reason (R) The size of the atom increases, and the outermost electron is more easily lost.

Ans. (a) Both (A) and (R) are true and (R) is the correct explanation of (A).

As we go down the group, the atomic size increases, reducing the effective nuclear pull on the valence electron, thus making it easier to lose electron and increasing its reactivity.

TYPE - 3 01 Mark

Fill in the Blanks

Q.1 Dobereiner's relationship is referred to as the .... (law of triads, periodic law).

Ans. law of triads

Q.2 Newland in 1866 arranged the elements in increasing order of their .... (atomic number, atomic masses).

Ans. atomic masses

Q.3 In Newlands' octave law every eighth element has properties similar to the .... element (first, second).

Ans. first

Q.4 Mendeleev arranged elements in horizontal rows and .... (horizontal columns, vertical columns).

Ans. vertical columns

Q.5 In Mendeleev's periodic table, eka-silicon and eka-aluminium were germanium and .... respectively (indium, gallium).

Ans. gallium

Q.6 The elements belonging the group 3 to 12 are called .... (transition elements, representative elements)

Ans. transition elements

Q.7 The ...... period is the shortest period. (first, second)

Ans. first

Q.8 Strontium belongs to second group and .... (fifth, sixth) period.

Ans. fifth

Q.9 The number of valence shell electrons increases by one unit as the .... increases (atomic mass, atomic number).

Ans. atomic number

Q.10 A metal present in period 3 and group 1 of the periodic table is .... (magnesium, sodium)

Ans. sodium

Q.11 The element with atomic number 12 belongs to group .... (2, 12).

Ans. 2

Q.12 Elements having a tendency to lose one or more electrons and form positive ions are called .... (metals, non-metals).

Ans. metals

Q.13 Elements of group 17 are called as .... (alkali metals, halogens).

Ans. halogens

Q.14 The lightest inert gas is .... (helium, neon).

Ans. helium

Q.15 .... is used to fill light bulbs (Helium, Argon).

Ans. Argon

TYPE - 4 — 01 Mark

Correct the Incorrect Statement

Q.1 Mendeleev's periodic table was arranged based on increasing atomic number.

Ans. **Modern periodic table** was arranged based on the increasing atomic number.

Q.2 Elements in the same period of the periodic table have the same number of valence electrons.

Ans. Elements in the same period of the periodic table have the same number of **shells**.

Q.3 The reactivity of non-metals increases as we move down a group in the periodic table.

Ans. The reactivity of non-metals **decreases** as we move down a group in the periodic table.

Q.4 All elements in group 1 are non-metals.

Ans. All elements of group 1 are **metals**.

Q.5 Noble gases are placed in group 17 of the periodic table.

Ans. Noble gases are placed in **group 18** of the periodic table.

TYPE - 5 — 01×05 = 05 Marks

Match the Columns

Q.1 Match the terms in Column I with their appropriate descriptions in Column II

	Column I		Column II
A.	Dobereiner's triads	1.	Properties repeat after 8 elements
B.	Newlands' law of octaves	2.	Atomic masses arranged in increasing order
C.	Mendeleev's Periodic law	3.	Groups of three elements with similar properties
D.	Modern Periodic law	4.	Reoccurrence of properties at regular intervals
E	Periodicity	5.	Properties depend on atomic number

Ans. A → (3), B → (1), C → (2), D → (5), E → (4).

Q.2 Match the terms in Column I with their appropriate descriptions in Column II.

Column II	Column II
A. Group 1 elements	1. Li, C, O
B. Group 18 elements	2. Alkali metals
C. Elements in period 2	3. S, Cl, Ar
D. Group 17 elements	4. Non-reactive and inert
E Elements in period 3	5. Halogens

Ans. A → (2), B → (4), C → (1), D → (5), E → (3).

TYPE - 6 — 01 Mark

Identify the Following

Q.1 What is the classification in which elements are grouped in a group of three known as?

Ans. Dobereiner's triad

Q.2 Name any two Dobereiner's triad, which are also found in modern periodic table.

Ans. Lithium, sodium, potassium and chlorine bromine, iodine.

Q.3 Elements *P*, *Q* and are the elements of Dobereiner's triad. If atomic mass of P is 7 and that of *R* is 39 what should be the atomic mass of *Q*?

Ans. $\frac{7 + 39}{2} = 23$

The atomic mass of $Q = 23$

Q.4 Name the classification of elements in which first and eighth elements had similar properties.

Ans. Newlands' law of octaves

Q.5 Which law states that "properties of elements are a periodic function of their atomic masses"?

Ans. Mendeleev's periodic law

Q.6 Name an element whose weight was corrected by Mendeleev.

Ans. Gold or Platinum

Q.7 Give one anomalous pair of elements found in Mendeleev's periodic table.

Ans. Cobalt and nickel

Q.8 Give the name of latest table in which elements are arranged in periods and groups.

Ans. Long form of periodic table

Q.9 What do you call vertical column and horizontal rows of modern periodic table?

Ans. Vertical columns are called **groups** and horizontal rows are called **periods**.

Q.10 Write number of elements in 2nd period.

Ans. 8 (eight)

Q.11 What is the longest period of periodic table?

Ans. 6th (sixth)

Q.12 Write the name of a group in which inert gases elements are present in the modern periodic table.

Ans. 18th group or zero group.

Q.13 What is the name of inner transition elements placed in sixth period?

Ans. Lanthanides

Q.14 How many elements are there in each lanthanides and actinides series?

Ans. Fourteen

Q.15 An element *X* is present at the left corner of modern periodic table. What would it be a metal or a non-metal?

Ans. A **metal** because left side of periodic table consists of metals, whereas right side of the periodic table mainly consists of non-metals.

Q.16 Give the name of elements which are placed at the bottom of long form of periodic table.

Ans. Lanthanides and actinides.

Q.17 What is the nature of metal oxide of group I^{st} and IInd element?

Ans. Basic nature

Q.18 Group I element are also known as

Ans. alkali metal

Q.19 Caesium belongs to which group of the modern periodic table?

Ans. Group I

Q.20 Write another name of group second element.

Ans. Alkaline earth metal

Q.21 Name the halogen which is liquid at room temperature.

Ans. Bromine

Q.22 Which inert gas is used in discharge tubes?

Ans. Neon

TYPE - 7 — 2 Marks

Short Answer Type I Questions

Q.1 What are the reasons for classification of element? Give any two.

Ans. Reasons for classification of elements.

1. It helps in studying the elements in an organised manner. **(1)**
2. It helps in correlating the properties of elements with the fundamental properties of all states of matter. **(1)**

Q.2 List any two demerits of Newlands' law of octaves?

Ans. Demerits of Newlands' law of octaves

- This classification did not work with heavier elements, i.e. those lying beyond calcium. **(1)**
- The position of hydrogen along with fluorine and chlorine was not justified on the basis of chemical properties. **(1)**

Q.3 On what basis, Mendeleev classified the elements? Also, state Mendeleev's law.

Ans. Mendeleev classified the elements on the basis of the **atomic masses**. **(1)**
His law states that "the properties of an element are the periodic function of their atomic masses". **(1)**

Q.4 (i) Why did Mendeleev left gap in his periodic table? Give example to justify.
(ii) Why position of hydrogen was not fixed in Mendeleev's periodic table ?

Ans. (i) Mendeleev left gap in his periodic table for the undiscovered elements which were not discovered at that time. e.g. Gallium and germanium. **(1)**

(ii) The electronic configuration of hydrogen resembles with alkali metals. It combines with halogen, oxygen and sulphur to give similar type of compounds as given by alkali metals. However, just like halogen, it exists in diatomic form and combines with metals and non-metals to forms covalent compounds.
Thus, its position was not fixed in the Mendeleev's periodic table. **(1)**

Q.5 Mendeleev devised the modern periodic table. He put elements in the same group if their properties were similar. One of the properties he used was the formation of the oxides of the elements.

When group I metals tarnish in air, different types of oxide are formed.

Element	Oxides formed	Formula
Lithium	Lithium oxide	Li_2O
Sodium	Sodium oxide Sodium peroxide	Na_2O Na_2O_2
Potassium	Potassium superoxide	KO_2
Rubidium	Rubidium superoxide	RbO_2

Mendeleev put all of these elements in group I.

(a) Do the formulae of the oxides given in the table show clearly that all of the elements belong in the same group?
Explain your answer.

(b) Do the formulae of the oxides given in the table show a trend down the group?
Explain your answer.

Ans. (i) (a) **Yes**. All the elements have a consistent 1 oxidation state in their oxides. **(1)**

(b) **Yes**. Alkali metals at the top of group forms only oxides. Sodium forms oxides and peroxides while alkali metals near the bottom of group tend to form superoxides. **(1)**

Q.6 Write major defects in modern periodic table?

Ans. Major defects in modern periodic table are

(i) Position of hydrogen is still not satisfactory, as its properties relate to both group 1 and group 17. **(1)**

(ii) It fails to accomdate the inner transition elements, i.e. the lanthanides and the actinides, into the main body of the periodic table. **(1)**

Q.7 Define the term valency. What is the valency of group 1 elements?

Ans. **Valency** of an element is the number of electrons that an atom of the element loses or gains or shares during a chemical reaction, in order to complete its octet or duplet.

The valency of group 1 elements is **1**.

e.g. $_3Li \rightarrow 2,1$

One electron is present in outermost shell of Li. By losing one electron, it can attain stable configuration therefore, valency of Li is 1. **(2)**

Q.8 Write the number of shells and valence electrons present in

(i) F (ii) S

Ans. (i) Electronic configuration of

$$\begin{matrix} & K & L \\ F = & 2 & 7 \end{matrix}$$

So, number of shell = 2

Valence electrons = 7 **(1)**

(ii) Electronic configuration of

$$\begin{matrix} & K & L & M \\ S = & 2 & 8 & 6 \end{matrix}$$

So, number of shell = 3

Valence electrons = 6 **(1)**

Q.9. Study the diagram given below.

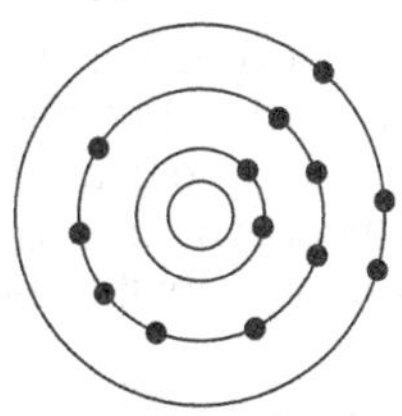

Write the name of element and give its valency.

Ans. Total number of electrons present in diagram are 13.

So, it is **aluminium (Al)**. Valency of aluminium (Al) is 3, as electronic configuration of aluminium is 2, 8, 3. So, it will lose 3 electrons to complete its octet. **(2)**

Q.10 Write number of elements in the

(i) 1st period (ii) 2nd period

Ans. (i) Number of elements in the first period are two. **(1)**

(ii) Number of elements in the second period are eight. **(1)**

Q.11 The diagram shows the part of the periodic table.

Group	13	14	15	16	17	18
						He
	B	C	N	O	F	Ne
	Al	Si	P	S	Cl	Ar

Answer the following questions from the given list of elements.

(i) Select a group of elements having valency zero.

(ii) Elements that have 6 valence electrons.

Ans. (i) He, Ne, Ar **(1)**

(ii) O, S **(1)**

Q.12 What is the number of elements in the

(i) first group, and

(ii) sixth period, of the modern periodic table?

Ans. (i) **Seven elements** are present in first group. **(1)**

(ii) **32 elements** are present in the sixth period of the modern periodic table. **(1)**

Q.13 Choose from the following elements to answer the questions below.

Lithium, Fluorine, Boron, Nitrogen, Phosphorus, Sulphur, Magnesium, Neon

(i) Element which has two shells and each one is completely filled.

(ii) Two elements that belong from same group.

Ans. (i) Neon **(1)**

(ii) Nitrogen and phosphorus **(1)**

Q.14 Give reason.

(i) Atomic number is considered to be a more appropriate parameter than atomic mass for classification of elements in a periodic table.

(ii) Alkali metals are good reducing agents.

Ans. (i) The properties of elements depend upon valence electrons in the atom, which in turn depends on the total number of electrons, e.g. atomic number. Therefore, atomic number is a more appropriate parameter than atomic mass for the classification of elements. **(1)**

(ii) Alkali metals have only one valence electron in their outermost shell.

Thus, it is easy for them to lose their outermost electron and attain a nearest noble gas configuration and become more stable. That's why they are good reducing agents. **(1)**

Q.15 Write reaction of sodium with hydrogen and oxygen.

Ans. Reaction of sodium with hydrogen forms **sodium hydride**.

$$2Na + H_2 \longrightarrow 2NaH$$ **(1)**

Reaction of sodium with oxygen forms **sodium oxide**.

$$4Na + O_2 \longrightarrow 2Na_2O$$ **(1)**

Q.16 Name the metals of group 1, arrange them in the order of

(i) in increasing reactivity

(ii) increasing tendency to lose electron

Ans. Group 1 elements are alkali metals

Lithium, sodium, potassium, rubidium

(i) Increasing order of reactivity

$$Li < Na < K < Rb$$

(As we move in a group from top to bottom, size of the metal increases, so they can easily lose electron. Hence, reactivity of metal increases.) **(1)**

(ii) Tendency to lose electrons

$$Li < Na < K < Rb$$

(as we move down the group, size of the atom increases, the effective nuclear charge on electron decreases, therefore, the outermost electron can easily be removed). **(1)**

Q.17 Amar was given an oxide '*XO*'. The metal *X* present in this oxide gives brick red colour in flame test. On heating *X* metal with nitrogen, it gives nitride.

(i) Identify the metal '*X*'.

(ii) What type of nitride will be formed by element '*X*'.

Ans. (i) The metal '*X*' is **calcium**. **(1)**

(ii) The nitride formed by calcium will be Ca_3N_2. **(1)**

Q.18 (i) Name all the elements of period two and arrange them in increasing order of non-metallic nature.

(ii) What happens to the number of valance electrons in atom of element as we move in a group from top to bottom?

Ans. (i) Lithium, beryllium, boron, carbon, nitrogen, oxygen, fluorine and neon. (These are arranged in the increasing order of their non-metallic nature)

Lithium and beryllium are metals, boron is a metalloid, while carbon, nitrogen, oxygen, fluorine, are non-metals. **(1)**

(ii) In a group from top to bottom, number of valence electrons remains same.

(e.g. All elements of group 1 have one valance electron, and all elements of group 2 have two valence electrons). **(1)**

Q.19 Complete the table.

Element	Electronic configuration	Colour	Physical state
F	2, 7	W	Gas
Cl	2, 8, 7	Greenish yellow	X
Br	2, 8, 18, 7	Y	Liquid
I	2, 8, 18, 18, 7	Violet	Z

Ans. *W* = Pale yellow, *X* = Gas, *Y* = Reddish brown, *Z* = Solid. **(½ × 4 = 2)**

Q.20 Sodium, aluminium have atomic numbers 11 and 13 respectively. They are separated by one element in the periodic table and have valency of one and three respectively. Chlorine and potassium are also separated by one element in the periodic table. Their atomic numbers are 17 and 19 respectively and yet both have valency one. Explain.

Ans. Sodium has atomic number 11, electronic configuration-2,8,1. So, its valency is 1. Aluminium (13) has electronic configuration-2, 8, 3 So, its valency is 3, whereas, chlorine has atomic number 17 and electronic configuration-2,8,7. So, chlorine reacts by gaining one electron and its valency is one. Potassium (atomic number 19) has electronic configuration 2, 8, 8,1. So, it reacts by losing one electron and its valency is 1. **(2)**

Q.21 What are the elements of group 17 called and also give their physical states?

Ans. Elements of group 17 are called **halogens**.

Physical states of members of halogen family are

- Fluorine and chlorine are gases.
- Bromine is liquid at room temperature.
- Iodine is a solid. **(2)**

Q.22. Sodium belongs to group 1, chlorine belongs to group 17, but both of them have same valency 1. Explain.

Ans. Sodium belongs to group 1 and has got one valance electron. Therefore, it reacts by losing that one electron and its valency is one.

Halogen belong to group 17, it has seven valence electrons. Therefore, it gains one electron to complete its valence shell and its valency is one.

Q.23 Name the first four halogen and arranged them in decreasing order of their reactivity.

Ans. The first four halogens are fluorine, chlorine, bromine and iodine. The increasing order of reactivity is

$$F > Cl > Br > I.$$

As in non-metals as we move down the group, the reactivity decreases. **(2)**

Q.24 (i) How many electrons are present in valence shell of inert gases?

(ii) Write two properties of group I elements.

Ans. (i) **Eight electrons** are present in valence shell of inert gases (except He, it has two valence electrons). **(1)**

(ii) Two properties of group I elements.

(a) They are soft metals. **(1/2)**

(b) They are good reducing agents. **(1/2)**

Q.25 (i) What are inert gas or noble gas?

(ii) Name a gas used in airships and balloons.

Ans. (i) Elements that have complete outermost shell are called **inert gas**. The are unreactive due to stable electronic configuration. They have been placed in group 18 of the periodic table. They have 8 electrons in their outermost orbits (except He, which has only 2). **(1)**

(ii) Helium. **(1)**

Q.26 Give reason.

(i) Helium is used in airships and balloons.

(ii) Noble gases are placed under a separate group in the periodic table.

Ans. (i) Helium is used in airships and balloons because it is both **light and unreactive.** **(1)**

(ii) Noble gases are not reactive due to their stable configuration. They are inert end hence they are placed in a separate group within the periodic table. **(1)**

Q.27 Name an element which has three shells, each shell is completely filled with electrons and also state its position in the periodic table.

Ans. Element is **argon**.

Position Third period, 18th group or zero group.

Electronic configuration is 2,8,8 (atomic number 18). **(2)**

Q.28 Give a suitable reason for each of the following assertions.

(i) Alkali metals and alkaline earth metals usually form electrovalent compounds.

(ii) Alkali metal and halogen do not occur free in nature.

(iii) Alkali metals are kept in inert solvent like, kerosene.

(iv) Inner gases do not form compound.

Ans. (i) Alkali metals have one valance electron and alkaline earth metals have two valance electrons, so they always react by losing electron and therefore always formed electrovalent bond. **(1/2)**

(ii) Alkali metals and halogen are very reactive elements, so they are always found in the form of compounds and not in free state in nature. **(1/2)**

(iii) Alkali metals are highly reactive elements. They react with the atmospheric moisture and oxygen even at low temperature. Therefore, they are stored in inert solvent. **(1/2)**

(iv) Inert gases have complete outer shell, so they do not react to form compounds. **(1/2)**

Q.29 You are provided with five elements, *A*, *B*, *C*, *D*, *E*, With atomic number 11, 12, 19, 20, 18. Identify the elements which will have similar chemical properties and why?

Ans. *A*-electronic configuration -2, 8, 1.

B-electronic configuration -2, 8, 2.

C-electronic configuration -2, 8, 8, 1.

D-electronic configuration 2, 8, 8, 2.

E-electronic configuration -2, 8, 8.

A and *C* have same number of valence electron, so they have same chemical properties.

Also, ***B* and *D***. have same number of valence electrons, so will have same chemical properties. **(2)**

TYPE - 8 — 03 Marks

Short Answer Type II Questions

Q.1 Can the following groups of elements be classified as Dobereiner's triad?

(i) Na, Si, Cl (ii) Be, Mg, Ca

(iii) Cl, Br, I

(Atomic mass of Be-9, Na-23, Mg-24, Si-28, Cl-35.5, Ca-40, Br-80, I-127.)

Explain by giving reason.

Ans. (i) **No**, because Si have approximately an average atomic mass of Na and Cl but they do not resemble in their properties. Na (23); Si (28); Cl (35.5)

$$\text{Atomic mass of Si} = \frac{23 + 35.5}{2}$$

$$= \frac{58.5}{2} = 29.25$$ **(1)**

(ii) **Yes**, Be (9); Mg (24); Ca (40)

$$\text{Atomic mass of Mg} = \frac{9 + 40}{2} = \frac{49}{2} = 24.5$$

It can be classified as Dobereiner's triads because the middle element of the triad had both atomic mass and properties similar to average of the two other elements of the triad. **(1)**

(iii) **Yes**, Cl(35.5), Br(80) and I(127)

$$\text{Atomic mass of Br} = \frac{35.5 + 127}{2} = 81.25$$

So, it can be classified as Dobereiner's triads because the middle element of the triad has both atomic mass and properties similar to average of the two other elements of the triad. **(1)**

Q.2 The three elements *A*, *B* and *C* with similar properties have atomic masses *X*, *Y*, and *Z* respectively. The mass of *Y* is approximately equal to the average mass of *X* and *Z*. What is such an arrangement of elements called as? Give one example of such a set of elements. Also give the reason why this arrangement was rejected?

Ans. This arrangement was given by scientist named **Dobereiner**.

e.g. Ca (40), Sr (88), Ba (137)

$$\text{Sr} = \frac{40 + 137}{2} = 88.5$$

Here, we can see that atomic mass of the middle element is the mean of other two elements.

The reason for rejection of this arrangement was that the classification was applicable only to a limited number of elements. Also the law did not fully apply even within the same family. **(3)**

Q.3 Elements have been arranged in the following sequence on the basis of their increasing atomic masses.

F, Na, Mg, Al, Si, P, S, Cl, K

(i) Pick two sets of elements which have similar properties.

(ii) The given sequence represents which law of classification of elements?

(iii) What is the limitation of this law?

Ans. (i) Here, the elements are arranged in the order of increasing atomic masses, so according to Newlands' law of octaves there is a repetition of properties in every eighth element as compared to the given element.

The two sets of elements which have similar properties are

Set I $\rightarrow$ F, Cl **Set II** $\rightarrow$ Na, K

(ii) The given sequence represents **Newlands' law of octaves.**

(iii) This classification fails for the heavier elements beyond calcium. **(1 × 3 = 3)**

Q.4 Many years ago, when grouping the known elements into a periodic table, Dmitri Mendeleev predicted that some elements had still to be discovered.

He gave one missing element the name 'eka-aluminium' and the symbol Ea. This element has been discovered now.

The element's electronic structure has four electron shells. The outer shell contains three electrons.

Use this information to complete table.

Information about element	
Name of element	eka-aluminium
Mendeleev's symbol	Ea
Group of the periodic table	
Period of the periodic table	
Charge on each ion	3+
Formula of its oxide	

Ans.

Information about element	
Name of element	eka-aluminium
Mendeleev's symbol	Ea
Group of the periodic table	Group III A or 13
Period of the periodic table	Period 4
Charge on each ion	3+
Formula of its oxide	Ea_2O_3

(3)

Q.5 The atomic number of an element is 19.

(i) Write the electronic configuration of the element.

(ii) Determine the valency of the element.

(iii) Write the formula of the oxide of the element.

Ans. The atomic number of an element is 19.

(i) Electronic configuration of the element having atomic number 19 is 2, 8, 8, 1.

(ii) Valency of the elements is **one**. As after loosing outermost shell electron, it gets stable electronic configuration.

(iii) Formula of the oxide of the element is K_2O. **(1 × 3 = 3)**

Q.6 Consider the part of periodic table given below and answer the following questions.

Period \ Group	1	2	13	14	15	16	17	18
I	*a*							*j*
II	*b*	*e*				*g*	*h*	*k*
III	*c*			*f*			*i*	*l*
IV	*d*							

(i) Which element has only one proton in its atom?

(ii) What is the valency of *'g'*?

(iii) How many valence electrons does *'g'* have?

Ans. (i) Element '*a*'.

(ii) Valency of *g* is = 8 – 6 = 2 (Group 16 elements have 6 valence electrons)

(iii) 6 electrons **(1 × 3 = 3)**

Q.7 An element *X* (atomic number 17) reacts with an element *Y* (atomic number 20).

(i) What is the position of elements *X* and *Y* in the periodic table?

(ii) What will be the nature of oxide of element *Y*? Identify the nature of bonding in the compound formed.

(iii) Also write valencies of these elements.

Ans. *X* is the non-metal, while *Y* is the metal.

Divalent halide = YX_2

(i) Position of *X* (2, 8, 7) - Group - 17, Period - 3

Position of *Y* (2,8, 8, 2)- Group - 2, Period - 4

(ii) Oxide of element *Y* (*YO*) is **basic** in nature as *Y* is an alkaline earth metal found in 2nd group of periodic table that forms basic oxides. It forms **ionic bond**.

(iii) *X* belongs to group 17 so, valency is 8 – 7 = 1 and *Y* belongs to group 2 so, valency is 2. **(1 × 3 = 3)**

Q.8 This question refers to elements of the periodic table with atomic numbers from 3 to 18. In the table below some elements are shown by letters, even though the letters are not the usual symbols of the elements.

3	4	5	6	7	8	9	10
A	B	C	D	E	F	G	H
11	12	13	14	15	16	17	18
I	J	K	L	M	N	O	P

(i) Which of these element have valency 4?

(ii) If A combines with F, what would be the formula of the resulting compound?

(iii) What is the electronic configuration of G?

Ans. (i) **D and L** have valency 4, as they are in group IVA and have 4 valence electrons. **(1)**

(ii) Valency of *A* [2, 1] is 1, so it loses one electron to attain a stable state.

Valency of F [2, 6] is –2, so it gains two electrons and attain a stable state. Hence, one F atom takes electron from two *A* atoms. Therefore, the formula of their compound will be $\mathbf{A_2F}$. **(1)**

(iii) Electronic configuration of G is **[2, 7]** as its atomic number is 9. **(1)**

Q.9 Write the name of elements based on the electronic configuration:

(i) 2, 8, 5 (ii) 2, 8, 8 (iii) 2, 8, 8, 1

Ans. (i) Phosphorus (P)

(ii) Argon (Ar)

(iii) Potassium (K) **(1 × 3 = 3)**

Q.10 Give the element which has

(i) thrice the number of electrons in second shell as in its first shell

(ii) only one shell which has two electrons

(iiii) 3 shells in total and 3 electrons in its valence shell.

Ans. (i) Oxygen, (O → 2, 6)

(ii) Helium (He → 2)

(iii) Aluminium (Al → 2, 8, 3) **(1 × 3 = 3)**

Q.11 Which of the following elements belong to

(i) same period? (ii) same group?

Explain giving reason.

Element	Atomic number
A	3
B	11
C	17

Ans. Electronic configuration of *A, B, C* are

	K	*L*	*M*
A	2	1	
B	2	8	1
C	2	8	7

(i) **Elements *B* and *C*** belong to the same period in the periodic table because both have same number of shells as electronic configuration of *B* and *C* are 2, 8, 1 and 2, 8, 7 respectively. **(2)**

(ii) **Elements *A* and *B*** belong to the same group as both have same number of valence electrons (i.e. one). **(1)**

Q.12 The position of elements A, B, C, D and E in the periodic table are shown below:

Group 1	Group 2	Group 17	Group 18
—	—	—	D
—	B	C	
A	—	—	E

(i) State which are metals and non-metals in this table.

(ii) State which is the most reactive (i) metal (ii) non-metal.

(iii) Which type of ion will be formed by elements A and C?

Ans. (i) Metals - A, B; Non-metal - C **(1)**

(ii) (a) Most reactive metal - A

(b) Most reactive non-metal - C **(1)**

(iii) A will form A^+ (cation).

C will form C^- (anion). **(1)**

Q.13 (i) What colour does sodium and potassium salt impart to the flame?

(ii) Why are alkali metals strong reducing agent?

(iii) How can we obtain alkali metals from their molten salts.

Ans. (i) The colour of the flame of sodium is golden yellow and the colour of the flame of potassium is pale violet.

(ii) Alkali metals lose their valence electrons easily. So, they are strong reducing agent.

(iii) Alkali metals are obtained by electrolysis of their molten salts. **(1 × 3 = 3)**

Q.14 Mention any three characteristics of halogens.

Ans. Three characteristics of halogens are

(i) They are highly reactive non-metallic elements. **(1)**

(ii) All the halogens are coloured. F_2 is yellow, Cl_2 is greenish yellow, Br_2 is reddish brown and I_2 is violet in colour. **(1)**

(iii) Most of the metals react with halogens to form metal halides as $2M + nX_2 \longrightarrow 2MX_n$

(Here, M = metal, n = valency of the metal, X = F, Cl, Br or I) **(1)**

Q.15 Arrange the following.

(i) Elements of group 1, in increasing order of reactivity.

(ii) Elements of group 17, in decreasing order of reactivity.

(iii) Al, Na, Mg in increasing order of valency.

Ans. (i) The increasing order of reactivity among group 1 elements is $\xrightarrow[\text{Reactivity increases}]{\text{Li < Na < K < Rb}}$ **(1)**

(ii) The elements of group 17 in decreasing order of reactivity.

$$\xrightarrow[\text{Reactivity decreases}]{\text{F > Cl > Br > I}}$$ **(1)**

(iii) Al, Na, Mg in increasing order of valency is

Element: Na < Mg < Al

Valency: 1 2 3 **(1)**

Q.16 Use the periodic table of the elements in answering the given below question.

(i) What common name is given to the element in

(a) Group 18 (b) Group 1

(ii) Write the formula of chloride formed that results from the reaction of an element M from group 2 with an element X from group 17.

Ans. (i) (a) Noble gases **(1)**

(b) Alkali metals **(1)**

(ii) MX_2 **(1)**

Q.17 What are the uses of noble gases?

Ans. Uses of noble gases.

(i) Helium is used in airships and balloons because it is both light and unreactive gas.

(ii) Argon is used to fill light bulbs because it will not react with the filament even at high temperature.

(iii) The best use of the noble gas is their use in 'neon' lights. The brightly coloured advertising light works when an electric discharge is passed in a tube containing a little amount of noble gas.

Different noble gases impart different colours. **(1 × 3 = 3)**

Q.18 The periodic table is a powerful tool for understanding the properties of elements. Fill in the blanks:

1. The modern periodic table is arranged based on the .... of elements.
2. Elements in Group 18 of the periodic table are called ....
3. The modern periodic table has 7 ....

Ans. 1. atomic number 2. noble gases 3. periods **(1 × 3 = 3)**

Q.19 Name the following with reference to the element of the first three periods of the periodic table.

(i) Noble gas with duplet arrangement of electrons.

(ii) Metalloid in period 3.

(iii) Element which imparts salt yellow colour during flame test.

Ans. (i) Helium **(1)**

(ii) Silicon **(1)**

(iii) Sodium **(1)**

TYPE - 9 04/05 Marks

Long Answer Type Questions

Q.1 Mendeleev predicted the existence of certain elements not known at that time and named two of them as eka-silicon and eka-aluminium.

(i) Name the elements which have taken the place of these elements.

(ii) Mention the group and the period of these elements in the long form periodic table.

(iii) Classify these elements as metals or non-metals or metalloids.

(iv) How many valence electrons are present in each one of them?

Ans. (i) Germanium as eka-silicon and gallium as eka-aluminium have taken the place of these elements.

(ii) Germanium - Group 14, Period 4
Gallium - Group 13, Period 4

(iii) Germanium is a metalloid and gallium is a metal.

(iv) In germanium, the number of valence electrons is 4 and in gallium, it is 3. **(1 × 4 = 4)**

Q.2 What are transition and inner transition elements? Give two characteristics of each.

Ans. (i) ***d*-block elements are known as transition elements.**

They include groups 3, 4, 5, 6, 7, 8, 9, 10, 11 and 12.

Characteristics of transition elements.

(a) All these elements are metals with high melting and boiling points.

(b) They are good conductors of heat and electricity. **(2)**

(ii) ***f*-block elements are called inner transition elements.**

The elements of the sixth and seventh periods of Group 3 or III B i.e. the lanthanides and the actinides, are collectively known as inner transition elements.

Characteristics of inner transition elements.

(a) They are heavy metals with high melting and boiling points.

(b) They show variable valencies. **(2)**

Q.3 Atomic number of a few elements are given below.
10, 20, 7, 14

(i) Identify the element with atomic number 7.

(ii) Identify the group number of the element of atomic number 10.

(iii) Identify the period of element of atomic mumber 7.

(iv) What would be the electronic configuration for the element of atomic mumber 20?

Ans. (i) The element with atomic number 7 is **nitrogen**.

(ii) Group number = 18
(Group no. = 10 + No. of valence electron)

(iii) The period is **2** (period no. is equal to number of shells).

(iv) Electronic configuration of calcium – *K L M N*
2 8 8 2

(1 × 4 = 4)

Q.4 Name the following.

(i) A halogen of period four.

(ii) Alkali metal of period four.

(iii) Smallest period.

(iv) Noble gas of period four.

Ans. (i) Bromine

(ii) Potassium

(iii) First period

(iv) Krypton **(1 × 4 = 4)**

Q.5 You are provided with a part of periodic table, the symbols, capital *A*, *B*, *C*, *D*, etc. are not the symbols of the elements.

Group 1	2	13	14	15	16	17	18
A	*C*	*D*	*E*	*F*	*G*	*H*	*I*
B						*K*	*J*

Answer the following questions with reference to the above periodic table.

(i) Give an element that forms a monovalent cation.

(ii) Give an element that forms a monovalent anion.

(iii) Give an element that forms a divalent anion.

(iv) Out of *K* and *H*, which is more reactive and why?

Ans. (i) *A*

(ii) *H*

(iii) *G*

(iv) *H* (reactivity of non-metals decreases down the group). **(1 × 4 = 4)**

Q.6 (i) "Hydrogen occupies a unique position in the modern periodic table". Justify the statement.

(ii) Give one use of

(a) Argon gas

(b) Neon gas

Ans. (i) In electronic configuration, hydrogen (1) resembles with alkali metals. Moreover, it combines with halogen, oxygen and sulphur to give similar type of compounds as given by alkali metals. e.g. (HCl, NaCl), (H_2O, Na_2O), (H_2S, Na_2S).

But just like halogens, it exists in diatomic form and combines with metals and non-metals to form covalent compounds. In the periodic table, a unique position has been given to the hydrogen. It is kept at the top left corner because of its unique characteristic. **(2)**

(ii) (a) Argon gas is used to provide an inert atmosphere in high temperature metallurgical process. **(1)**

(b) Neon gas is used in discharge tubes. **(1)**

Q.7 **(i) A metal *M* forms an oxide having the formula *MO*. It belongs to 2nd period in the modern periodic table. Write its atomic number and valency.**

(ii) Write the reaction of alkaline earth metal with

(a) oxygen (b) water (c) dil. HCl

Ans. (i) Since, the metal form *MO* type oxide, it belongs to second group and have configuration 2, 2 because it has two shells. Thus, atomic number of the element is 4 and its valency is 2. **(2)**

(ii) (a) Alkaline earth metals reacts with oxygen to form respective oxides.

$$2M + O_2 \longrightarrow 2MO$$

(where, *M* = any alkaline earth metals)

(b) They reacts with water to produce a base and hydrogen gas.

$$\underset{\text{Alkaline earth metal}}{M} + 2H_2O \longrightarrow \underset{\text{Alkali}}{M(OH)_2} + H_2\uparrow$$

(c) $M + \underset{\text{Dil.}}{2HCl} \longrightarrow MCl_2 + H_2\uparrow$ **(3)**

Q.8 **The position of three elements *A*, *B* and *C* in the periodic table are shown below.**

Group 16	Group 17
—	—
—	A
—	—
B	C

(i) State whether *A* is a metal or non-metal.

(ii) State whether *C* is more reactive or less reactive than *A*.

(iii) *B* will form Na_2B with sodium. Explain.

(iv) Which type of ion, cation or anion, will be formed by *A* ?

(v) Write name of first element of group 17.

Ans. (i) *A* is a **non-metal** (*A* belongs to group 17 and has 7 valence electrons so, it is a non-metal because it will gain an electron to complete its octet).

(ii) **C is less reactive than** A. (reactivity of non-metals decreases down the group as tendency to gain electron decreases).

(iii) *B* belongs to group-16, so it has 6 valence electrons, and it can gain two electrons to complete its octet, so its valency is 2. Sodium belongs to group -1 and has a valency of 1. Thus, the compound formed between Na and *B* will have Na_2B formula.

(iv) As discussed in part (i) that element *A* has a tendency to gain electron to complete its octet. It needs to take up one electron, so it will form **anion (A^-)**.

(v) First element of group 17 is **fluorine (F)**. **(1 × 5 = 5)**

Q.9 **(i) Properties of the elements are given below. Where would you locate the following elements in the periodic table?**

(a) A soft metal stored in kerosene.

(b) An element with variable (more than one) valency stored in water.

(c) An element which is tetravalent (valency 4) and forms the basis of organic chemistry.

(d) An element which is an inert gas with atomic number 2.

(ii) Write the chemical formula of sodium oxide.

Ans. (i) (a) Group 1, Period 3 (Na)

(b) Group 15, Period 3 (P)

(c) Group 14, Period 2 (C)

(d) Group 18, Period 1 (He) **(1 × 4 = 4)**

(ii) Chemical formula of sodium oxide is Na_2O. **(1)**

Q.10 **The table given below shows the mass number and number of neutrons of four elements, *P*, *Q*, *R* and *S*.**

Elements	P	Q	R	S
Mass number	12	20	23	35
Number of neutrons	6	10	12	18

(i) Write the atomic number of *P*, *Q*, *R* and *S*.

(ii) Write down electronic configuration of *P*, *Q*, *R* and *S*.

(iii) To which period *P*, *Q*, *R* and *S* belong?

(iv) To which group *P*, *Q*, *R* and *S* belong?

(v) Name which amongst *P*, *Q*, *R* and *S* is a halogen.

Ans.

	Elements	P	Q	R	S
(i)	Atomic number	(12 – 6) = 6	(20 – 10) = 10	(23 – 12) = 11	(35 – 18) = 17
(ii)	Electronic configuration	2, 4	2, 8	2, 8, 1	2, 8, 7
(iii)	Period	2nd	2nd	3rd	3rd
(iv)	Group	IV A or 14	Zero or 18	I A or 1	VII A or 17

(v) **S** is a halogen. **(1 × 5 = 5)**

Q.11 Given the name and symbol of the following elements which occupy each of the following positions in the periodic table.

(i) Period 2, group III A
(ii) Period 2, group VI A
(iii) Period I, group I A
(iv) Period 3, group VII A
(v) Period 3, group zero

Ans. (i) The element in period 2, group III A is: **Boron**
(ii) The element in period 2, group VI A is: **Oxygen**
(iii) The element in period 1, group I A is: **Hydrogen**
(iv) The element in period 3, group VII A is: **Chlorine**
(v) The element in period 3, group zero is: **Argon** **$(1 \times 5 = 5)$**

Q.12 Write the electronic configuration of the element $^{35}_{17}T$ and answer the following questions.

(i) What is the group number of *T*?
(ii) What is the period number of *T*?
(iii) How many valence electrons are there in an atom of *T*?
(iv) What is the valency of *T*?
(v) Is it a metal or a non-metal?

Ans. The electronic configuration of $^{35}_{17}T$ is 2, 8, 7.

(i) Group number of *T* is **VIIA or 17** [∵ it has 7 valence electrons].
(ii) Period number of *T* is **third period** [∵ it has 3 shells].
(iii) Valence electrons in *T* are **seven** [from electronic configuration].
(iv) Valency of *T* is **1** [∵ it needs to gain one electron to complete its octet].
(v) *T* is a **non-metal** [∵ is has a tendency to accept electrons]. **$(1 \times 5 = 5)$**

TYPE - 10 — 03 Marks

Case-Based Questions

Q.1 Ramesh was studying about the properties of an element *M* which belongs to group I of the periodic table. He observed that during flame test, its salt imparted pale violet colour.

(i) Identify the element *M* and write its electronic configuration.
(ii) How does *M* react with water?
(iii) Why is element *M* kept in kerosene oil and not in air?

Ans. (i) Element *M*: Potassium (K)
Electronic configuration: 2, 8, 8, 1

(ii) *M* reacts violently with water to produce alkali and hydrogen gas.

$$2M + 2H_2O \longrightarrow \underset{\text{(Alkali)}}{2MOH} + H_2$$

(iii) Element *M* reacts rapidly and violently with atmospheric oxygen to from metal oxides, thus it is kept in kerosene oil and not in air.

$$4M + O_2 \longrightarrow 2M_2O$$ **$(1 \times 3 = 3)$**

Q.2 An element *Y* is placed in Group 17 and Period 2 of the periodic table.

(i) Identify the element *Y*. Write its electronic configuration.
(ii) What is the valency of this element? Explain.
(iii) Compare its reactivity with other elements in Group 17.

Ans. (i) Element *Y*: Fluorine (F).
Electronic configuration: 2, 7.

(ii) The valency of fluorine is **1**.
It needs one electron to complete its octet.

(iii) Fluorine is the most reactive halogen in Group 17 because it has the smallest atomic size and highest electron egativity. **$(1 \times 3 = 3)$**

Q.3 An element *X* has an atomic number of 19 and is placed in Group 1 of the modern periodic table.
Answer the following questions.

(i) Identify the element *X*. What is its electronic configuration?
(ii) Which period does it belong to? Justify your answer.
(iii) Predict the nature of the oxide of this element.

Ans. (i) Element *X* : potassium (K) .
Electronic configuration: 2, 8, 8, 1.

(ii) Period: It belongs to the **4**th **period**.
The number of electronic shells occupied by electrons are four (*K*, *L*, *M* and *N* shells).

(iii) Potassium forms an oxide with the formula **K_2O** which is **basic** in nature. **$(1 \times 3 = 3)$**

STUDY OF THE FIRST ELEMENT-HYDROGEN

Hydrogen is the **lightest element** known to us, it is thus placed at the first position in the periodic table. The atomic number of hydrogen is 1 and it has **no neutrons**. It is represented by the symbol H. It was discovered by **Cavendish** and named by **Lavoisier**.

Position of Hydrogen in the Periodic Table

Hydrogen belongs to first group and first period of the periodic table. Hydrogen shows dual nature, since it resembles the alkali metals of **group IA (1)** and the halogens of **group VIIA (17)**.

Similarity of Hydrogen with Alkali Metals and Halogens

	Similarity of hydrogen with alkali metals [Group 1 (IA)]	**Similarity of hydrogen with halogens [Group 17 (VIIA)]**
Electronic configuration	There is 1 electron in the valence shell. e.g. H = 1; Li = 2,1; Na = 2,8,1; K = 2,8,8,1	One electron less than the nearest noble gas. e.g. H = 1 (He = 2); F = 2,7 (Ne = 2,8); Cl = 2,8,7 (Ar = 2,8,8)
Ion formation	Electropositive character exhibited. e.g. $H - 1e^- \longrightarrow H^+$ $Li - 1e^- \longrightarrow Li^+$ $Na - 1e^- \longrightarrow Na^+$	Electronegative character exhibited. e.g. $H + 1e^- \longrightarrow H^-$ $F + 1e^- \longrightarrow F^-$ $Cl + 1e^- \longrightarrow Cl^-$
Valency	Electrovalency of one exhibited. H^+, Li^+, Na^+	Electrovalency and covalency of 1 exhibited.
Reactions	Strong affinity for non-metals like O, S, Cl, i.e. both have a tendency to react with certain non-metals. **Hydrogen forms** H_2O, H_2S, HCl **Sodium forms** Na_2O, Na_2S, NaCl	Both of them react with alkali. e.g. NaH, CaH_2, NaCl, $CaCl_2$.
Physical state	—	Like halogen (F and Cl), hydrogen too is a gas.
Reducing agent	Acts as a reducing agent. **Hydrogen** $CuO + H_2 \longrightarrow Cu + H_2O$ **Sodium** $CuO + 2Na \longrightarrow Cu + Na_2O$	—

	Similarity of hydrogen with alkali metals [Group 1 (IA)]	Similarity of hydrogen with halogens [Group 17 (VIIA)]
Atomicity	—	Diatomic molecules are formed (two atoms linked by a single bond). **Hydrogen** $H \overset{\times}{\bullet} H$ or $H—H \longrightarrow H_2$ **Chlorine** $:\ddot{Cl}\overset{\times}{\bullet}\overset{\times\times}{\underset{\times\times}{Cl}}\overset{\times}{\times}$ or $Cl—Cl \longrightarrow Cl_2$
Burning	Burns with oxygen to form oxides. • Hydrogen burns with **pop sound** to form neutral oxide (water). $2H_2 + O_2 \longrightarrow 2H_2O$ • Sodium burns vigorously to form sodium oxide. $2Na + O_2 \longrightarrow 2Na_2O$ • Hydrogen also forms peroxide like sodium. $H_2 + O_2 \longrightarrow H_2O_2$ $2Na + O_2 \longrightarrow Na_2O_2$	—

Properties different from Alkali Metals as well as Halogens

- Hydrogen has only one shell, while in alkali metals and halogens, there are more than one shell.
- Oxides of alkali metals are basic, while those of halogens are generally acidic. Oxide of hydrogen, i.e. water (H_2O) is, however a neutral oxide.
- Hydrogen is less electropositive than alkali metals and less electronegative than halogens.

Preparation of Hydrogen from Water

Action of metals on water in different states or at different temperature produces hydrogen gas. The reactions are as follows

(i) Action of Active Metals with Cold Water

Active metals like **sodium**, **potassium** and **calcium** being highly reactive, reacts with cold water producing bases (hydroxides of metals) and **hydrogen gas**.

$$\underset{\text{Metal}}{2M} + \underset{\text{Cold water}}{2H_2O} \longrightarrow \underset{\text{Metal hydroxide}}{2MOH} + \underset{\text{Hydrogen}}{H_2\uparrow} \quad \text{(where, } M = \text{Na or K)}$$

$$\underset{\text{Calcium}}{Ca} + \underset{\text{Water}}{2H_2O} \longrightarrow \underset{\text{Calcium hydroxide}}{Ca(OH)_2} + \underset{\text{Hydrogen}}{H_2\uparrow}$$

The reaction with active metals is **exothermic**, and the reactions of sodium and potassium are violent and may result in explosion.

(ii) Action of Hot Water on Magnesium

Magnesium reacts with hot water slowly to produce magnesium hydroxide with the evolution of hydrogen gas.

$$\underset{\text{Magnesium}}{Mg} + \underset{\text{Hot water}}{2H_2O} \xrightarrow{\Delta} \underset{\text{Magnesium hydroxide}}{Mg(OH)_2} + \underset{\text{Hydrogen}}{H_2\uparrow}$$

Magnesium burns in steam with an intense white light, liberating hydrogen gas and white ash, i.e. magnesium oxide. e.g.

$$Mg + \underset{\text{(Steam)}}{H_2O} \longrightarrow \underset{\text{Magnesium oxide}}{MgO} + H_2\uparrow$$

(iii) Action of Steam on Metals

Metals like magnesium, aluminium, iron and zinc reacts with steam to form oxides of metals and evolve hydrogen gas. e.g.

$$\underset{\text{Aluminium}}{2Al} + \underset{\text{Steam}}{3H_2O} \xrightarrow{800^\circ C} \underset{\text{Aluminium oxide}}{Al_2O_3} + \underset{\text{Hydrogen}}{3H_2\uparrow}$$

$$Zn + \underset{\text{(steam)}}{H_2O} \longrightarrow ZnO + H_2$$

$$3Fe + \underset{\text{(steam)}}{4H_2O} \rightleftharpoons \underset{\text{Iron oxide}}{Fe_3O_4} + 4H_2 \uparrow$$

This reaction with iron is reversible. If hydrogen formed is not removed, the iron oxide formed is reduced back to iron.

(iv) Action of Steam on Non-metals

When steam is passed over red hot coke, water gas ($CO + H_2$) is formed.

$$\underset{\substack{\text{Carbon} \\ \text{(Red hot coke)}}}{C} + \underset{\text{Steam}}{H_2O(g)} \longrightarrow \underbrace{CO + H_2}_{\text{Water gas}}$$

Application of Activity Series in the Preparation of Hydrogen

The arrangement of metals in decreasing order of reactivity is called **activity series of metals.**

K	—	Potassium	
Na	—	Sodium	Highly reactive
Ca	—	Calcium	↑
Mg	—	Magnesium	
Al	—	Aluminium	
Zn	—	Zinc	
Fe	—	Iron	
Ni	—	Nickel	
Sn	—	Tin	
Pb	—	Lead	
H	—	Hydrogen	
Cu	—	Copper	
Hg	—	Mercury	
Ag	—	Silver	
Au	—	Gold	
Pt	—	Platinum	Less reactive

Hydrogen, though a non-metal is included in the series due to its ability to form positive ion.

- Metals present on the top of the series are active metals.
- The ability of metals to reduce water to hydrogen decreases on going down the series.
- The tendency of any metal to get oxidised decreases down the series. So, potassium is the most readily oxidised metal.
- Electropositive character and reducing power of metals decreases down the series.
- A metal higher up in the series displaces a metal below it from the salt solution of latter and *vice-versa* does not takes place.

i.e. $CuSO_4(aq) + Zn(s) \longrightarrow ZnSO_4\,(aq) + Cu$

MAKE IT EASY

PSC mazintl (e.g. P = Potassium, S = Sodium, C = Calcium, M = Magnesium, A = Aluminium, Z = Zinc, I = Iron, N = Nickel, T = Tin, L = Lead).

Displacement of Hydrogen from Dilute Acids

- Few metals which are **more active than hydrogen** in activity series (or reactivity series) **displaces hydrogen from acids.**
- Metals such as Zn, Fe, Al and Mg (above hydrogen in the activity series) react with dil. H_2SO_4 or HCl at room temperature, liberating hydrogen and forming their respective salts. e.g.

$$\underset{\text{Zinc}}{Zn} + \underset{\text{Sulphuric acid}}{H_2SO_4} \longrightarrow \underset{\text{Zinc sulphate}}{ZnSO_4} + \underset{\text{Hydrogen gas}}{H_2\uparrow}$$

$$\underset{\text{(Aluminium)}}{2Al} \quad 6HCl \longrightarrow 2AlCl_3 + 3H_2 \uparrow$$

$$\underset{\text{(Magnesium)}}{Mg} + H_2SO_4 \longrightarrow MgSO_4 + H_2 \uparrow$$

$$\underset{\text{(Iron)}}{Fe} + 2HCl \longrightarrow FeCl_2 + H_2 \uparrow$$

- On the other hand, **metals** which are **less reactive than hydrogen** like copper and silver (below hydrogen in the activity series) has **no effect on acid**. e.g.

$$Cu + H_2SO_4 \longrightarrow \text{No reaction}$$

- **Potassium**, **sodium** and **calcium** react with dilute H_2SO_4 and HCl but the reaction is **explosive** and thus is feasible.
- Nitric acid is not used to form hydrogen because it is a strong oxidising agent and it oxidises the hydrogen gas to form water. Only magnesium and manganese react with very dilute nitric acid to form H_2.

$$M + 2HNO_3 \longrightarrow \underset{\text{Metal nitrate}}{M(NO_3)_2} + H_2 \uparrow \qquad \text{(where, } M = \text{Mg and Mn)}$$

Displacement of Hydrogen from Alkalis

- Powdered form of active metals like aluminium, zinc and lead, when boiled with alkalis (like NaOH , KOH) evolve hydrogen gas.

$$\underset{\text{Aluminium}}{2Al} + \underset{\text{Sodium hydroxide}}{2NaOH} + \underset{\text{Water}}{2H_2O} \longrightarrow \underset{\text{Sodium } meta \text{ aluminate}}{2NaAlO_2} + 3H_2 \uparrow$$

$$\underset{\text{Aluminium}}{2Al} + \underset{\text{Potassium hydroxide}}{2KOH} + \underset{\text{Water}}{2H_2O} \longrightarrow \underset{\text{Potassium } meta \text{ aluminate}}{2KAlO_2} + 3H_2 \uparrow$$

$$\underset{\text{Zinc}}{Zn} + \underset{\text{Sodium hydroxide}}{2NaOH} \longrightarrow \underset{\text{Sodium zincate}}{Na_2ZnO_2} + H_2 \uparrow$$

$$\underset{\text{Zinc}}{Zn} + \underset{\text{Potassium hydroxide}}{2KOH} \longrightarrow \underset{\text{Potassium zincate}}{K_2ZnO_2} + H_2 \uparrow$$

$$\underset{\text{Lead}}{Pb} + \underset{\text{Sodium hydroxide}}{2NaOH} \longrightarrow \underset{\text{Sodium plumbite}}{Na_2PbO_2} + H_2 \uparrow$$

$$\underset{\text{Lead}}{Pb} + \underset{\text{Potassium hydroxide}}{2KOH} \longrightarrow \underset{\text{Potassium plumbite}}{K_2PbO_2} + H_2 \uparrow$$

- Metals like zinc, lead and aluminium react with both acids and alkalis to produce hydrogen and salts. This is **unique nature** of these metals. Their oxides and hydroxides have both basic and acidic nature. Therefore, they are called **amphoteric oxides** or **hydroxides**.

Laboratory Preparation of Hydrogen Gas

- In laboratory, hydrogen is mainly prepared by treating zinc granules either with dilute sulphuric acid or dilute hydrochloric acid.

$$\underset{\text{Zinc}}{Zn} + \underset{\text{Dil. sulphuric acid}}{H_2SO_4} \longrightarrow \underset{\text{Zinc sulphate}}{ZnSO_4} + \underset{\text{Hydrogen}}{H_2 \uparrow}$$

$$Zn + \underset{\text{Dil. hydrochloric acid}}{2HCl} \longrightarrow \underset{\text{Zinc chloride}}{ZnCl_2} + H_2 \uparrow$$

- Zinc metal is preferred over other active metals as hydrogen gas is produced slowly in the reaction and hence, it is easy to collect the gas in this case.
- Also, zinc granules are preferred for this reaction over pure zinc because the impurity present in zinc granules is copper, whose catalysing effect speeds up the rate of reaction.

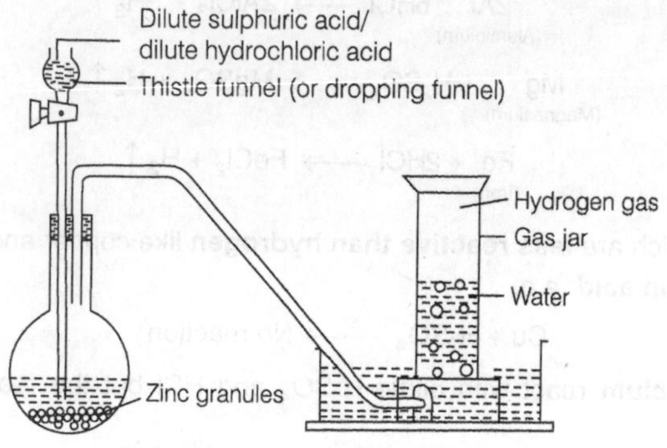

Laboratory preparation of hydrogen

Collection of Hydrogen

- Hydrogen is collected by **downward displacement of water** as it is very virtually insoluble in water.
- Hydrogen forms an explosive mixture with air, thus it is not collected by downward displacement of air, even though it is lighter than air.
- Main impurities that are usually found in hydrogen gas are phosphine (PH_3), arsine (AsH_3), hydrogen sulphide (H_2S), sulphur dioxide (SO_2), oxides of nitrogen, carbon dioxide (CO_2), water vapour (H_2O), etc.

Removal of Impurities

- To remove the impurities, hydrogen gas is treated with following compounds or reagents.

Reagents/Compounds	Impurities removed
Silver nitrate solution (*aq.* $AgNO_3$) e.g. $\underset{\text{Arsine}}{AsH_3} + 6AgNO_3 \longrightarrow \underset{\text{Silver arsenide}}{Ag_3As} + 3AgNO_3 + 3HNO_3$ $\underset{\text{Phosphine}}{PH_3} + 6AgNO_3 \longrightarrow \underset{\text{Silver phosphide}}{Ag_3P} + 3AgNO_3 + 3HNO_3$	PH_3, AsH_3
Lead nitrate solution (*aq.* $Pb(NO_3)_2$) e.g. $Pb(NO_3)_2 + \underset{\text{Hydrogen sulphide}}{H_2S} \longrightarrow \underset{\text{Lead sulphide}}{PbS} + 2HNO_3$	H_2S
Potassium hydroxide solution (*aq.* KOH) e.g. $\underset{\text{Sulphur dioxide}}{SO_2} + 2KOH \longrightarrow \underset{\text{Potassium sulphite}}{K_2SO_3} + H_2O$ $\underset{\text{Carbon dioxide}}{CO_2} + 2KOH \longrightarrow \underset{\text{Potassium carbonate}}{K_2CO_3} + H_2O$ $\underset{\text{Nitrogen dioxide}}{2NO_2} + 2KOH \longrightarrow \underset{\text{Potassium nitrite}}{KNO_2} + KNO_3 + H_2O$	SO_2, CO_2 and oxides of nitrogen (acidic gases)
Anhydrous calcium chloride ($CaCl_2$), caustic potash stick or phosphorous pentaoxide remove water vapour as they act as **drying agent**.	

- Concentrated sulphuric acid is a good drying agent but it is not used to dry hydrogen as it reacts with hydrogen, thus defeating the purpose of the reaction.

$$\text{Conc. } H_2SO_4 + H_2 \longrightarrow 2H_2O + SO_2$$

- Also, concentrated sulphuric acid is not used in the preparation of hydrogen gas because it is a good oxidising agent and will produce SO_2 on reaction with zinc.

$$Zn + \underset{\text{Conc.}}{2H_2SO_4} \longrightarrow \underset{\text{Zinc sulphate}}{ZnSO_4} + SO_2\uparrow + 2H_2O$$

Industrial Preparation of Hydrogen Gas By Bosch Process

Various steps involved in this process are as follows

1. Production of Water Gas: Coal Gasification

On passing super-heated steam over red hot coke or coal at 1000° C in the presence of Ni as catalyst, a mixture of carbon monoxide (CO) and dihydrogen (H_2) is obtained. This reaction is endothermic.

$$C(s) + H_2O(g) \xrightarrow[Ni]{1000°C} \underbrace{CO(g) + H_2(g)}_{\text{Water gas}}$$

2. Reduction of Steam by Water Gas

In order to remove CO and to increase the production of hydrogen from water gas, CO of the water gas is oxidised to CO_2 by mixing it with more steam at 673 K in the presence of iron chromate or ferric oxide and little chromium oxide (at 450°C) as catalyst. This reaction is exothermic.

$$\underbrace{CO(g) + H_2(g)}_{\text{Water gas}} + \underset{\text{Steam}}{H_2O(g)} \xrightarrow[Fe_2O_3,\ Cr_2O_3]{450°C} CO_2(g) + 2H_2(g)$$

3. Separation of Carbon Dioxide (CO_2) and Carbon Monoxide (CO)

(i) **Carbon dioxide** can be removed either by passing the mixture, (i.e. $CO_2 + H_2$), through cold water under high pressure. As the result most of the CO_2 is dissolved in cold water leaving behind hydrogen. It can also be removed by passing the mixture ($CO_2 + H_2$) through potassium hydroxide solution, which removes carbon dioxide by reacting with it and hydrogen remain unreactive.

$$2KOH + CO_2 \longrightarrow K_2CO_3 + H_2O$$

(ii) **Carbon monoxide** is removed by passing hydrogen gas into ammoniacal cuprous chloride solution.

$$CuCl + CO + 2H_2O \longrightarrow CuCl \cdot CO \cdot 2H_2O$$

Thus, hydrogen gas is left behind.

Tests for Hydrogen

- Impure Hydrogen gas burns with a pop sound.
- Pure hydrogen burns in air with pale blue flame to form colourless liquid water, which turns anhydrous copper sulphate white to blue.

Oxidation and Reduction Reactions

Oxidation

It is the process in which oxygen is added to a substance or the process in which hydrogen is removed from a substance.

e.g.

$$\underset{\text{Copper}}{2Cu} + \underset{\text{Oxygen}}{O_2} \xrightarrow{\text{Heat}} \underset{\text{Copper (II) oxide (Black)}}{2CuO}$$

$$\underset{\text{Hydrogen sulphide}}{H_2S} + \underset{\text{Chlorine}}{Cl_2} \longrightarrow \underset{\text{Hydrochloric acid}}{2HCl} + \underset{\text{Sulphur}}{S}$$

Reduction

It is the process in which oxygen is removed from a substance or the process in which hydrogen is added to a substance.

e.g.

$$\underset{\text{Potassium chlorate}}{2KClO_3(s)} \xrightarrow{\Delta} \underset{\text{Potassium chloride}}{2KCl(s)} + \underset{\text{Oxygen}}{3O_2(g)}$$

$$\underset{\text{Sodium}}{2Na} + \underset{\text{Hydrogen}}{H_2} \longrightarrow \underset{\text{Sodium hydride}}{2NaH}$$

- If a substance gains oxygen during a reaction, it is said to be oxidised. If a substance loses oxygen during a reaction, it is said to be reduced.
- The substance which can bring about oxidation of other substances is called an **oxidising agent**.
- The substance which can bring about reduction of other substances is called a **reducing agent**.

EXAM ORIENTED QUESTIONS

TYPE - 1 01 Mark

Multiple Choice Questions

Q.1 Water upon reaction with sodium metal produce
(a) acidic solution (b) basic solution
(c) amphoteric solution (d) neutral solution

Ans. (b) Basic solution (sodium reacts with water to form sodium hydroxide).

Q.2 An experiment is carried out to find the ability of metals to reduce water to hydrogen gas.

Four metals are placed in separate beakers is containing water in them (under precautions).

The result are shown as

Metal	Na	Cu	Al	Zn
Water	✓	×	✓	✓

Key : ✓ = reaction observed
× = no reaction observed

What is the order of reactivity of these metals?

Reactivity $\longrightarrow$
(a) Cu, Zn, Al, Na
(b) Na, Al, Zn, Cu
(c) Cu, Na, Zn, Al
(d) Cu, Al, Zn, Na

Ans. (a) The ability of metals to reduce water to hydrogen gas decreases on going down the activity series.

$$Na > Al > Zn > Cu$$

Q.3 Which of the following would displace hydrogen from acid?
(a) Copper (b) Mercury
(c) Platinum (d) None of these

Ans. (d) None of these

Q.4 Zinc metal reacts with sulphuric acid
(a) explosively (b) fast
(c) slowly (d) does not react

Ans. (c) slowly

Q.5 Hydrogen is evolved by the action cold dil.HNO_3 on
(a) Fe (b) Cu
(c) Mg (d) Al

Ans. (c) Mg

Q.6 Consider the following reaction of displacement of hydrogen from dilute acids.

$$Mn + xHNO_3 \underset{\text{Dilute nitric acid}}{\longrightarrow} Mn(NO_3)_2 + yH_2\uparrow$$

What are the values of x and y?

	x	y		x	y
(a)	1	1	(b)	2	1
(c)	1	2	(d)	2	2

Ans. (b) $Mn + 2HNO_3 \longrightarrow Mn(NO_3)_2 + H_2\uparrow$

So, $x = 2$ and $y = 1$.

Q.7 Which of the following metals is commonly used for preparing hydrogen in the lab?
(a) Sodium (b) Zinc
(c) Copper (d) Gold

Ans. (b) Zinc (as granulated zinc).

Q.8 Which of the following solution is used to remove phosphine impurity from hydrogen gas?
(a) Lead nitrate (b) Silver nitrate
(c) Lead chloride (d) Silver chloride

Ans. (b) Silver nitrate

Q.9 Impurities can be removed from hydrogen by passing it through certain solutions.

Which of the following solution could be used to remove AsH_3 and H_2S impurities?

P. AsH_3 : $AgNO_3$ solution; H_2S : $Pb(NO_3)_2$ solution
Q. AsH_3 : $Pb(NO_3)_2$ solution; H_2S : $AgNO_3$ solution
R. AsH_3 : KOH solution; H_2S : $Pb(NO_3)_2$ solution
(a) Only P (b) Only Q
(c) Only R (d) both P and R

Ans. (a) Silver nitrate ($AgNO_3$) solution is used to remove arsine (AsH_3) impurity and lead nitrate ($AgNO_3$) solution is used to remove hydrogen sulphide (H_2S) impurity from hydrogen gas.

Q.10 Carbon dioxide in Bosch process is separated as
(a) $CaCO_3$ (b) $NaHCO_3$
(c) Na_2CO_3 (d) H_2CO_3

Ans. (d) H_2CO_3 (CO_2 is passed through cold water at high pressure, so it forms H_2CO_3).

Q.11 Solubility of hydrogen in water is
(a) very low (b) moderate
(c) high (d) cannot be determined

Ans. (a) very low

Q.12 Which substance in the given reaction is getting oxidised?

$$3C + Fe_2O_3 \longrightarrow 3CO + 2Fe$$

(a) C (b) Fe_2O_3

(c) CO (d) Fe

Ans. (a) C is oxidised (as it gains oxygen).

Q.13 Which of the statement about the reaction below is incorrect?

$$2PbO(s) + C(s) \longrightarrow 2Pb(s) + CO_2(g)$$

(a) Lead is getting reduced.

(b) Carbon is getting oxidised.

(c) Lead oxide is getting reduced.

(d) Cannot be predicted.

Ans. (a) Lead is getting reduced.

Q.14 A metal oxide that is reduced by hydrogen is

(a) Al_2O_3 (b) CuO (c) CaO (d) Na_2O

Ans. (b) CuO.

$$CuO + H_2 \longrightarrow Cu + H_2O$$

TYPE - 2 01 Mark

Assertion-Reason Questions

Directions (Q. Nos. 1-5) In the following questions statements are given Assertion and Reason.

(a) Both (A) and (R) are true and (R) is the correct explanation of (A).

(b) Both (A) and (R) are true but (R) is not the correct explanation of (A).

(c) (A) is true but (R) is false.

(d) (A) is false but (R) is true.

Q.1 Assertion (A) Hydrogen is the smallest element in the periodic table.

Reason (R) Hydrogen has the lowest atomic mass of 1.008 u.

Ans. (a) Both (A) and (R) are true and (R) is the correct explanation of (A).

Hydrogen has the lowest atomic mass, 1.008 u, making it the lightest element in the periodic table.

Q.2 Assertion (A) Hydrogen gas can be prepared by the reaction of a metal with an acid.

Reason (R) The reaction of metals like zinc, magnesium and calcium with acids like hydrochloric acid or sulphuric acid produces hydrogen gas.

Ans. (a) Both (A) and (R) are true and (R) is the correct explanation of (A).

When metal like zinc reacts with hydrochloric acid, zinc chloride and hydrogen gas are produced due to the displacement of hydrogen by zinc.

Q.3 Assertion (A) Granulated zinc is used for laboratory preparation of hydrogen gas.

Reason (R) Granulated zinc has greater surface area.

Ans. (c) (A) is true but (R) is false.

Granulated zinc is preferred over pure zinc because the copper present as impurity, speeds up the rate of reaction.

Q.4 Assertion (A) Hydrogen is collected by the downward displacement of air.

Reason (R) Hydrogen is lighter than air.

Ans. (d) (A) is false but (R) is true.

Hydrogen is collected by the downward displacement of water. It forms an explosive mixture with air and therefore cannot be collected by downward displacement of air even though it is lighter than air.

Q.5 Assertion (A) Concentrated sulphuric acid is a good durying agent.

Reason (R) It is used to dry the hydrogen by removing water vapour.

Ans. (c) (A) is true but (R) is false.

Concentrated sulphuric acid is a good drying agent but it is not used to dry hydrogen as it reacts with hydrogen and thus, defeating the purpose of the reaction.

$$H_2SO_4 + H_2 \longrightarrow 2H_2O + SO_2 \uparrow$$

TYPE - 3 01 Mark

Fill in the Blanks

Q.1 Hydrogen is placed in same group as the .... (alkali, alkaline earth) metals.

Ans. alkali

Q.2 Hydrogen literally means .... producer. (acid, water)

Ans. water

Q.3 .... is a less reactive metal. (Iron, Gold)

Ans. Gold

Q.4 .... burns with a pop sound and is absorbed by metals like palladium. (Hydrogen, Carbon dioxide)

Ans. Hydrogen

Q.5 Carbon dioxide present as impurity in hydrogen gas is removed using .... solution. (aqueous KOH, ammoniacal cuprous chloride)

Ans. aqueous KOH

Q.6 .... is used as drying agent to remove moisture from hydrogen gas (Anhyd. $CaCl_2$, Anhyd. $MgCl_2$).

Ans. Anhyd. $CaCl_2$

Q.7 Water gas is a mixture of .... and hydrogen. (carbon dioxide, carbon monoxide)

Ans. carbon monoxide

Q.8 Conc. H_2SO_4 reacts with hydrogen to release .... gas. (sulphur dioxide, hydrogen sulphide).

Ans. sulphur dioxide

TYPE - 4 — 01 Mark

Correct the Incorrect Statement

Q.1 All metals which are below in the activity series gives hydrogen when reacted with an acid.

Ans. All the metals which are **above** hydrogen in the activity series gives hydrogen when reacted with acid.

Q.2 Conc. H_2SO_4 reacts with zinc to liberate hydrogen.

Ans. **Zinc** reacts with **dilue H_2SO_4** to liberate hydrogen.

Q.3 Very dilute nitric acid reacts with iron to produce hydrogen.

Ans. Very dilute nitric acid reacts with **magnesium and manganese** to produce hydrogen.

Q.4 Hydrogen is dried by passing it through conc. H_2SO_4.

Ans. Hydrogen is dried by passing it through **anhydrous calcium chloride, caustic potash or phosphorus pentoxide.**

Q.5 Hydrogen is separated from CO by passing the mixture through caustic soda solution.

Ans. Hydrogen is separated from CO by passing the mixture through **ammmonical cuprous chloride** solution.

Q.6 $KMnO_4$ and $K_2Cr_2O_7$ are used as reducing agents.

Ans. $KMnO_4$ and $K_2Cr_2O_7$ are used as **oxidising agents**.

TYPE - 5 — 01×05 = 05 Marks

Match the Columns

Q.1 Match the following columns.

Column I (Element)	Column II (Properties)
A. Aluminium	1. Does not displace hydrogen.
B. Copper	2. Used in laboratory preparation of hydrogen.
C. Potassium	3. Form amphoteric oxide.
D. Platinum	4. Most reactive metal.
E. Zinc	5. Least reactive metal than hydrogen.

Ans. A → (3), B → (1), C → (4), D → (5), E → (2).

Q.2 Match the following columns.

Column I	Column II
A. Arsine (AsH_3) and phosphine (PH_3)	1. Collected over mercury
B. Hydrogen sulphide	2. Fused calcium chloride or caustic potash stick
C. Sulphur dioxide (SO_2) carbon dioxide (CO_2), nitrogen dioxide (NO_2) all acidic gases.	3. Lead nitrate solution
D. Water vapour	4. Silver nitrate solution
E. Purified H_2 gas	5. Caustic potash solution

Ans. A → (4), B → (3), C → (5), D → (2), E → (1).

TYPE - 6 — 01 Mark

Identify the Following

Q.1 Name the gas produced by reacting active metal with water.

Ans. Hydrogen gas

Q.2 Name a metal that react reversibly with steam.

Ans. Iron

Q.3 Write the name of compound formed, when zinc reacts with KOH.

Ans. Potassium zincate (K_2ZnO_2)

Q.4 How is hydrogen gas collected?

Ans. Downward displacement of water.

Q.5 Name a solution used to remove arsine and phosphine.

Ans. Silver nitrate

Q.6 Write the name of a solution that absorbs hydrogen sulphide.

Ans. Lead nitrate

Q.7 Name the process which is used to manufacture hydrogen gas on industrial scale.

Ans. Bosch process

Q.8 Which gas is formed when steam is passed over red hot coke?

Ans. Water gas ($CO + H_2$)

Q.9 Name a solvent used to dissolve carbon monoxide gas.

Ans. Ammoniacal cuprous chloride solution.

Q.10 Name of a liquid which can acts a both oxidising and reducing agent.

Ans. Hydrogen peroxide

TYPE - 7

02 Marks

Short Answer Type I Questions

Q.1 Write any two similarities of hydrogen and halogens.

Ans. Electronic configuration: Hydrogen and halogens have one electron less than the nearest inert gas.

H = 1 [He = 2]

F = 2, 7 [Ne = 2, 8]

Cl = 2, 8, 7 [Ar = 2, 8, 8]

Valency: Both have valency 1. **(1)**

Thus, they accept one electron to attain the electronic configuration of the nearest inert gas. **(1)**

Q.2 What do you observe when sodium is added to water?

Ans. (i) It melts, forming a silvery globule, which darts about on the surface of water. **(1)**

(ii) It catches fire and burn with a golden yellow flame. **(1)**

Q.3 Give two observations when potassium is added to water.

Ans. (i) Potassium melts, forming a grey silver globule that darts about on the surface of water. **(1)**

(ii) It catches fire and burns with a lilac-coloured flame. **(1)**

Q.4 (i) Potassium should not be used for preparation of hydrogen.

(ii) Why are sodium amalgam and potassium amalgam generally used to prepare hydrogen from water?

Ans. (i) Potassium is not used for preparation of hydrogen because the reaction of water with potassium is highly exothermic and explosive. **(1)**

(ii) Sodium amalgam and potassium amalgam reacts smoothly with water. Therefore, it is safe to prepare hydrogen from their amalgams. **(1)**

Q.5 (i) Given an example of metal which can be used for preparing hydrogen from (i) cold water and (ii) hot water.

(ii) Write the balanced equation for each case.

Ans. (i) (a) Potassium

(b) Magnesium **(1)**

(ii) Potassium reacts with water to give potassium hydroxide and hydrogen gas.

$$2K + 2H_2O \longrightarrow 2KOH + H_2\uparrow$$

Magnesium reacts slowly with boiling water and forms a base (magnesium hydroxide), liberating hydrogen gas.

$$Mg + 2H_2O \longrightarrow Mg(OH)_2 + H_2\uparrow$$ **(1)**

Q.6 (i) Magnesium, aluminium and zinc reacts with steam, the reaction stops after sometime. Explain?

(ii) How are the products of reaction of magnesium with boiling water and steam different?

Ans. (i) This is because the oxides of magnesium, aluminium and zinc, i.e. magnesium oxide, aluminium oxide and zinc oxide sticks to the surface of these respective metals and do not further allow this steam to come into contact with a metal. This stops the reaction.

(ii) Magnesium reacts with boiling water to give magnesium hydroxide and hydrogen gas, whereas when magnesium reacts with steam magnesium oxide and hydrogen are formed. **(1)**

Q.7 You are provided with the list of metals mentioned below in the box

K, Al, Na, Fe, Zn

(i) From the above list, name two metals which react with cold water.

(ii) Select the least reactive metal from the list and under what conditions it shows reaction with water?

Ans. (i) **Potassium (K) and sodium (Na)** reacts with cold water. **(1)**

(ii) **Iron (Fe)** is the least reactive metal from the list. Red hot iron shows reaction only with steam. **(1)**

Q.8. A student takes Cu and Zn strips, separately in two test tubes labelled as I and II. He adds 2 mL of dilute hydrochloric acid solution to each test tube, under the observation of his teacher.

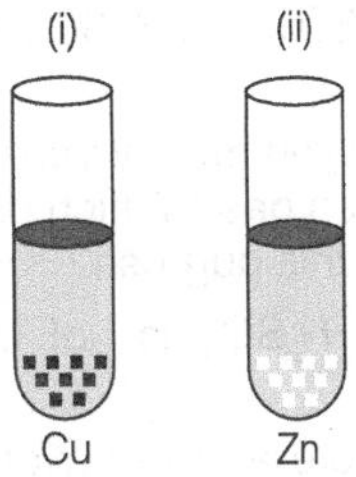

Write the reactions taking place in both the test tubes I and II

Ans. Test tube I : $Cu + HCl(dil.) \longrightarrow$ No reaction **(1)**

Test tube II : $Zn + 2HCl(dil.) \longrightarrow ZnCl_2 + H_2\uparrow$ **(1)**

Q.9 The following diagram represents the laboratory preparation of a colourless gas. Study the diagram and answer the following questions.

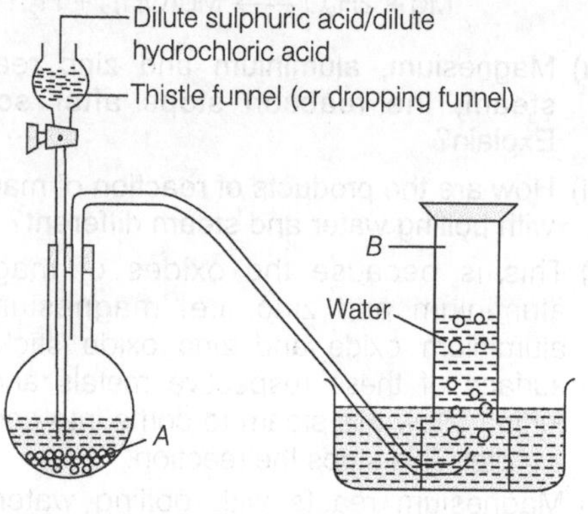

(i) Metal *A* reacts with acid to produce gas *B*. Identify *A* and *B*.

(ii) Why the end of the thistle funnel should be dipped under acid?

Ans. (i) *A* = Zinc granules

B = Hydrogen gas **(1)**

(ii) The end of the thistle funnel should be dipped under acid to **prevent gas from escaping** from the thistle funnel. **(1)**

Q.10. Give a suitable reason for the following assertions.

(i) Purified and dried hydrogen gas is collected over mercury.

(ii) Dilute sulphuric acid cannot be replaced by concentrated sulphuric acid in the preparation of hydrogen gas.

Ans. (i) Purified and dried hydrogen gas is collected over a mercury because hydrogen is free from water vapour and mercury does not react with hydrogen. **(1)**

(ii) We do not use concentrated sulphuric acid because concentrated sulphuric acid is a strong oxidiser and it will produce sulphur dioxide gas. **(1)**

$$Zn + \underset{\text{(Conc.)}}{2H_2SO_4} \longrightarrow ZnSO_4 + SO_2 + 2H_2O$$

Q.11. **(i) How would you modify your apparatus to collect dry hydrogen gas? Which drying agent would you employ for this purpose?**

(ii) Why conc. H_2SO_4 is not used to dry hydrogen gas?

Ans. (i) To collect pure and dry hydrogen gas, mercury is used.

The most suitable agent for drying hydrogen is anhydrous calcium chloride, caustic potash strick or phosphorus pentoxide. **(1)**

(ii) Conc. H_2SO_4 is a good drying agent but it is not used to dry hydrogen gas as it reacts with hydrogen and defeating the purpose of the reaction. **(1)**

Q.12 How can production of hydrogen from water gas be increased during Bosch process?

Ans. To increase the production of hydrogen from water gas, CO of the water gas is removed by oxidation of CO to CO_2 by mixing it with more steam at 673 K in the presence of iron chromate or ferric oxide and little chromium oxide (at 450°C) as catalyst.

$$\underbrace{CO(g) + H_2(g)}_{\text{Water gas}} + \underset{\text{Steam}}{H_2O\,(g)} \xrightarrow[Fe_2O_3 + Cr_2O_3]{450°C} CO_2(g) + 2H_2(g)$$

(2)

Q.13 Identify the substance that are oxidised and the substances that are reduced in the following reactions.

(i) $4Na(s) + O_2(g) \longrightarrow 2Na_2O(s)$

(ii) $CuO(s) + H_2(g) \longrightarrow Cu(s) + H_2O(l)$

Ans. (i) $Na(s) + O_2(g) \longrightarrow 2Na_2O$

So, **Na is oxidised and O_2 is reduced.** **(1)**

(ii) $CuO(s) + H_2(g) \longrightarrow Cu(s) + H_2O(l)$

CuO has lost oxygen and forms Cu.

So, **Cu is reduced while H_2 has gained oxygen hence, it is oxidised.** **(1)**

Q.14 Choose the appropriate term from the list given below to complete the following reaction.

Oxidising agent, Reducing agent, Oxidation, Reduction

$$\underset{(a)}{CuO} + \underset{(c)}{H_2} \longrightarrow Cu + H_2O$$

(d): $H_2 \rightarrow H_2O$; (b): $CuO \rightarrow Cu$

Ans. (a) : Oxidising agent (b) : Reduction **(1)**

(c) : Reducing agent (d) : Oxidation **(1)**

TYPE - 8 03 Marks

Short Answer Type II Questions

Q.1 Comment on the position of hydrogen in the periodic table.

Ans. The first element of the periodic table is hydrogen. Its valence shell has a single electron, and its atomic number is 1. As a result, it is a member of the periodic table's first group and first period. Hydrogen's characteristics are different from those of the other members of the Ist group, which is contrary to expectations.

The fundamental reason for this is because while some of hydrogen's characteristics are comparable to those of the Group 1 elements (alkali metals), others are more like those of the Group 17 (halogens) elements. **(3)**

Q.2 Compare hydrogen with alkali metals on the basis of
(i) Ion formation
(ii) Reducing power
(iii) Reaction with oxygen

Ans. (i) **Ion formation** Hydrogen forms cation like alkali metals by losing an electron.

$$H \longrightarrow H^+ + e^-$$
$$Na \longrightarrow Na^+ + e^- \quad \textbf{(1)}$$

(ii) **Reducing power** Hydrogen acts as a good reducing agents like alkali metals.

$$CuO + H_2 \longrightarrow Cu + H_2O$$
$$CuO + 2Na \longrightarrow Cu + Na_2O \quad \textbf{(1)}$$

(iii) **Reaction with oxygen** Hydrogen like alkali metals burns in air to form oxides.

$$2H_2 + O_2 \longrightarrow 2H_2O$$
$$4Li + O_2 \longrightarrow 2Li_2O \quad \textbf{(1)}$$

Q.3 How do active metals like sodium, potassium and calcium react with water? Explain your observations.

Ans. Reactive metals like potassium, sodium and calcium react with cold water, forming their corresponding hydroxides and evolving hydrogen gas. Their reactions are exothermic.

(i) $2K + 2H_2O \longrightarrow 2KOH + H_2$
(ii) $2Na + 2H_2O \longrightarrow 2NaOH + H_2$
(iii) $Ca + 2H_2O \longrightarrow Ca(OH)_2 + H_2$ **(1 × 3 = 3)**

Q.4 (i) What conditions are required for iron to react with water?
(ii) Give the balanced equation of the reaction.
(iii) What will happen if the products are not allowed to escape?

Ans. (i) Iron does not react with water directly. Red hot iron reacts with steam to produce triferric tetraoxide and hydrogen gas. **(1)**
(ii) $3Fe + 4H_2O \rightleftharpoons Fe_3O_4 + 4H_2 \uparrow$ **(1)**
(iii) If the hydrogen formed (product) is not removed then the iron oxide formed is reduced back to iron as it is a reversible reaction. **(1)**

Q.5 A small piece of calcium metal is put into a small trough containing water. There is effervescence and white turbidity is formed. After some time calcium start floating on surface of water.
(i) Name the gas formed in the reaction. How would you test the gas?
(ii) Write an equation for the reaction.
(iii) What do you observe when a few drops of red litmus solution are added to the turbid solution?

Ans. (i) **Hydrogen gas** is formed in the reaction. It can be tested by bringing burning splinter near to it. Hydrogen burns with a pop sound in oxygen. **(1)**
(ii) $Ca + 2H_2O \longrightarrow Ca(OH)_2 + H_2$ **(1)**
(iii) The red litmus solution **turns blue** as it is a basic solution (alkaline) because of presence of calcium hydroxide.

Q.6 With the help of metal of your choice write the balanced equations for preparing hydrogen in the following cases:
(i) Cold water (ii) Hot water
(iii) Steam

Ans. (i) Calcium is preferred for collecting hydrogen from cold water as the reaction is less vigorous than sodium and potassium.

$$Ca + 2H_2O \longrightarrow Ca(OH)_2 + H_2 \quad \textbf{(1)}$$

(ii) Magnesium is preferred for collecting hydrogen from hot water.

$$Mg + 2H_2O \longrightarrow Mg(OH)_2 + H_2 \quad \textbf{(1)}$$

(iii) Aluminium is preferred for collecting hydrogen from steam.

$$2Al + 3H_2O \xrightarrow{800^\circ C} Al_2O_3 + 3H_2 \quad \textbf{(1)}$$

Q.7 Complete the flowchart by identifying 'X', 'Y' and 'Z'.

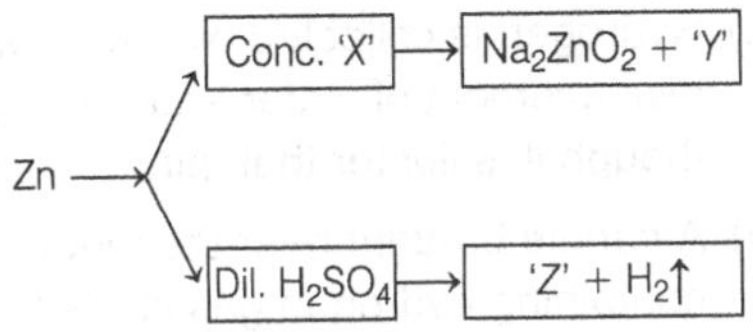

Ans. 'X' : Conc. NaOH $Y : H_2$ $Z : ZnSO_4$ **(1 × 3 = 3)**

Q.8 Why is it safe to store acid in a copper container but not in an iron container?

Ans. Iron lies above hydrogen in the activity series, hence, it displaces hydrogen from an acid when the acid is kept in an iron container.

$$\underset{\text{Iron}}{Fe} + \underset{\text{Sulphuric acid}}{H_2SO_4} \longrightarrow \underset{\text{Iron sulphate}}{FeSO_4} + \underset{\text{Hydrogen}}{H_2 \uparrow}$$

In this process iron corrodes and hence, wall of container deplete.

Whereas, copper is less reactive than hydrogen, hence it cannot react with acid to displace hydrogen.

And thus, the copper container remains harmless and can be used as a container to store acid.

$$\underset{\text{Copper}}{Cu} + \underset{\text{Sulphuric acid}}{H_2SO_4} \longrightarrow \text{No reaction} \quad \textbf{(3)}$$

Q.9 **Name any two alkalis that can be used to prepare hydrogen with metals. Give balanced equations for the same. Why are the metals you have used considered to the have unique nature?**

Ans. The two alkalies that can produce hydrogen with metals are **sodium hydroxide (NaOH) and potassium hydroxide (KOH)**. **(1)**

$$Zn + 2NaOH \longrightarrow \underset{\text{Sodium zincate}}{Na_2ZnO_2} + H_2$$

$$Pb + 2KOH \longrightarrow \underset{\text{Potassium plumbite}}{K_2PbO_2} + H_2 \quad \textbf{(1)}$$

Metals such as zinc, lead and aluminium have a unique nature because they react with acids and also with hot concentrated alkalis to form hydrogen gas and a soluble salt. **(1)**

Q.10 **Complete the following equations.**

(i) $Fe + HCl \rightarrow$ ___ + ___

(ii) $Zn + NaOH \rightarrow$ ____ + ____

(iii) $Al + KOH + H_2O \rightarrow$ ____ + ____

Ans. (i) $Fe + 2HCl \longrightarrow FeCl_2 + H_2$ **(1)**

(ii) $Zn + 2NaOH \longrightarrow Na_2ZnO_2 + H_2$ **(1)**

(iii) $2Al + 2KOH + 2H_2O \longrightarrow 2KAlO_2 + 3H_2$ **(1)**

Q.11 **Give reasons**

(i) **Hydrogen is collected by the downward displacement of water and not of air, even though it is lighter than air.**

(ii) **A candle brought near the mouth of a jar containing hydrogen gas starts burning but is extinguished when pushed inside the jar.**

(iii) **Apparatus for laboratory preparation of hydrogen should be air-tight and away from a naked flame.**

Ans. (i) Hydrogen is collected by the downward displacement of water because it is insoluble in water and it forms an explosive mixture with air. **(1)**

(ii) Hydrogen is a combustible gas, but it does not support combustion. When a candle is brought near the mouth of a jar containing hydrogen, it burns with the help of oxygen present in the atmosphere.
But when the candle is pushed inside the jar, oxygen supply gets cuts off hence the fire gets extinguished. **(1)**

(iii) Apparatus for laboratory preparation of hydrogen should be air-tight and away from a naked flame because mixture of hydrogen and air explodes violently, when brought near a flame. **(1)**

Q.12 (i) **Why zinc granules are preferred over pure zinc for the preparation of hydrogen in labs?**

(ii) **Arrange the following metals in increasing order of their reactivity toward water: sodium, magnesium, zinc, calcium, iron.**

(iii) **Name any four metals that can not displace hydrogen from dilute acid.**

Ans. (i) Because zinc granules include copper impurities that function as a catalyst and increases the rate of the reaction between zinc and dilute acid. **(1)**

(ii) Sodium > Calcium > Magnesium > Zinc > Iron **(1)**

(iii) The metals are copper, mercury, gold and silver. **(1)**

Q.13 **During laboratory preparation of hydrogen, some impurities may be present with hydrogen. The purification setup is shown below for the removal of different impurities. Three different solution (*X*, *Y* and *Z*) can be used. Identify *X*, *Y* and *Z* respectively.**

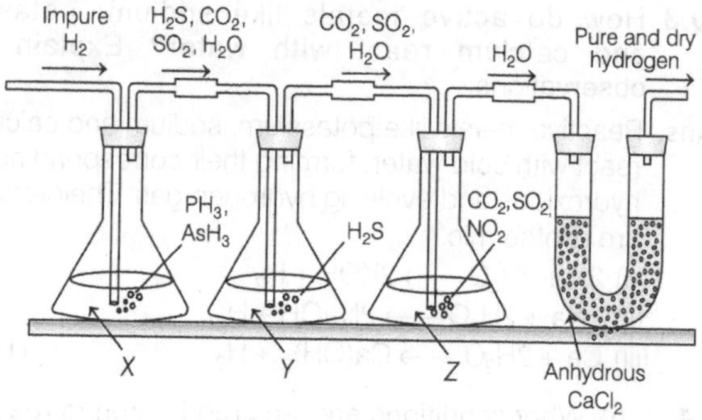

Ans. $X = AgNO_3$ solution, $Y = Pb(NO_3)_2$ solution

$Z =$ KOH solution **(1 × 3 = 3)**

Q.14 **The following table is related to an industrial process of preparation of hydrogen.**

Name of the process	Reactant	Catalyst	Final product
(i)	$(CO + H_2) + H_2O$	(ii)	(iii)

Identify (i), (ii) and (iii).

Ans. (i) Bosch process (ii) Fe_2O_3

(iii) $CO_2 + 2H_2$ **(1 × 3 = 3)**

Q.15 (i) **Write the equation involved for the laboratory preparation of hydrogen.**

(ii) **How is the hydrogen gas collected?**

(iii) **Write the confirmatory test for hydrogen gas.**

Ans. (i) Hydrogen is prepared in the laboratory by the action of dilute hydrochloric acid on granulated zinc.

$$Zn + 2HCl \longrightarrow ZnCl_2 + H_2 \uparrow \quad \textbf{(1)}$$

(ii) Hydrogen gas is collected by **downward displacement of water**. **(1)**

(iii) Hydrogen gas evolved is colourless, odourless and neutral to litmus. Hydrogen gas burns with a pale blue flame when a burning splinter is brought near it. **(1)**

Q.16 **Complete the table given below by observing the nature of the examples of some reagents.**

$K_2Cr_2O_7$	–	Solid
Carbon monoxide	Reducing agent	–
Hydrogen peroxide	–	Liquid

Ans.

$K_2Cr_2O_7$	Oxidising agent	Solid
Carbon monoxide	Reducing agent	Gas
Hydrogen peroxide	Oxidising and reducing agent	Liquid

(1 × 3 = 3)

TYPE - 9 04/05 Marks

Long Answer Type Questions

Q.1 **Which of the acid, sulphuric acid, concentrated sulphuric acid, nitric acid and concentrated nitric acid, would you choose for the preparation of hydrogen gas? Explain why you would not use the rejected acid?**

Ans. The most preferable acid is dilute sulphuric acid.
Concentrated sulphuric acid is not used because concentrated sulphuric acid produces sulphur dioxide gas.
Nitric acid is not used because it is an oxidising agent, so it oxidise hydrogen to form water and the purpose of the reaction gets defeated.
Concentrated nitric acid is also an oxidising agent. It also produces water in place of hydrogen and also nitrogen dioxide gas. **(4)**

Q.2 **(i) How is hydrogen obtained from**
(a) dilute sulphuric acid
(b) sodium hydroxide
(c) potassium hydroxide
Give one equation in each case.
(ii) What happens when aluminium reacts with steam? Give a balanced equation.

Ans. (i) (a) When metal reacts with dilute sulphuric acid, hydrogen is obtained along with metal salts.

e.g. $\underset{\text{Magnesium}}{Mg(s)} + \underset{\text{Dil. sulphuric acid}}{H_2SO_4(aq)} \longrightarrow \underset{\text{Magnesium sulphate}}{MgSO_4(aq)} + H_2(g)\uparrow$

(b) When zinc reacts with sodium hydroxide, sodium zincate is formed and hydrogen gas is evolved.

$\underset{\text{Zinc}}{Zn(s)} + \underset{\text{Sodium hydroxide}}{2NaOH(aq)} \longrightarrow \underset{\text{Sodium zincate}}{Na_2ZnO_2(aq)} + H_2(g)\uparrow$

(c) When lead reacts with potassium hydroxide, potassium plumbite is formed and hydrogen gas is evolved.

$\underset{\text{Lead}}{Pb(s)} + \underset{\text{Potassium hydroxide}}{2KOH(aq)} \longrightarrow \underset{\text{Potassium Plumbite}}{K_2PbO_2(aq)} + H_2(g)\uparrow$ **(1 × 3 = 3)**

(ii) Reaction of aluminium with steam results in the formation of hydrogen gas. But this reaction is not completed due to formation of hard Al_2O_3 layer. However, at higher temperature the coating breaks.

$\underset{\text{Aluminium}}{2Al} + \underset{\text{Steam}}{3H_2O} \xrightarrow{800^\circ C} \underset{\text{Aluminium oxide}}{Al_2O_3} + \underset{\text{Hydrogen}}{3H_2\uparrow}$ **(1)**

Q.3 **Answer the following questions with regard to laboratory preparation of hydrogen.**
(i) Name the reactant taken for the preparation of hydrogen in flat bottom flask.
(ii) Which chemical is added through thistle funnel?
(iii) How is hydrogen collected?
(iv) Why is hydrogen collected by the above stated method ?

Ans. (i) Reactant used for the preparation of hydrogen in flat bottom flask is **granulated zinc**. **(1)**

(ii) **Dilute sulphuric acid or dilute HCl** is added through thistle funnel. **(1)**

(iii) Hydrogen is collected by **downward displacement of water**. **(1)**

(iv) It is collected by above stated method because
(a) it is almost insoluble in water.
(b) it forms an explosive mixture with air. **(1)**

Q.4 **List any four precautions that must be taken during laboratory preparation of hydrogen gas.**

Ans. Following precautions must be taken while preparing the hydrogen gas in laboratory.

- The apparatus used should be airtight, otherwise gas will leak from the set up.
- There should be no flame near the apparatus as hydrogen is highly flammable.
- Make sure all the air has escaped from the setup as the mixture of hydrogen gas and air is highly explosive.
- The end of the thistle funnel must be dipped in acid, otherwise gas will also escape through the thistle funnel. **(1 × 4 = 4)**

Q.5. (i) Complete the following reactions:

(a) $C(s) + H_2O(g) \xrightarrow{Ni, \Delta}$

(b) $Zn(s) + NaOH(aq) \xrightarrow{Heat}$

(c) $(CO + H_2) + H_2O \xrightarrow[450°C]{Fe_2O_3}$

(ii) What do you understand by the term 'water gas'?

Ans. (i) (a) $\underset{\text{Carbon}}{C(s)} + \underset{\text{Water}}{H_2O(g)} \xrightarrow{Ni, \Delta} \underbrace{CO(g) + H_2(g)}_{\text{Water gas}}$

(b) $\underset{\text{Zinc}}{Zn(s)} + \underset{\text{Sodium hydroxide}}{2NaOH(aq)} \xrightarrow{Heat} \underset{\text{Sodium zincate}}{Na_2ZnO_2(aq)} + H_2(g)$

(c) $(CO + H_2) + H_2O \xrightarrow[450°C]{Fe_2O_3} CO_2 + 2H_2$ **(3)**

(ii) **Water gas** Mixture of CO and H_2 is known as synthesis gas or water gas. Reaction of steam on hydrocarbons or coke at high temperatures in the presence of catalyst yields water gas.

e.g. $\underset{\text{Red hot coke}}{C(s)} + \underset{\text{Steam}}{H_2O(g)} \xrightarrow[Ni]{\Delta} \underbrace{CO(g) + H_2(g)}_{\text{Water gas}}$ **(1)**

Q.6 **Give the difference between oxidation and reduction with examples.**

Ans. **Oxidation** is defined as a chemical process which involves either the addition of oxygen to the substance or loss of hydrogen from the substance. **(1)**

e.g.

Oxidation ($H_2S \to S$)

$\underset{\text{Hydrogen sulphide}}{H_2S} + Cl_2 \longrightarrow \underset{\text{Hydrogen chloride}}{2HCl} + \underset{\text{Sulphur}}{S}$

Oxidation ($Cu \to CuO$)

$\underset{\text{Copper}}{2Cu} + \underset{\text{Oxygen}}{O_2} \longrightarrow \underset{\text{Copper oxide}}{2CuO}$ **(1)**

Reduction is defined as a chemical process which involves either the addition of hydrogen to the substance or loss of oxygen from the substance. **(1)**

Reduction ($Na \to NaH$)

e.g. $\underset{\text{Sodium}}{2Na} + \underset{\text{Hydrogen}}{H_2} \longrightarrow \underset{\text{Sodium hydride}}{2NaH}$

Reduction ($ZnO \to Zn$)

$\underset{\text{Zinc oxide}}{ZnO} + \underset{\text{Hydrogen}}{H_2} \longrightarrow \underset{\text{Zinc}}{Zn} + \underset{\text{Water}}{H_2O}$ **(1)**

Q.7 Name the following.

(i) A gas that act as oxidising agent as well as a reducing agent.

(ii) A solid oxidising agent.

(iii) An oxidising agent that does not contain oxygen.

(iv) A coloured gas that act as an oxidising agent.

Ans. (i) Sulphur dioxide gas (ii) Manganese dioxide (iii) Chlorine gas (iv) Chlorine gas **(1 × 4 = 4)**

Q.8 **Give reasons why are the following substances not used to prepare hydrogen gas?**

(i) Sodium and potassium

(ii) Calcium and magnesium

(iii) Mercury and copper

(iv) Aluminium

(v) Iron

Ans. (i) Sodium and potassium reacts violently with acid and catch fire.

(ii) Calcium and magnesium are very expensive.

(iii) Copper and mercury are less reactive than hydrogen, so cannot displace hydrogen from acid.

(iv) Aluminium has a protective coating of aluminium oxide on the surface of the metal, which prevents aluminium from further getting reacted.

(v) Reaction of iron with steam is reversible and also iron contains a lot of impurities. So, the hydrogen prepared by reaction of iron contains a lot of impurities of hydrogen sulphide and sulphur dioxide gas. **(1 × 5 = 5)**

Q.9 (i) **From the knowledge of activity series, name a metal which shows the following properties:**

(a) It displaces hydrogen from hot water.

(b) It displaces hydrogen from dilute HCl.

(c) It forms a base which is insoluble in water.

(ii) Complete the following word equations:

(a) Sodium hydroxide + zinc → Hydrogen + ...

(b) Calcium + water → Calcium hydroxide + ...

Ans. (i) (a) Magnesium (b) Zinc (c) Calcium **(1 × 3 = 3)**

(ii) (a) Sodium hydroxide + zinc → Hydrogen + sodium zincate

(b) Calcium + water → Calcium hydroxide + hydrogen **(1 × 2 = 2)**

Q.10 **During the laboratory preparation of hydrogen gas, some impurities may be present in the gas. List any common impurities that might be present in hydrogen gas. How can these impurities be removed from hydrogen gas?**

Ans. During the laboratory preparation of hydrogen gas the impurities present are

(i) hydrogen sulphide (H_2S)

(ii) sulphur dioxide (SO_2)

(iii) oxides of nitrogen

(iv) phosphine (PH_3)

(v) arsine (AsH_3)

(vi) carbon dioxide

(vii) water vapour **(2)**

Impurities can be removed from hydrogen by passing it through:

1. **Silver nitrate solution** [to remove arsine and phosphine].

$AsH_3 + 6AgNO_3 \rightarrow Ag_3As + 3AgNO_3 + 3HNO_3$

$PH_3 + 6AgNO_3 \rightarrow Ag_3P + 3AgNO_3 + 3HNO_3$

2. **Lead nitrate solution** [to remove hydrogen sulphide].

$Pb(NO_3)_2 + H_2S \rightarrow PbS + 2HNO_3$

3. **Caustic potash solution** [to remove sulphur dioxide, carbon dioxide and oxides of nitrogen].

$SO_2 + 2KOH \longrightarrow K_2SO_3 + H_2O$

$CO_2 + 2KOH \longrightarrow K_2CO_3 + H_2O$

$2NO_2 + 2KOH \longrightarrow KNO_2 + KNO_3 + H_2O$ **(3)**

Q.11 **State, giving reasons, whether the substances printed in bold letters have been oxidised or reduced.**

(i) $PbO + CO \longrightarrow Pb + CO_2$

(ii) $2Mg + O_2 \longrightarrow 2MgO$

(iii) $H_2S + Cl_2 \longrightarrow 2HCl + S$

(iv) $Cl_2 + H_2S \longrightarrow 2HCl + S$

(v) $CuO + H_2 \longrightarrow Cu + H_2O$

Ans. (i) PbO is **reduced**, due to removal of oxygen.

(ii) Mg is **oxidised**, due to addition of oxygen.

(iii) H_2S is **oxidised**, as hydrogen is removed and added to sulphur.

(iv) Chlorine is **reduced**, due to addition of hydrogen to form HCl.

(v) CuO is **reduced**, due to removal of oxygen atom. **(5)**

TYPE - 10   03 Marks

Case-Based Questions

Q.1 **Priya is studying the Bosch Process as part of her chemistry syllabus. The Bosch Process is an important industrial method for the production of hydrogen gas (H_2). The hydrogen produced is essential for various industrial applications, including ammonia production, oil refining and fuel cells.**

The reaction takes place at high temperatures, and the products are hydrogen gas (H_2) and carbon dioxide (CO_2).

(i) What is the first step in the Bosch Process?

(ii) Which catalyst is used in the Bosch Process and what is the reaction involved?

(iii) How is the by-product, CO_2 separated from the H_2 gas.

Ans. (i) The first step in the Bosch Process is passing steam (H_2O) over hot coke (carbon) at high temperature (1000 °C) to form water gas.

$$\underset{\text{Hot coke}}{C} + \underset{\text{Steam}}{H_2O} \xrightarrow{1000°C} \underset{\text{Water gas}}{(CO + H_2)} - \Delta$$ **(1)**

(ii) Water gas is mixed with excess steam and passed over heated **ferric oxide, which acts as a catalyst, and chromic oxide Cr_2O_3, which acts as a promoter.**

$$\underset{\text{Water gas}}{(CO + H_2)} + \underset{\text{Steam}}{H_2O} \xrightarrow[450°C]{Fe_2O_3} CO_2 + 2H_2 + \Delta$$ **(1)**

(iii) The above mixture, i.e. $CO_2 + H_2$, is passed at high pressure through cold water under pressure (30 atm), or through caustic potash solution, which dissolves the more soluble carbon dioxide, leaving hydrogen. **(1)**

Q.2 **Ramesh was studying redox reactions and came across the following reactions**

1. $2Mg + O_2 \longrightarrow 2MgO$
2. $H_2S + Cl_2 \longrightarrow 2HCl + S$

(i) Identify which species are getting oxidised in the given reactions with respect to gaining oxygen or losing hydrogen.

(ii) Write a balanced chemical equation where potassium (K) undergoes oxidation.

Ans. (i) Species getting oxidised :

In reaction 1 : **Mg** (gains oxygen to form MgO).

In reaction 2 : **H_2S** (loses hydrogen to form S). **(2)**

(ii) Reaction where K underoges oxidation is:

$4K + O_2 \longrightarrow 2K_2O$ (Potassium reacts with oxygen to form potassium oxide). **(1)**

07

STUDY OF GAS LAWS

The state of matter in which inter-particle attraction is weak and inter-particle space is so large that the particles become completely free to move randomly in the entire available space is known as the **gaseous state**.

Behaviour and Characteristic Properties of Gases

The kinetic molecular theory of gases explains the behaviour and characteristic properties of gases. The main assumption of this theory are as follows.

- Gases are made up of tiny particles (molecules) moving in all possible directions at all possible speeds.
- Due to negligible force of attraction, the gas molecules are free to move in whole space available, so gases neither have **definite shape nor definite volume**.
- The moving particles of a gas collide with each other and also with the walls of the container. Due to these collisions, gas molecules exert **pressure in all directions**.
- There is large intermolecular spaces between gas molecules, so gases are **highly compressible**.
- On decreasing pressure and increasing temperature, gases show increase in volume, thus gases are **highly expansible**.
- Gases have large intermolecular spaces between their molecules. Therefore, gases have very **low density**.
- Inter-molecular spaces in a gas are very large. When two gases are brought in contact with each other, their molecules mix with each other in such a manner that a homogeneous gaseous mixture is formed, i.e. **gases have a tendency to mix with one another** and this process is called **diffusion**.
- On cooling, the kinetic energy of the molecules of a gas is reduced and on applying pressure on a cooled gas, the molecules come closer, thus **gases can be liquefied**.

Molecular Motion

According to the kinetic model, particles (molecules) of gases are in constant random motion, so they possess kinetic energy.

- The **average kinetic energy** of a particle (molecule) is **directly proportional** to its **absolute temperature**.
- As temperature increases, molecular motion increases and when temperature decreases, molecular motion also decreases.
- The temperature at which the molecular motion completely stops (theoretical concept) is called **absolute zero**.
- The force exerted on a unit area of the wall of the container is equal to the **pressure of the gas**.

Gas Laws

The behaviour of a gas under known conditions of pressure, volume and temperature is described by laws known as **gas laws**.

The behaviour of gases can be described by three standard variables, i.e. **volume** (V), **pressure** (p) and **temperature** (T).

REVISION NOTES

- The **volume (V)** of a gas is the space occupied by that gas. The space occupied by a gas is equal to the volume of its container. It can be expressed in **mL** or **cm^3** and **dm^3** or **L**.

$$1 m^3 = 1000 dm^3 = 1000 L \quad \text{and} \quad 1 L = 1000 cm^3 = 1000 mL$$
$$1 mL = 1 cm^3 \text{(cubic centimeter)} \quad \text{and} \quad 1 L = 1 dm^3 \text{(cubic decimetre)}$$

- The **pressure (p)** of a gas is the force that the gas exerts per unit area on the walls of its container. The pressure exerted by air (present in the atmosphere) on the surface of the earth is called **atmospheric pressure**. It can be expressed in **mm of Hg**, **cm of Hg**, **atmosphere (atm)**, **Pascal Pa** or **kPa**.

$$1 \text{ atmosphere (atm)} = 76 \text{ cm of Hg} = 760 \text{ mm of Hg} = 760 \text{ torr} = 101.325 \text{ kPa}$$

- The **temperature (T)** of a gas is defined as the degree of hotness of that gas. Several scales that are used to measure temperature are **°C** (degree Celsius), **K** (Kelvin) and **°F**(degree Fahrenheit).
- Standard unit to measure temperature in **Kelvin**. The temperature is always used in 'K' because (theoretically) the lowest attainable temperature is 0 K. So, temperature is never negative and all temperature in Kelvin scale are positive.

Boyle's Law (Pressure-Volume Relationship)

It states that "volume of a given mass of a dry gas is inversely proportional to its pressure at constant temperature."

- A gas occupies volume V at temperature T and pressure p, then

$$\boxed{p \propto 1/V} \quad \text{or} \quad p = k\,(1/V)$$

Here, k = proportionality constant

$$pV = k$$

- Let, V_1 be the volume of a given mass of gas at pressure p_1 and at a given temperature T_1. When the pressure is changed to p_2 at the same temperature, let the volume become V_2.

According to Boyle's law,

$$p_1V_1 = k \quad \text{...(i)}$$
$$p_2V_2 = k \quad \text{...(ii)}$$

From Eqs. (i) and (ii), we get,

$$\boxed{p_1V_1 = p_2V_2}$$

Graphical Representation of Boyle's Law

- The p/V graph for Boyle's law are called **isotherm** because they are drawn at constant temperature.

(i) ***V* vs $\frac{1}{p}$**

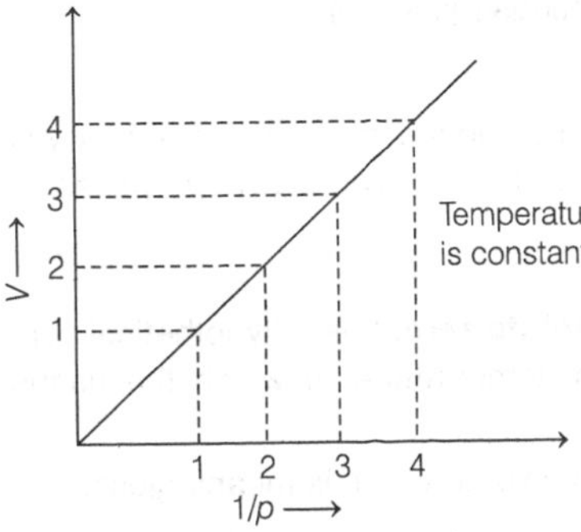

Variation in volume (V) plotted against 1 / p at constant temperature

(ii) ***V* vs *p***

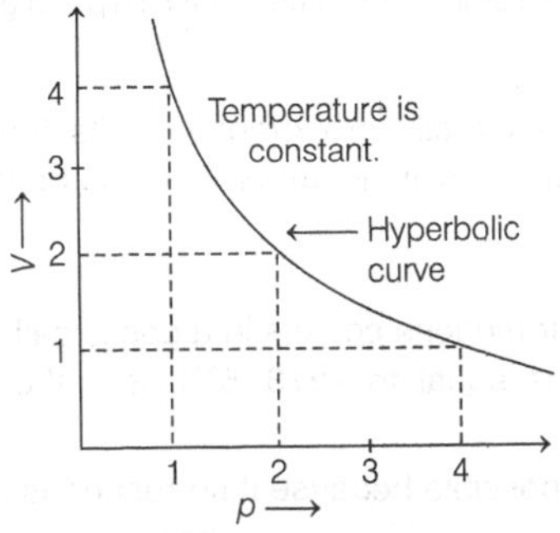

Variation in volume (V) plotted against pressure (p) at constant temperature

(iii) ***pV* vs *p***

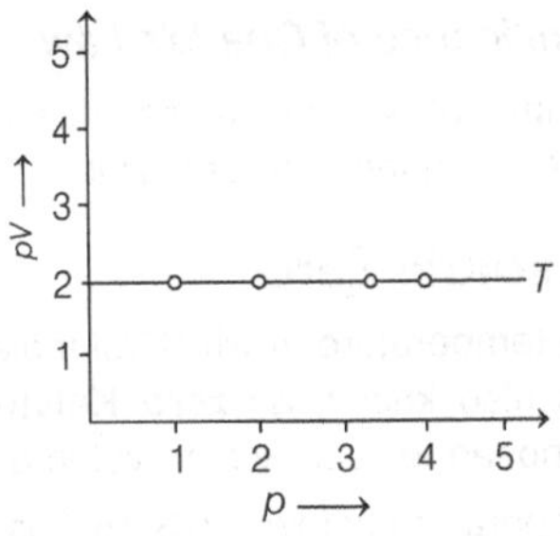

Variation in pV plotted against pressure (p) at constant temperature

Significance of Boyle's Law

- On increasing pressure, volume decreases. The gas becomes denser. Thus, at constant temperature the density of a gas is directly proportional to its pressure.

$$\boxed{\textbf{Density} \propto \textbf{Pressure (at constant temperature)}}$$

- At high altitudes, the atmospheric pressure is low thus, air is less dense. This results in less availability of oxygen for breathing. Therefore, a mountaineer has to carry oxygen cylinders with them.

Charle's Law (Temperature-Volume Relationship)

It states that "pressure remaining constant, the volume of a given mass of a dry gas increases or decreases by 1/273 of its original volume at 0°C for each 1°C increase or decrease in temperature."

$$V_{t^\circ C} = V_0\left(1+\frac{t}{273}\right) \text{(At constant pressure)}$$

Or

Volume of a given mass of a dry gas is directly proportional to its absolute temperature (in Kelvin), if pressure remains constant.

$$V \propto T \quad \text{or} \quad \frac{V}{T} = \text{Constant}$$

i.e.

$$\boxed{\frac{V_1}{T_1} = \frac{V_2}{T_2}} \quad (p = \text{Constant})$$

According to this equation,

- if the temperature is doubled, the volume would be doubled.
- if it is reduced by half, the volume would be reduced by half.

Graphical Representation of Charle's Law

The plot of volume *vs* temperature at constant pressure are called **isobars** or **isoplestics**. When volume of fixed mass of a gas is plotted with temperature at different constant pressures, we get straight line in each case.

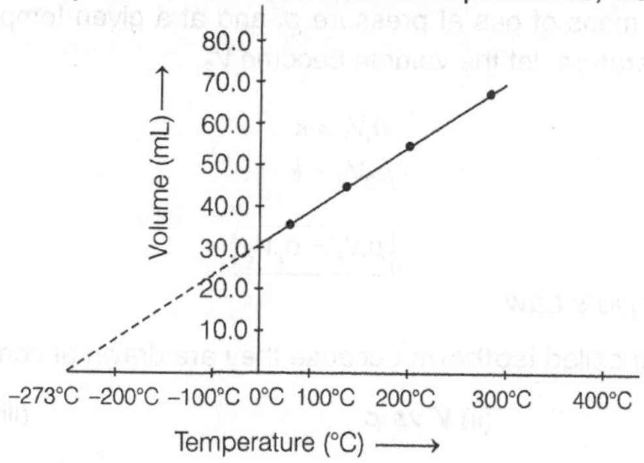

Graph showing volume-temperature relationship in a gas (at constant pressure)

Significance of Charle's Law

Volume of a given mass of a gas is directly proportional to its temperature, hence density decreases with an increase in temperature. This is the reason why hot air is filled into balloons used for meteorological purposes.

Absolute Zero

The temperature at which all molecular motions ceases in a gas is called **absolute zero**. It is a hypothetical concept. It is also known as **zero Kelvin**. It is equal to –273.15°C. It is the lowest temperature at which the gases are supposed to occupy zero volume.

Temperature below –273.15°C is not possible because it corresponds to zero volume which is meaningless.

$$V = V_0\left(\frac{273+t}{273}\right)$$

$$\text{Volume at } -273^\circ C = V_0\left(\frac{273-273}{273}\right) = 0$$

Thus, it can be concluded that the volume of a gas would be reduced to zero at – 273° C.

However, this is not possible, because gas is a state of matter and hence, must have some definite mass and volume.

Absolute or Kelvin Scale of Temperature

The temperature scale with its zero at –273°C and each degree equal to one degree on the Celsius scale is called **Kelvin** or **the absolute scale of temperature**.

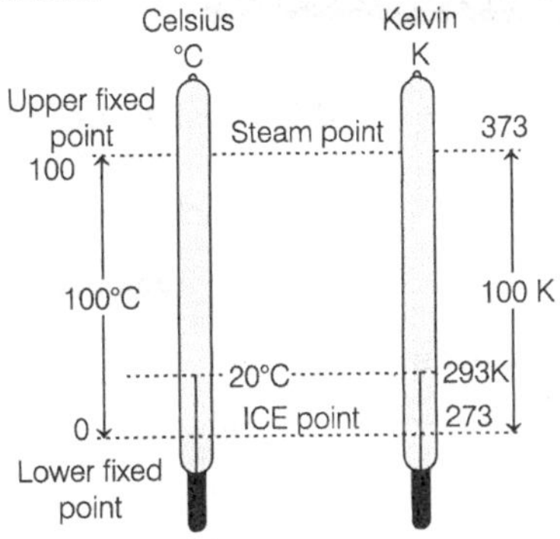

Conversion of Temperature from Celsius Scale to Kelvin Scale and *Vice-Versa*

- The value of temperature present on the Celsius scale can be converted to Kelvin scale by adding 273 to it.

  e.g. $$25°\text{C} = 25 + 273 = 298\text{ K}$$

- The value of temperature present on the Kelvin scale can be converted to Celsius scale by subtracting 273 from it.

  e.g. $$25\text{ K} = 25 - 273 = -248°\text{ C}$$

Gas Equation

On combining Boyle's law and Charles' law, we get a single equation, which is called **gas equation**. This equation gives the simultaneous effect of pressure and temperature on the volume of a gas.

According to Boyle's law, $$\boxed{V \propto \frac{1}{p}}$$

According to Charle's law, $$\boxed{V \propto T}$$

Now, on combining the two laws, *volume of a given mass of a gas varies inversely with pressure and directly with absolute temperature.*

$$V \propto \frac{1}{p} \times T \Rightarrow V = \frac{T}{p} \times \text{constant} \Rightarrow \frac{pV}{T} = \text{constant}$$

Accordingly, if the volume of a given mass of a gas changes from V_1 or V_2, its pressure from p_1 to p_2, and its temperature from T_1 to T_2, then

$$\boxed{\frac{p_1V_1}{T_1} = \frac{p_2V_2}{T_2}}$$

The above mathematical expression is called the **gas equation**.

Standard Temperature and Pressure (S.T.P.)

- Since, volume of a gas changes remarkably with change in temperature and pressure, it becomes necessary to choose standard values of temperature and pressure to which gas volumes can be referred.
- The standard values chosen are 0°C or 273K for temperature, and 1 atmospheric unit (atm) or 760 mm Hg for pressure. These standard values are known as **Standard Temperature and Pressure** (S.T.P.).

  Standard temperature = 0° C = 273K

  Standard pressure = 760 mm Hg = 76 cm Hg = 1 atm = 760 torr

Effect of Moisture on Pressure

If a gas is collected over water then it is moist and also contains water vapour.

The partial pressure of water vapour at any temperature and pressure is known as its **aqueous tension**.

$$\boxed{\text{Total pressure of gas observed} = \text{Pressure of dry gas} + \text{Aqueous tension}}$$

EXAM ORIENTED QUESTIONS

TYPE - 1   01 Mark

Multiple Choice Questions

Q.1 On applying the pressure, the intermolecular spaces can be reduced. This assumption explains the
(a) fixed volume of gases.
(b) partial pressure exerted by the gases.
(c) compressibility of gases.
(d) All of the above

Ans. (c) compressibility of gases.

Q.2 Gases expand and occupy all the space available to them. Which of the following assumption explain this behaviour correctly?
(a) There is very less force of attraction between gas molecules.
(b) Gas molecules are considered as negligible masses.
(c) Collisions of the gas molecules are perfectly elastic.
(d) All of the above

Ans. (a) There is very less force of attraction between gas molecules.

Q.3 The theory that attempts to elucidate the behaviour of gases is known as ...... of gases.
(a) valence bond theory
(b) kinetic molecular theory
(c) Both (a) and (b)
(d) None of the above

Ans. (b) kinetic molecular theory

Q.4 Kinetic energy of the molecules of a gas is directly proportional to
(a) pressure (b) volume
(c) temperature (d) potential energy

Ans. (c) temperature

Q.5 At any particular time different particles in the gas have ......I......speed and hence ......II......kinetic energies.
Here, I and II refer to
(a) I $\rightarrow$ same, II $\rightarrow$ same
(b) I $\rightarrow$ different, II $\rightarrow$ same
(c) I $\rightarrow$ different, II $\rightarrow$ different
(d) I $\rightarrow$ same, II $\rightarrow$ different

Ans. (c) I $\rightarrow$ different, II $\rightarrow$ different

Q.6 Physical behaviour of gases can be described by some standard variables.
Which line of the table is correct?

	Volume	Speed	Temperature	Pressure
(a)	✓	×	✓	✓
(b)	✓	✓	✓	×
(c)	×	✓	×	✓
(d)	✓	×	×	✓

Key
✓ = standard variable
× not a standard variable

Ans. (a) Volume, temperature and pressure are three standard variables.

Q.7 The pressure exerted by the gas is due to
(a) the repulsion between gas molecules
(b) the attraction between gas molecules
(c) collision of the particles with the walls of the container
(d) Both (a) and (b)

Ans. (c) Collision of the particles with the walls of the container.

Q.8 A unit of pressure is ....
(a) kilogram
(b) atmosphere
(c) cubic centimetre
(d) litre

Ans. (b) atmosphere

Q.9 6 atmosphere = '*X*' torr. Here, *X* is
(a) 5760 (b) 3876
(c) 2769 (d) 4560

Ans. (d) 1 atmosphere = 760 torr
So, 6 atmosphere = $6 \times 760 = 4560$ torr

Q.10 The Kelvin temperature scale is also known as
(i) absolute temperature scale
(ii) thermodynamic scale
Choose the correct option.
(a) Only (i)
(b) Only (ii)
(c) Both (i) and (ii)
(d) Neither (i) nor (ii)

Ans. (c) Both (i) and (ii)

Q.11 The given graph represents the Boyle's law.

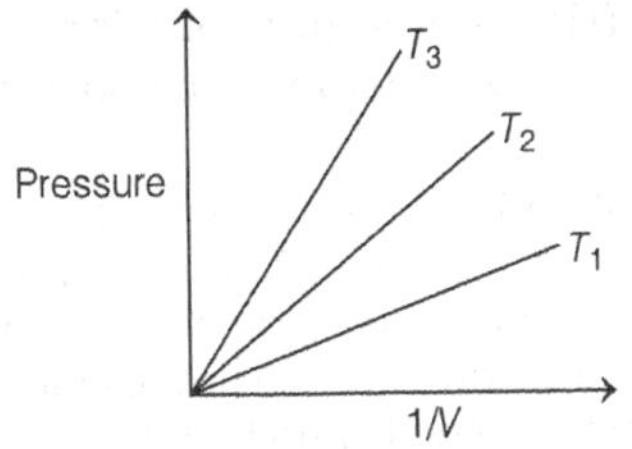

Choose the correct relation between T_1, T_2 and T_3.

(a) $T_1 = T_2 = T_3$
(b) $T_1 > T_2 > T_3$
(c) $T_3 > T_2 > T_1$
(d) No specific relation

Ans. (c) $T_3 > T_2 > T_1$

Q.12 Boyle's law is valid for

(i) $pV = \text{constant}$ (ii) $\frac{p_1}{V_2} = \frac{p_2}{V_1}$

(iii)

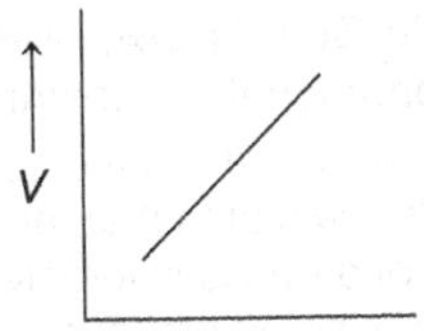

Which of the following is the correct option?

(a) (i) and (iii) (b) (i) and (ii)
(c) (ii) and (iii) (d) (i), (ii) and (iii)

Ans. (b) (i) and (ii)

Q.13 The graph of pV *vs* p for a gas is

(a) straight line passing through origin
(b) straight line parallel to x-axis
(c) hyperbolic
(d) parabolic

Ans. (b) straight line parallel to x-axis.

Q.14 Observe the given graph and choose the correct graphical representation of Boyle's law.

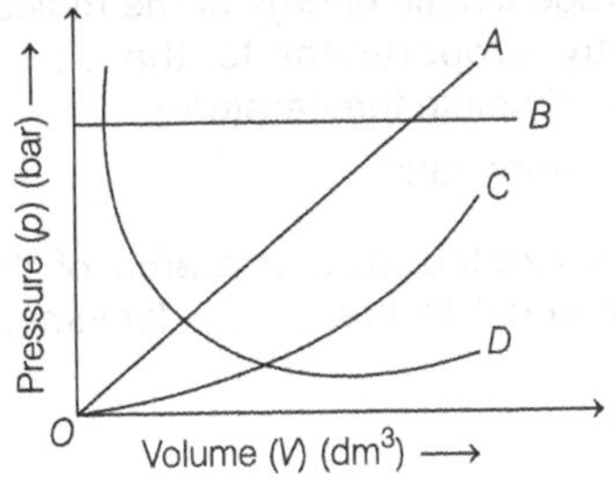

(a) *A* (b) *B*
(c) *C* (d) *D*

Ans. (d) (hyperbolic curve)

Q.15 The following graph represents isotherm for Boyle's law.

Complete the given graph by identifying *X* and *Y*.

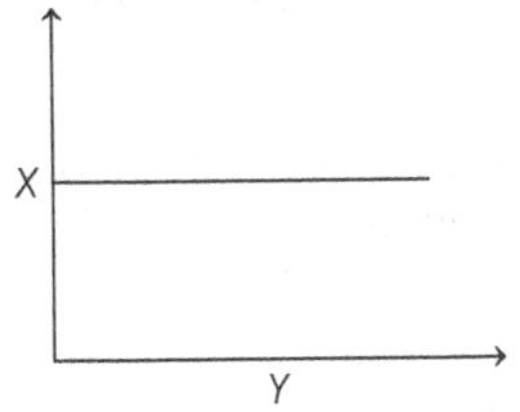

	X	Y		X	Y
(a)	pV	p	(b)	V	p
(c)	$1/V$	p	(d)	V	$1/p$

Ans. (a) pV v/s p

Q.16 If pressure is increased by 4 times for a fixed mass of a gas, its volume will become

(a) 2 times (b) 1/4 times
(c) 6 times (d) no change

Ans. (b) According to Boyle's law,

$$p_1V_1 = p_2V_2 \ (T = \text{constant})$$

$$p_1 = p, \quad p_2 = 4p$$

$$V_1 = v \quad V_2 = ?$$

$$p \times v = 4p \times V_2$$

$$V_2 = \frac{pv}{4p} \Rightarrow V_2 = \frac{v}{4}$$

Q.17 Which of the following does not represent the isotherm for Boyle's law?

(a) V *vs* $1/p$ (b) V *vs* p
(c) pV *vs* p (d) V *vs* T

Ans. (d) V *vs* T (isotherms are graph plotted at constant temperature)

Q.18 Volume-temperature relationship at constant pressure is given by

(a) Gay-Lussac's law (b) Boyle's law
(c) Charles' law (d) Dalton's law

Ans. (c) Charles' law

Q.19. The following graph represents Charle's law.

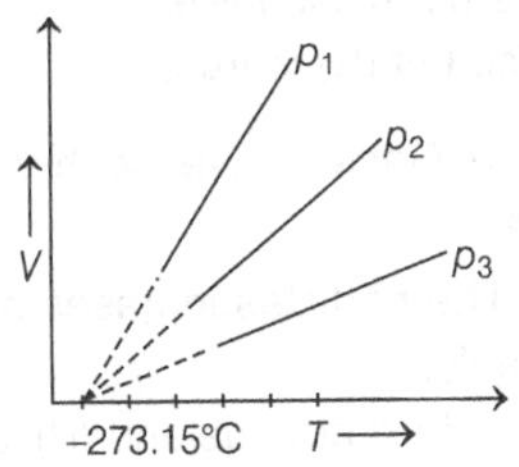

The correct relation between p_1, p_2 and p_3 is

(a) $p_1 = p_2 = p_3$ (b) $p_1 < p_2 < p_3$
(c) $p_1 > p_2 > p_3$ (d) $p_1 = 2p_2 = 3p_3$

Ans. (b) $p_1 < p_2 < p_3$

Q.20 On the basis of theoretical concept, the temperature at which the molecular motion completely stop is
(a) 273°C (b) absolute zero
(c) 273 K (d) – 173 K

Ans. (b) absolute zero

Q.21 The temperature scale with zero at – 273.15°C and whose each degree is equal to 1° on Celsius scale is called
(a) centigrade scale
(b) celsius scale
(c) absolute scale of temperature
(d) millimetre of mercury

Ans. (c) absolute scale of temperature or Kelvin scale.

Q.22 58°C in Kelvin is equal to
(a) 334 K (b) 332 K
(c) 331 K (d) 330 K

Ans. (c) $°C \xrightarrow{+273} K$

$\therefore 58° C = 58 + 273 K = 331 K$

Q.23 A mathematical expression describing the simultaneous effects of changes in temperature, pressure and volume of a given mass of a gas is called
(a) Boyle's law
(b) Charles' law
(c) Avogadro's law
(d) Ideal gas equation

Ans. (d) Ideal gas equation

TYPE - 2 01 Mark

Assertion-Reason Questions

Directions (Q. Nos. 1-5) In the following questions statement are given Assertion and Reason.
(a) Both (A) and (R) are true and (R) is the correct explanation of (A).
(b) Both (A) and (R) are true but (R) is not the correct explanation of (A).
(c) (A) is true but (R) is false.
(d) (A) is false but (R) is true.

Q.1 Assertion (A) Gases have neither fixed shape nor fixed volume.

Reason (R) The particles in gases are widely spaced and move freely.

Ans. (a) Both (A) and (R) are true and (R) is the correct explanation of (A). The particles in gases have high kinetic energy, allowing them to move freely and spread out, which leads to gases having neither a fixed shape nor volume.

Q.2 Assertion (A) Gases exhibit the property of diffusion.

Reason (R) The intermolecular spaces in gas molecules are very large as compared to solids and liquids.

Ans. (a) Both (A) and (R) are true and (R) is the correct explanation of (A). Gases have a natural tendency to mix with another or to exhibit diffusion because the intermolecular spaces in gas molecules are very large as compared to solids and liquids.

Q.3 Assertion (A) The kinetic energy of particles increases with an increase in temperature.

Reason (R) As temperature is lowered, the particles move faster and their kinetic energy increases.

Ans. (c) (A) is true but (R) is false. Kinetic energy is directly related to temperature; as temperature increases, particles move faster and possess more kinetic energy.

Q.4 Assertion (A) The volume of a gas decreases when the pressure is increased at constant *T*.

Reason (R) According to Boyle's law, pressure and volume are inversely proportional at constant *T*.

Ans. (a) Both (A) and (R) are true and (R) is the correct explanation of (A). Boyle's law states that, at constant temperature, the volume of a gas is inversely proportional to its pressure, so as pressure increases, the volume decreases.

Q.5 Assertion (A) At absolute zero, the volume of a gas is non-zero.

Reason (R) At absolute zero, the motion of particles ceases completely.

Ans. (d) (A) is false but (R) is true. Absolute zero is the temperature at which gas particles have no kinetic energy and the volume of a gas is zero (theoretically).

TYPE - 3 01 Mark

Fill in the Blanks

Q.1 The average kinetic energy of the molecules of a gas is directly proportional to the .... (absolute pressure, absolute temperature).

Ans. absolute temperature

Q.2 The force exerted on a unit area of the wall of the vessel is equal to the .... (volume, pressure) of the gas.

Ans. pressure

Q.3 The SI unit of pressure is .... (Pascal, Newton).

Ans. pascal

Q.4 An increase in the pressure of a gas at constant temperature causes a ...... in the volume of gas (Increase, decrease).

Ans. decrease

Q.5 If the pressure is doubled, the volume would be .... (halved, doubled).

Ans. halved

Q.6 Pressure remaining constant, the volume of a given mass of a dry gas increases or decreases by ...... (273, 1/273) of its original volume at 0°C for each 1°C increase or decrease temperature.

Ans. 1/273

Q.7 If the temperature is reduced to half, the volume would also reduce to .... (double, half).

Ans. half

Q.8 All temperature on Kelvin scale are .... (negative, positive).

Ans. positive

Q.9 The magnitude of each degree on Kelvin scale is same as on ...... (Fahrenheit, Centigrade) scale.

Ans. centigrade

Q.10 Kelvin zero is equal to ...... (0°C, – 273°C).

Ans. – 273°C

Q.11 The melting point of ice is .... (0 K, 273 K).

Ans. 273 K

Q.12 ...... is known as the steam point (273 K, 373 K).

Ans. 373 K

Q.13 Standard temperature is .... (0°C, 100°C).

Ans. 0°C

TYPE - 4 — 01 Mark

Correct the Incorrect Statement

Q.1 The molecules of gas move only in one direction.

Ans. The molecules of gas move in **all possible** directions.

Q.2 The force exerted per unit area on the wall of the container is equal to the density of the gas.

Ans. The force exerted per unit area on the wall of the container is equal to the **pressure** of the gas.

Q.3 According to Boyle's law, the volume of a given mass of a dry gas is directly proportional to its pressure at constant temperature.

Ans. According to Boyle's law, the volume of a given mass of a dry gas is **inversely** proportional to its pressure at constant temperature.

Q.4 Atmospheric pressure is very high at high altitudes, so air is less dense.

Ans. Atmospheric pressure is very **low** at high altitudes, so air is less dense.

Q.5 Fahrenheit scale is also called the absolute scale of temperature.

Ans. **Kelvin** scale is also called he absolute scale of temperature.

TYPE - 5 — 01×05 = 05 Marks

Match the Columns

Q.1 Match the following columns.

	Column I		Column II
A.	cm^3	1.	Pressure
B.	Kelvin	2.	273 K
C.	torr	3.	Volume
D.	ice point	4.	373 K
E.	Steam point	5.	Temperature

Ans. (A)→3, (B)→5, (C)→1, (D)→2, (E)→4.

Q.2 Match the following columns.

	Column I (Temperature in Celsius)		Column II (Temperature in Kelvin)
A.	17°C	1.	273 K
B.	20°C	2.	0 K
C.	–273°C	3.	290 K
D.	0°C	4.	298 K
E.	25°C	5.	293 K

Ans. (A)→3, (B)→5, (C)→2, (D)→1, (E)→4.

TYPE - 6 — 01 Mark

Identify the Following

Q.1 Which law states that pressure and volume are inversely related?

Ans. Boyle's law

Q.2 What is the general term used for the graph plotted at constant temperature?

Ans. Isotherm

Q.3 What type of graph is formed when volume is plotted against temperature at constant pressure in Charles' law?

Ans. Straight line

Q.4 What is the relationship between Kelvin and degree Celsius?

Ans. K = °C + 273

Q.5 What is the value to 25 K in Celsius?

Ans. −248° C

TYPE - 7 — 02 Marks

Short Answer Type I Questions

Q.1 Give a suitable reason for each the following assertions.

(i) Gases show diffusion.

(ii) Gases are highly compressible.

Ans. (i) There are large intermolecular spaces between the molecules of a gas. When two gases are brought in contact, the molecules of one gas occupies the vacant spaces of the other gas, therefore gases show the property of diffusion. **(1)**

(ii) As there are large intermolecular spaces between the molecules. On applying pressure, the vacant spaces between the molecules decreases, the molecules come closer and occupy less space. Thus, we can say gases can be compressed. **(1)**

Q.2 State Boyle's law and give its mathematical expression.

Ans. **Boyle's law** Volume of a given mass of a dry gas is inversely proportional to its pressure at constant temperature.

Mathematical expression of Boyle's law:

Suppose a gas occupies volume V_1 when its pressure is p_1, then

$$V_1 \propto \frac{1}{p_1} \text{ or } V_1 = \frac{k}{p_1}$$

or $p_1V_1 = k = \text{constant}$

If V_2 is the volume occupied when the pressure is p_2 at the same temperature, then

$$V_2 \propto \frac{1}{p_2}$$

or $$V_2 = \frac{k}{p_2}$$ **(1)**

or $p_2V_2 = k = \text{constant}$

$\therefore p_1V_1 = p_2V_2 = k$; at constant temperature

This is called **Boyle's law equation.** **(1)**

Q.3 Explain Boyle's law on the basis of kinetic theory of gases.

Ans. According to kinetic theory of gas, the pressure of a gas depends on the number of molecules that strike the wall of the container. Greater the number of particles that strike the wall of the container, more will be the pressure of the gas.

If we decrease the volume of the gas, whereas temperature is kept constant, more molecules will go and strike the walls of the container. Therefore, pressure of the gas will increase.

Similarly, if we increase the volume of given mass of a gas temperature, when temperature is kept constant then lesser particles will go and strike the wall of the container. Therefore, pressure of the gas is decreased. **(2)**

Q.4 Calculate the minimum pressure required to compress 500 dm³ of air at 1 bar to 200 dm³ at 30°C?

Ans. Given, $p_1 = 1\text{bar}, p_2 = ?, V_1 = 500\text{ dm}^3, V_2 = 200\text{ dm}^3$

$$\therefore \quad p_1V_1 = p_2V_2$$

$$\Rightarrow \quad p_2 = \frac{p_1V_1}{V_2}$$

$$= \frac{1\text{ bar} \times 500\text{ dm}^3}{200\text{ dm}^3} = 2.5\text{ bar}$$ **(2)**

Q.5 A gas occupies 1500 cm³ volume, at pressure of 720 mm of Hg. Find the pressure at which its volume will be 1000 cm³. Assume that temperature remains constant.

Ans. Initial pressure, $p_1 = 720$ mm of Hg

Initial volume, $V_1 = 1500\text{cm}^3$

Final volume, $V_2 = 1000\text{cm}^3$

Final pressure, $p_2 = ?$

According to Boyle's law, $p_1V_1 = p_2V_2$

$$720 \times 1500 = p_2 \times 1000$$

$$\Rightarrow \quad p_2 = \frac{720 \times 1500}{1000} = 1080\text{ mm of Hg}$$ **(2)**

Q.6 A gas occupies a volume of 250 mL at 745 mm Hg and 25°C. What additional pressure is required to reduce the gas volume to 200 mL at the same temperature?

Ans. Given, initial volume, $V_1 = 250$ mL

Initial pressure, $p_1 = 745$ mm Hg

Final volume, $V_2 = 200$ mL

Final pressure, $p_2 = ?$

Additional pressure, $p = ?$

$$\therefore \quad p_1V_1 = p_2V_2$$

$$745 \text{ mm Hg} \times 250 \text{ mL} = p_2 \times 200 \text{ mL}$$

$$p_2 = \frac{745 \text{ mm Hg} \times 250 \text{ mL}}{200 \text{ mL}}$$

$$= 931.25 \text{ mm Hg}$$

Additional pressure $= p_2 - p_1$

$= 931.25 - 745 = 186.25$ mm Hg **(2)**

Q.7 Complete the following table by using the appropriate gas law at constant temperature, 30°C.

	Pressure (p)	Volume (V)
Case I	4.5 atm	10 mL
Case II	9 atm	$V = ?$

Ans. Using Boyle's law, $p_1V_1 = p_2V_2$

$$4.5 \text{ atm} \times 10 \text{ mL} = 9 \text{ atm} \times V$$

$$V = \frac{45}{9} \Rightarrow V = 5 \text{ mL}$$ **(2)**

Q.8 The molecular theory accounts for the pressure exerted by a gas in a closed vessel as a result of the gas molecules striking on the walls of the vessel. How will the pressure changes, if

(i) the volume is made half of original value, maintaining the temperature constant?

(ii) temperature is doubled maintaining the volume constant?

Ans. (i) When the volume is halved, the number of gas molecules striking per unit area of the walls of the vessel is doubled. Thus, the pressure is doubled as per the Boyle's law. **(1)**

(ii) When the temperature is doubled, the average kinetic energy of the gas molecules is doubled. Thus, the pressure is doubled. **(1)**

Q.9 State Charles' law and give its mathematical expression.

Ans. Charles' law Volume of a given mass of a dry gas is directly proportional to its absolute (Kelvin) temperature, if the pressure remains constant.

Mathematical expression of Charles' law

Suppose, a gas occupies V_1 cm^3 at T_1 temperature and V_2 cm^3 at T_2 temperature, then by Charle's law,

$$V_1 \propto T_1$$

$$V_1 = kT_1 \qquad (k \text{ is constant})$$

$$\frac{V_1}{T_1} = \frac{V_2}{T_2} = k \text{ (at constant pressure)}$$

This is called **Charles' law equation.** **(2)**

Q.10 A gas is enclosed in a vessel at standard temperature. Find out the temperature at which the volume of enclosed gas will be 1/6 of its initial volume. (Given that the pressure remain constant)

Ans. Suppose that the initial volume of gas, $V_1 = x$

Final volume, $V_2 = x / 6$

Initial temperature, $T_1 = 0°\text{C} = 0 + 273\text{K} = 273\text{K}$

Final temperature, $T_2 = ?$

Applying Charles' law, $\frac{V_1}{T_1} = \frac{V_2}{T_2}$

$$\Rightarrow \quad \frac{x}{273} = \frac{x}{6 \times T_2}$$

$$T_2 = \frac{273x}{6 \times (x)} = 45.5 \text{ K}$$ **(2)**

Q.11 State the laws which are represented by the given graphs.

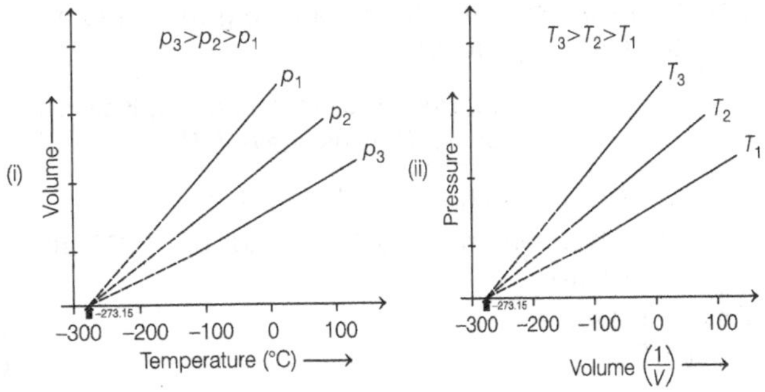

Ans. (i) The first graph represents the **Charles' law**, i.e. graph of volume *versus* temperature, at constant pressure which states that volume of a given mass of a dry gas is directly proportional to its absolute temperature. **(1)**

(ii) The second graph represents the **Boyle's law**, i.e. graph of pressure *vs* reciprocal of volume, at constant temperature. This states that volume of a given mass of a dry gas is inversely proportional to its pressure at constant temperature. **(1)**

Q.12 Explain, why

(i) temperature –273°C is a theoretical temperature, but cannot be achieved?

(ii) Kelvin temperature is always positive?

Ans. (i) At –273°C, volume of a gas becomes zero. But it is not possible because gas is a state of matter and cannot have zero volume. Thus, –273°C is a theoretical temperature, which cannot be achieved. **(1)**

(ii) Kelvin scale of temperature starts from zero, which is equal to –273°C. Temperature below –273°C is not possible. Thus, Kelvin temperature is always positive. **(1)**

Q.13 Convert the following.
(i) 38 K to °C
(ii) −250°C to K

Ans. (i) 38 K = 38 − 273 = −235°C **(1)**
(ii) −250°C = −250 + 273 = 23 K **(1)**

Q.14 In Kelvin scale what is the
(i) boiling point of water?
(ii) melting point of ice?

Ans. (i) 373 K (ii) 273 K **(1 × 2 = 2)**

Q.15 State one difference and similarity between the Celsius scale and Kelvin scale.

Ans. The difference is that the temperature on Kelvin scale is always positive while temperature on Celsius scale may be negative, zero or positive. **(1)**
The similarity is that, the magnitude of each degree on Celsius scale is same as on Kelvin scale. **(1)**

Q.16 Choose the correct term from the given list to answer the following questions.

Volume, Pressure, Temperature, Kelvin scale, Celsius scale, STP.

(i) Which term has SI unit of Pascal?
(ii) Which term represent the condition of 0°C and 1 atm?

Ans. (i) Pressure **(1)**
(ii) STP **(1)**

TYPE - 8 03 Marks

Short Answer Type II Questions

Q.1 List important characteristics of a gas based upon kinetic theory of gases (Mention any three).

Ans. (i) Gases have neither fixed shape nor fixed volume.
(ii) Gases have negligible attractive forces between the molecules of a gas.
(iii) Gases exert pressure in all the directions.
(iv) Gases have low density.
(v) Gases have high compressibility.
(vi) Gases easily undergo diffusion. **(3)**

Q.2 Write an experiment to show the pressure-volume relationship of a gas.

Ans. Take a 10 mL syringe fitted with a piston and move the piston upward to mark 10 mL.
Cover the adhesive tape over its nozzle. Fit this nozzle tightly into a hole in the rubber stopper as shown in given figure.

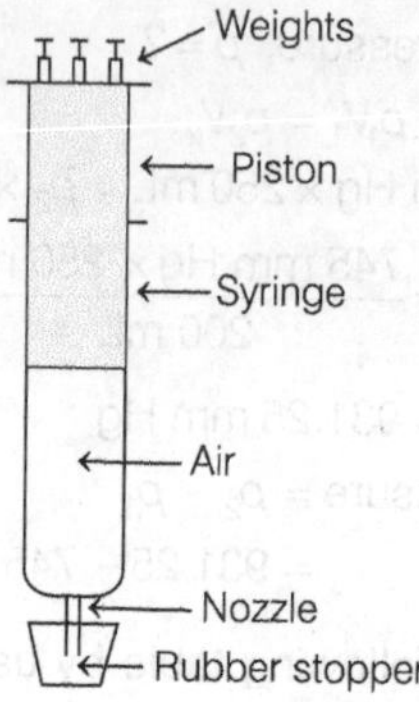

On putting some weight on the piston (pressure increases), the piston moves downward and volume of the air in the syringe decreases.
Then put some more weight, the piston moves further downwards and the volume of the air is further reduced.
Similarly, if the weights on the piston are gradually decreased, the piston moves upwards and volume of air starts increasing. **(3)**

Q.3 Determine the pressure of a gas in mm Hg, when the volume of gas initially is 250 mL and is expanded to 1000 mL at the final pressure of 0.4 atmosphere. Assume that temperature during the reaction remains constant.

Ans. Given, initial volume, $V_1 = 250$ mL
Final volume, $V_2 = 1000$ mL
Initial pressure, $p_1 = ?$
Final pressure, $p_2 = 0.4$ atm
Applying Boyle's law, $p_1V_1 = p_2V_2$

$$p_1 \times 250 = 0.4 \times 1000$$

$$\Rightarrow \quad p_1 = \frac{0.4 \times 1000}{250} = 1.6 \text{ atm}$$

$\because$ 1 atm = 760 mm Hg
$\therefore$ 1.6 atm = (1.6 × 760) mm Hg
= 1216 mm Hg **(3)**

Q.4 The volume occupied by a gas was 5.6 dm^3 at 2 atmospheric pressure. If the pressure is increased by 20%, calculate the new volume of the gas, at constant temperature.

Ans. Initial volume of gas, $V_1 = 5.6\ dm^3$
Initial pressure of gas, $p_1 = 2$ atm
Increase in p = 20% of initial pressure $= 2 \times \frac{20}{100}$

$$= \frac{4}{10} = 0.4 \text{ atm}$$

Final pressure, $p_2 = 0.4 + 2 = 2.4$ atm

Final volume, $V_2 = ?$

Applying Boyle's law, $p_1V_1 = p_2V_2$

$$2 \times 5.6 = 2.4 \times V_2$$

$$\Rightarrow \quad V_2 = \frac{5.6 \times 2}{2.4} = 4.67 \text{ dm}^3$$ **(3)**

Q.5 88 cm^3 of nitrogen is at a pressure of 770 mm of Hg. Calculate the change in volume if the pressure is raised to 880 mm of Hg, when temperature is kept constant.

Ans. $V_1 = 88 \text{ cm}^3$

$V_2 = ?$

$p_1 = 770$ mm of Hg

$p_2 = 880$ mm of Hg (T constant)

According to Boyle's law,

$p_1V_1 = p_2V_2$ (T constant)

$$88 \times 770 = V_2 \times 880$$

$$V_2 = \frac{88 \times 770}{880} = 77 \text{ cm}^3$$

Decrease in volume $= 88 - 77 = 11$ cm^3 **(3)**

Q.6 561 dm^3 of a gas at STP is to be filled in a 748 dm^3 flask. Calculate the percentage change in the pressure required, temperature is kept constant.

Ans. $V_1 = 561 \text{dm}^3$ $\quad V_2 = 748 \text{ dm}^3$

$p_1 = 1$ atm $\quad p_2 = ?$ (Temperature constant)

According to Boyle's law,

$p_1V_1 = p_2V_2$ (T constant)

$$561 \times 1 = p_2 \times 748$$

$$p_2 = \frac{561}{748}$$

$$\Delta p = 1 - \frac{561}{748} = \frac{748 - 561}{748}$$

$$\Delta p = \frac{187}{748}$$

$$\% \text{ change} = \frac{187}{748} \times 100 = 25\%$$ **(3)**

Q.7 A cylinder of 20 litres capacity contains a gas at 100 atm pressure. How many flasks of 200 cm^3 capacity can be filled from it at 1 atm pressure, temperature remaining constant?

Ans. 20 L volume at 100 atm has to be converted to 1 atm.

$V_1 = 20$ L

$V_2 = ?$

$p_1 = 100$ atm

$p_2 = 1$ atm

Using Boyle's law,

$$p_1V_1 = p_2V_2$$

$$100 \times 20 = 1 \times V_2$$

$$V_2 = 2000 \text{ L} = 2000 \times 1000 \text{ cm}^3$$

$$= 20,00,000 \text{ cm}^3$$

No. of containers

$$= \frac{\text{Total volume}}{\text{Volume of one container at same conditions}}$$

$$= \frac{2000000}{200} = 10000 \text{ flasks}$$ **(3)**

Q.8 How did Charles' law state the concept of absolute scale of temperature?

Ans. From the Charles' law, at constant pressure, the volume of a given mass of a gas increases or decreases by $\frac{1}{273}$ of its volume at 0°C for each 1°C rise or fall in temperature.

Suppose V_0 be the volume of a fixed mass of a gas at 0°C and its pressure is p.

$\therefore$ At constant pressure, volume of gas (V) at t° C is

$$V_{t°\text{C}} = V_0 + \frac{1}{273} \times V_0 t$$

Volume of a gas at −273° C (at constant pressure),

$$V_{(-273°\text{C})} = V_0 + \frac{1}{273} \times V_0(-273)$$

$$= V_0 - V_0 = 0$$

The temperature −273° C is called **absolute zero.** **(3)**

Q.9 A gas occupies a volume of 120 cm^3 at 27.3 K. What volume it will occupy at 0°C; pressure remaining constant?

Ans. Given, initial volume, $V_1 = 120 \text{cm}^3$

Initial temperature, $T_1 = 27.3$ K

Final volume, $V_2 = ?$

Final temperature, $T_2 = 0° \text{C} = 273 \text{K}$

By Charles' law, $\frac{V_1}{T_1} = \frac{V_2}{T_2}$ (p constant)

$$\Rightarrow \quad \frac{120}{27.3} = \frac{V_2}{273}$$

$$\Rightarrow \quad V_2 = \frac{120 \times 273}{27.3} = 1200 \text{ cm}^3$$ **(3)**

Q.10 At what temperature in centigrade will the volume of a gas at 0°C double itself with pressure remains constant?

Ans. Let the volume of the gas at 0°C $= V$ mL

Thus, we have $V_1 = V$ mL, $V_2 = 2V$ mL

$T_1 = 0 + 273 = 273 \text{ K}, T_2 = ?$

By Charles' law, $\frac{V_1}{V_2} = \frac{T_1}{T_2} \Rightarrow \frac{V_1}{T_1} = \frac{V_2}{T_2}$

On substituting the corresponding values, we get

$$\frac{V}{273} = \frac{2V}{T_2}$$

$$\Rightarrow \quad T_2 = \frac{2V \times 273}{V} = 546 \text{ K}$$

$$\therefore \quad T_2 = 546 - 273 = 273°\text{C}$$ **(3)**

Q.11 **State the following.**

(i) The volume of a gas at 0 K.

(ii) The STP conditions.

(iii) The absolute temperature of a gas at 7°C.

Ans. (i) The volume of a gas at 0 K is **zero.** **(1)**

(ii) 1 atmospheric pressure and 0°C (273 K) temperature. **(1)**

(iii) 7°C + 273 = 280 K. **(1)**

Q.12 **Convert the following temperature to Celsius scale.**

(i) 426 K **(ii) 105 K**

(iii) 250 K **(iv) 338 K**

(v) 285 K **(vi) 728 K**

Ans. [$T°\text{C} = \text{K} - 273$]

(i) 426 K = 426 − 273 = 153° C

(ii) 105 K = 105 − 273 = − 168° C

(iii) 250 K = 250 − 273 = − 23° C

(iv) 338 K = 338 − 273 = 65° C

(v) 285 K = 285 − 273 = 12° C

(vi) 728 K = 728 − 273 = 455° C **(½ × 6 = 3)**

Q.13 **At 25°C and 760 mm of Hg pressure, a gas occupies 600 mL volume. What will be its pressure at a height where temperature is 10°C and volume of the gas is 640 mL?**

Ans. Given, that

$p_1 = 760$ mm Hg

$V_1 = 600$ mL

$T_1 = 25°\text{C} = 25 + 273 = 298$ K

and $p_2 = ?$

$V_2 = 640$ mL

$T_2 = 10°\text{C} = 10 + 273 = 283$ K

According to Gas equation, $\frac{p_1V_1}{T_1} = \frac{p_2V_2}{T_2}$

On substituting the corresponding values, we get

$$p_2 = \frac{(760 \text{ mm Hg}) \times (600 \text{ mL}) \times (283 \text{ K})}{(640 \text{ mL}) \times (298 \text{ K})}$$

$= 676.6$ mm Hg **(3)**

Q.14 **6 dm^3 of dry gas is present at temperature of 27°C and pressure of 700 mm of Hg. Determine the volume of gas at STP.**

Ans. Initial volume, $V_1 = 6 \text{ dm}^3$

Final volume, $V_2 = ?$

Initial pressure, $p_1 = 700$ mm of Hg

Final pressure, $p_2 = 760$ mm of Hg

Initial temperature, $T_1 = 27 + 273 = 300$ K

Final temperature, $T_2 = 273$ K

Applying ideal gas equation,

$$\frac{p_1V_1}{T_1} = \frac{p_2V_2}{T_2}$$

$$\frac{700 \times 6}{300} = \frac{760 \times V_2}{273}$$

or $$V_2 = \frac{700 \times 6 \times 273}{300 \times 760} = 5.03 \text{ dm}^3$$ **(3)**

Q.15 **Nitrogen is collected over water. The pressure observed was 700 mm of Hg at temperature of 300 K and a volume of 100 cm^3. Determine the volume of dry nitrogen gas at STP. (Take aqueous tension at 27°C is 15 mm of Hg)**

Ans. Initial pressure, $p_1 = 700 - 15 = 685$ mm of Hg

Final pressure, $p_2 = 760$ mm of Hg

Initial volume, $V_1 = 100 \text{ cm}^3$

Final volume, $V_2 = ?$

Initial temperature, $T_1 = 300$ K

Final temperature, $T_2 = 273$ K

Applying ideal gas equation,

$$\frac{p_1V_1}{T_1} = \frac{p_2V_2}{T_2}$$

$$\frac{685 \times 100}{300} = \frac{760 \times V_2}{273}$$

or $$V_2 = \frac{685 \times 100 \times 273}{300 \times 760} = 82.02 \text{ cm}^3$$ **(3)**

Q.16 **22.4 L of a gas weigh 44 g at STP. Calculate weight of the gas if it occupies a volume of 20 L at 27°C and 700 mm Hg of pressure.**

Ans. Given Mass of 22.4 L of a gas at STP = 44 g

(*So convert the given value also at STP*)

$V_1 = 20$ L

$T_1 = 27°\text{C} = 300$ K

$p_1 = 700$ mm of Hg

$V_2 = ?$

$T_2 = 273$ K

$p_2 = 760$ m of Hg

Using gas equation,

$$\frac{p_1V_1}{T_1} = \frac{p_2V_2}{T_2}$$

$$\frac{700 \times 20}{300} = \frac{760 \times V_2}{273}$$

$$\Rightarrow \quad V_2 = \frac{700 \times 20 \times 273}{300 \times 760} = 16.76 \text{ L}$$

Mass of 22.4 L of a gas at STP = 44 g

Mass of 1 L of a gas at STP = $\frac{44}{22.4}$ g

Mass of 16.76 L of a gas at STP = $\frac{44}{22.4} \times 16.76$

= 32.9 g

(3)

Q. 17 Calculate the volume occupied by 2g of hydrogen at 27°C and 4 atm pressure, if at STP it occupies 22.4 L. Volume of 2 g = 22.4 L at STP

Ans. $V_1 = 22.4$ L

$V_2 = ?$

$T_1 = 273$ K

$T_2 = 27 + 273$ K $= 300$ K

$p_1 = 1$ atm

$p_2 = 4$ atm

According to gas equation

$$\frac{p_1V_1}{T_1} = \frac{p_2V_2}{T_2}$$

$$\frac{1 \times 22.4}{273} = \frac{4 \times V_2}{300 \text{ K}}$$

$$V_2 = \frac{22.4 \times 1 \times 300}{273 \times 4}$$

$= 6.15$ L **(3)**

Q.18 Calculate the final volume of a gas '*X*' if the original pressure of the gas at S.T.P is doubled and its temperature is increased three times.

Ans. $p_1 = 1$ atm

$p_2 = 2 \times 1 = 2$ atm

$T_1 = 273$ K

$T_2 = 3 \times 273$ K

$V_1 = V$

$V_2 = ?$

Using gas equation,

$$\frac{p_1V_1}{T_1} = \frac{p_2V_2}{T_2}$$

$$\frac{1 \times V}{273} = \frac{2 \times V_2}{3 \times 273}$$

$$V_2 = \frac{3 \times 273 \times V}{2 \times 273} = 1\frac{1}{2} = \frac{3}{2}\text{V}$$

One and a half times the initial volume. **(3)**

Q.19 Write the value of

(i) standard pressure in

(a) mm of Hg (b) cm of Hg

(c) atm (d) torr

(ii) Standard temperature in

(a) °C (b) K

Ans. (i) Standard pressure

(a) 760 mm of Hg

(b) 76 cm of Hg

(c) 1 atmosphere

(d) 760 torr **($\frac{1}{2} \times 4 = 2$)**

(ii) Standard temperature

(a) 0°C

(b) $273 + 0 = 273$K **($\frac{1}{2} \times 2 = 1$)**

TYPE - 9 — 04/05 Marks

Long Answer Type Questions

Q.1 **(i) Explain Charles' law on the basis of the kinetic theory of gases.**

(ii) Give difference between absolule zero and absolute scale of temperature.

Ans. (i) According to kinetic theory of gas, the pressure of gas depends upon the number of gas particles that strike the walls of the container.

It the temperature of the gas increases, the kinetic energy of the particles increases due to which more particles go and strike the wall of the container thereby increasing the pressure.

Thus, when the temperature increases the volume of the gas increases so that a constant pressure can be maintained. **(2)**

(ii) The temperature (−273 K) at which the molecular motion completely ceases (theoretical concept), on the Kelvin scale, is called absolute zero. **(1)**

The temperature scale with its zero at −273.15° C and whose each degree is equal to the one degree on the Celsius scale, is called the Kelvin or absolute scale of temperature. **(1)**

Q.2 Give reason for the following statements.

(i) It is necessary to specify the temperature and pressure while stating volume of a gas.

(ii) Gas fills the vessel completely in which it is kept.

(iii) Inflating a balloon seems to violate Boyle's law.

(iv) Mountaineers carry oxygen cylinders with them.

Ans. (i) This is due to the fact that volume of a gas changes with the change in temperature or pressure.

The relation it follows is $\frac{p_1V_1}{T_1} = \frac{p_2V_2}{T_2}$

(ii) The gas particles have very low intermolecular force of attraction and rapidly move in all directions. Therefore, they completely fill the vessel in which they are kept.

(iii) Boyle's law is valid for a definite mass of a gas in a closed container. In this case the mass of air inside the balloon rapidly increases as the air is blown into the balloon. Hence, it is not violating the Boyle's law.

(iv) This is because at higher altitudes (at mountains), the density of oxygen is less. Thus, due to less density of oxygen it is available in less amount for breathing. Hence, mountaineers carry oxygen cylinders with them. **(1 × 4 = 4)**

Q.3 Name the following.

(i) Theory that help in explaining the relationship between p, V and T.

(ii) Process of gradual mixing of two substances.

(iii) Term used for degree of hotness of gas.

(iv) Theoretical concept of temperature at which the molecular motion completely ceases.

Ans. (i) Kinetic theory of gases

(ii) Diffusion

(iii) Temperature

(iv) Absolute zero **(1 × 4 = 4)**

Q.4 (i) Derive the expression for gas equation.

(ii) A certain mass of a gas occupies 4 L at 27°C and 200 Pascal. Calculate the temperature when the volume and pressure become half of their initial value.

Ans. (i) The gas equation gives us a fixed relation amongst volume, pressure and temperature.

According to Boyle's law,

$$V \propto \frac{1}{p} \quad \ldots(i)$$

and according to Charles' law,

$$V \propto T \quad \ldots(ii)$$

Combining Eqs. (i) and (ii)

$$V \propto \frac{1}{p} \times T$$

$$\Rightarrow \quad V = \frac{T}{p} \times \text{constant}$$

$$\Rightarrow \quad \frac{pV}{T} = \text{constant}$$

Accordingly, if the volume of a given mass of a gas changes from V_1 to V_2, its pressure from p_1 to p_2 and its temperature from T_1 to T_2, then

$$\frac{p_1V_1}{T_1} = \frac{p_2V_2}{T_2}$$

This is the expression for gas equation. **(2)**

(ii) Given, $p_1 = 200$ Pa, $p_2 = 100$ Pa

$V_1 = 4$ L, $V_2 = 2$ L, $T_1 = 300$ K, $T_2 = ?$

Using gas equation,

$$\frac{p_1V_1}{T_1} = \frac{p_2V_2}{T_2}$$

$$\Rightarrow \quad \frac{200 \times 4}{300} = \frac{100 \times 2}{T_2}$$

$$T_2 = \frac{100 \times 2 \times 300}{4 \times 200}$$

$$\therefore \quad T_2 = 75\,\text{K}$$ **(2)**

Q.5 (i) Define the following terms:

(a) Isotherm (b) Isobar

(ii) Draw the graphs for the following reactions.

(a) pV vs p (b) p vs V

(c) p vs $\frac{1}{V}$ (d) V vs T

Ans. (i)(a) **Isotherm** A state where temperature remains constant (graph of Boyle's law is also termed as isotherm as it is drawn at constant of temperature). **(1/2)**

(b) **Isobar** A state where pressure remains constant (graph of Charles' law is also termed as isobar as it is drawn at constant pressure). **(1/2)**

(ii)

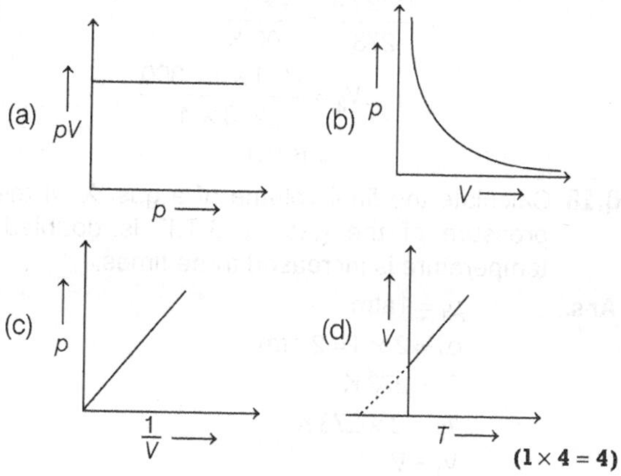

(1 × 4 = 4)

Q.6 (i) Explain the following.

(a) Gases have low densities.

(b) Gases are highly expandable.

(c) Gases exert pressure in all directions.

(ii) 150 cm^3 of hydrogen is collected over water at 27°C and 750 mm Hg pressure. Find the volume of dry gas at STP if the vapour pressure at 27°C is 48 mm Hg.

Ans. (i)(a) Since, the number of molecules per unit volume in a gas is very less as compared to solids and liquids they have large intermolecular spaces therefore, gases have very low density.

(b) Particles of gases have very less intermolecular force of attraction, when pressure is reduced the particles quickly move apart.

(c) Since, the particles of gases are in random motion, due to this they collide with each other and as a result they strike with the walls of container. Thus, gases exert pressure in all direction. **(1 × 3 = 3)**

(ii) $V_1 = 150 \text{ cm}^3$ $V_2 = ?$

$T_1 = 300 \text{ K}$, $T_2 = 273 \text{ K}$

$p_1 = 750 - 48 = 702$ mm of Hg

$p_2 = 760$ mm of Hg

Using gas equation,

$$\frac{p_1V_1}{T_1} = \frac{p_2V_2}{T_2}$$

$$\Rightarrow \quad V_2 = \frac{p_1V_1T_2}{p_2T_1}$$

$$V_2 = \frac{702 \times 150 \times 273}{760 \times 300} = 126.08 \text{ cm}^3$$ **(2)**

Q.7 (i) Mention whether the volume of a given mass of a gas increases or decreases if

(a) pressure increases, while temperature remain constant.

(b) temperature decreases and pressure remains constant.

(ii) 370 cc of moist hydrogen measured at 19°C and 859 mm pressure. Calculate the volume of dry hydrogen at STP. The vapour pressure of water at 19°C is 9 mm.

Ans. (i) (a) decreases (b) decreases **(1 × 2 = 2)**

(ii) $V_1 = 370 \text{cc}$, $V_2 = ?$

$T_1 = 19^\circ\text{C} = 19 + 273 = 292 \text{ K}$, $T_2 = 273 \text{ K}$

$p_1 = 859 - 9 = 850 \text{ mm}$, $p_2 = 760 \text{ mm}$

Using gas equation, $\frac{p_1V_1}{T_1} = \frac{p_2V_2}{T_2}$

$$\Rightarrow \quad V_2 = \frac{p_1V_1T_2}{p_2T_1}$$

$$\Rightarrow \quad V_2 = \frac{850 \times 370 \times 273}{760 \times 292}$$

$$V_2 = 386.89 \text{ cc}$$ **(3)**

Q.8 Give the scientific term for each of the following.

(i) The behaviour of a gas under known conditions of pressure, volume and temperature at this is described by these laws.

(ii) The process of gradual mixing of two substances kept in close contact by molecular motion.

(iii) The temperature at which the molecular motion completely ceases.

(iv) The pressure exerted by air present in the atmosphere on the surface of the Earth.

(v) Partial pressure of water vapour in gas when the gas is collected over water.

Ans. (i) Gas laws

(ii) Diffusion

(iii) Absolute zero

(iv) Atmospheric pressure

(v) Aqueous tension **(1 × 5 = 5)**

TYPE - 10 — 03 Marks

Case-Based Questions

Q.1 Ravi and Kavya were studying gas laws in their laboratory. They were doing an experiment using balloon. At 27°C, they found the volume of the gas in balloon is 4.8 L. Similarly they have taken five readings and recorded them in tabular form as shown below.

Temperature	Volume (in L)
27°C	4.8
77°C	5.6
127°C	6.4
177°C	7.2
227°C	8.0

(i) What will be the nature of graph between V and T(K)?

(ii) Check whether the line passes through the origin.

(iii) Which gas law is obeyed by the above data?

Ans. (i) The graph between V and T(K) is a straight line.

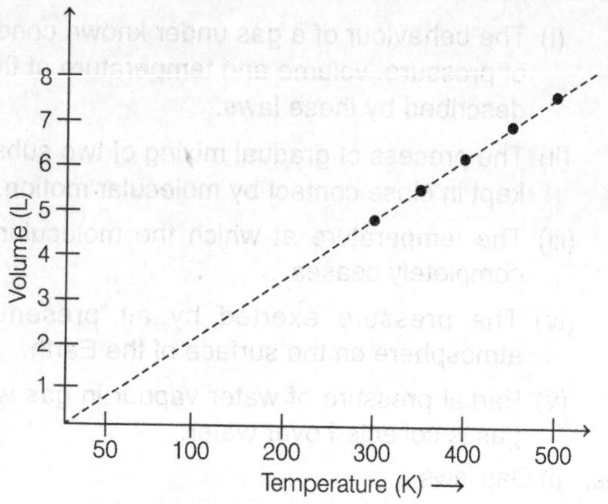

(ii) Yes, as we can see in the graph, the line passes through the origin.

(iii) The above data obeys Charles' law (volume-temperature relationship). **(1 × 3 = 3)**

Q.2 **A football is inflated to the recommended pressure and volume on a warm summer day at 30°C.**

When the same football is taken out on a cold winter morning at –10°C, players observe that it feels deflated and less bouncy despite being properly inflated earlier. This phenomenon is based on the kinetic theory of gases.

(i) What is the kinetic theory of gases?

(ii) How would the decreased temperature in winters affect the pressure inside the football?

(iii) Convert –10°C and 30°C into Kelvin.

Ans. (i) The kinetic theory of gases states that gas molecules are in constant random motion, and their average kinetic energy is directly proportional to the absolute temperature.

(ii) As the temperature decreases in winter, the kinetic energy of the gas molecules inside the football reduces. This causes fewer collisions with the inner walls of the football, leading to a decrease in internal pressure and a less bouncy ball.

(iii) To convert Celsius (°C) to Kelvin (K), use the formula.

$$K = °C + 273$$

For –10° C

$$K = -10 + 273 = 263 \text{ K}$$

For 30°C

$$K = 30 + 273 = 303 \text{ K}$$

(1 × 3 = 3)

08

ATMOSPHERIC POLLUTION

- Earth is surrounded by a layer of various gases, called **atmosphere**.
- Addition of some undesirable substances into our surroundings, which have adverse effect on plants and animals, including human beings is called **environmental pollution**. These undesirable substance are called **pollutants**.
- On the basis of origin or sources, pollutants are of two types, i.e. natural and man-made.

Air Pollution

An increase in the composition of harmful or undesirable substances in the air is called **air pollution** (atmospheric pollution). These undesirable and harmful substances are called **air pollutants**.

- **Smog** is a pollutant which is formed by combination of oxides of nitrogen and sulphur and of partially oxidised hydrocarbons and their derivatives. It forms a dark, thick, dust and soot laden fog.

Smog = Smoke + Fog

- Carbon monoxide is also a harmful air pollutant, produced by incomplete combustion of fuels in homes, factories and automobiles. It combines with haemoglobin more strongly than oxygen to form carboxyhaemoglobin. This reduces the oxygen-carrying capacity of blood, which causes retardation and dizziness.

Oxides of Nitrogen as Air Pollutants

Sources

(i) By burning of fuels in **furnaces** at high temperature.

(ii) When fuel burns in an **internal combustion** engine of automobile.

(iii) Atmospheric nitrogen and oxygen reacts during an **electric discharge**.

Harmful Effects

(i) It causes **irritation in mucous membrane.**

(ii) High concentrations of NO_2 may cause **serious lung diseases**.

(iii) Nitrogen dioxide causes serious injury to **vegetation,** it damages plant leaves.

(iv) It is one of the cause of **photochemical smog**, which causes eye irritation, nasal and throat infections.

Oxides of Sulphur as Air Pollutants

Sources

By burning of fuels like coal and petroleum.

Harmful Effects

(i) It causes **headache, vomiting** and even death due to respiratory failure.

(ii) It mixes with water to form sulphuric acid, which is the cause of **acid rain**.

(iii) It **destroys vegetation** and weakens building materials.

(iv) It mixes with smoke and fog to **form smog**.

Acid Rain

- Sometimes rain water is more acidic than normal, such rain is called **acid rain.**
- pH of acid rain usually ranges between 5.6 and 3.5, but it can also be as low as 2.
- When gases like sulphur dioxide (SO_2), nitrogen dioxide (NO_2) are released in air due to burning of fossil fuels, they mix with water vapour in the atmosphere and forms acid as sulphuric acid (H_2SO_4) and nitric acid (HNO_3).
- These acids get mixed with rain forming acid rain.

Formation of Nitric Acid

- Nitrogen and oxygen combine in the presence of thunder and lightning to form nitrogen oxide.
- Nitrogen oxide then gets oxidised in the atmosphere to form nitrogen dioxide. Nitrogen dioxide combines with water to form a mixture of nitrous acid and nitric acid.

$$N_2 + O_2 \xrightarrow[\text{(3000°C)}]{\text{High temperature}} \underset{\text{(Nitrogen oxide)}}{2NO}$$

$$2NO + O_2 \longrightarrow \underset{\text{(Nitrogen dioxide)}}{2NO_2}$$

$$2NO_2 + H_2O \longrightarrow \underset{\text{(Nitrous acid)}}{HNO_2} + \underset{\text{(Nitric acid)}}{HNO_3}$$

Formation of Sulphuric Acid

- Sulphur dioxide can also be oxidised to sulphur trioxide.

$$2SO_2 + O_2 \longrightarrow \underset{\text{(Sulphur trioxide)}}{2SO_3}$$

- Sulphur trioxide reacts with water vapour to form sulphuric acid.

$$SO_3 + H_2O \longrightarrow \underset{\text{(Sulphuric acid)}}{H_2SO_4}$$

Impact of Acid Rain

(i) **Changes the acidity of soil** The acids present in acid rain such as nitric acid, nitrous acid, sulphuric acid and sulphurous acid increases the acidity of soil.

(ii) **Affects water bodies and marine organisms** The water of lakes and rivers becomes acidic and may no longer support aquatic life.

(iii) **Material damage** It increases corrosion of metals, disintegrates paper and leather, and weakens building materials such as marble, limestone, slate, mortar, statues and sculptures. The Taj Mahal is facing this serious problem.

(iv) **Impact on living things** Acid rain damages forests. It gets absorbed by plants and animals directly or indirectly and thus enters the food chain, affecting humans. It can affect a person's breathing at sufficiently high concentrations.

Reducing the Impact of Acid Rain

- By **reducing the emission of oxides of sulphur and nitrogen**, this can be done by using coal or oil with low sulphur content or by using catalytic converters in cars.
- By **using a scrubber**, a device that absorbs gaseous pollutants.

Global Warming

- The increase in temperature of earth above its normal temperature is called **global warming**. It occurs due to increase in concentration of **greenhouse gases.**
- The gases such as carbon dioxide (CO_2), methane, water vapour, oxide of nitrogen, etc., that prevents the escape of heat from earth, are called **greenhouse gases.**
- If concentration of the greenhouse gases increase above a certain level, they prevent the outflow of heat from the earth, leading to an increase in earth's temperature, known as **global warming**.

Sources of Greenhouse Gases

(i) **Water vapour** The main sources of water vapour are industrial exhaust, vehicular exhaust, burning of fuels and volcanic eruptions.

(ii) **Carbon dioxide (CO_2)** Respiration, burning of fossil fuels for energy, decomposition of limestone, volcanic eruptions, etc., all processes proceed with the liberation of carbon dioxide into the atmosphere.

(iii) **Hydrocarbons (Methane, CH_4)** These are obtained by the incomplete combustion of fossil fuels in automobile engines and by anaerobic decomposition of organic matter or vegetation.

(iv) **Oxides of nitrogen** Combustion of fossil fuels such as coal, oil, gasoline, etc., in automobile engines and power plants at high temperature produces oxides of nitrogen.

Advantages of Greenhouse Effect

- It helps in maintaining the optimum temperature necessary for survival.
- It is necessary for evaporation of water and formation of clouds, leading to rain.

Effects or Consequences of Global Warming

- Due to global warming, glaciers and polar ice caps have started to melt, and gradually this may lead to an **increase in sea level**.
- Global warming will cause **more water to evaporate from water bodies**, thus forming more water vapour. Since, water vapour also contributes to green house effect, global warming will further increase.
- Global warming can lead to **changes in rain pattern and thus shift in crop zones**. For example, the wheat producing zones will shift from Russia and Canada to the less fertile polar regions.

Methods of Reducing Global Warming

(i) By minimising the use of automobiles.

(ii) By promoting afforestation.

(iii) By making smoking illegal in public places.

(iv) By avoiding burning of dry leaves, wood, etc.

(v) By creating awareness about global warming.

Ozone Depletion

Ozone (O_3) is a light bluish gas which is found in the upper layer of atmosphere (stratosphere). It is formed from oxygen in the presence of UV rays.

$$\underset{\text{Oxygen}}{3O_2(g)} \xrightarrow{\text{UV rays}} \underset{\text{Ozone}}{2O_3(g)}$$

- Ozone forms a thick layer in the upper region of atmosphere known as **ozone layer**.
- Ozone layer absorbs the harmful ultraviolet (UV) radiations coming from the sun. Thus, it protects life on earth from the harmful effects of UV rays.

$$O_2(g) \xrightarrow{\text{UV}} \underset{\substack{\text{(Nascent}\\\text{oxygen)}}}{O(g)} + O(g)$$

$$O_2(g) + O \underset{}{\overset{\text{UV}}{\rightleftharpoons}} O_3(g)$$

$$\text{Net reaction}: 3O_2 + \text{UV} \longrightarrow 2O_3$$

- Decrease in the quantity of ozone in upper layers of the atmosphere is called **depletion of ozone**, which leads to the formation of an **ozone hole**.
- Due to the formation of ozone hole, UV rays of the sun reach the earth and cause diseases like skin cancer.

Chemicals Responsible for Destruction of Ozone Layer

(i) **Chlorofluorocarbons or CFCs** These are man-made compounds which are very stable and are decomposed by UV rays. These compounds reach the ozone layer and deplete it by reacting with it.

(ii) **Fuel of planes** On burning of plane fuels, different gases like nitric oxide are emitted in the atmosphere which reacts with ozone and reduces its quantity.

(iii) **Use of industrial chemicals** The chemicals used in industries like methyl chloride (CH_3Cl), methyl bromide (CH_3Br), carbon tetrachloride (CCl_4), etc., are decomposed by UV-rays to give highly reactive species which depletes the ozone layer by reacting with it.

EXAM ORIENTED QUESTIONS

TYPE - 1 01 Mark

Multiple Choice Questions

Q.1 Which of the following is the source of man-made pollution?

(a) Coal power plant (b) Forest fires
(c) Volcanoes (d) Decaying vegetation

Ans. (a) Coal power plant

Q.2 Which type of pollutant in the left had column is linked correctly to the health impact in the right hand column?

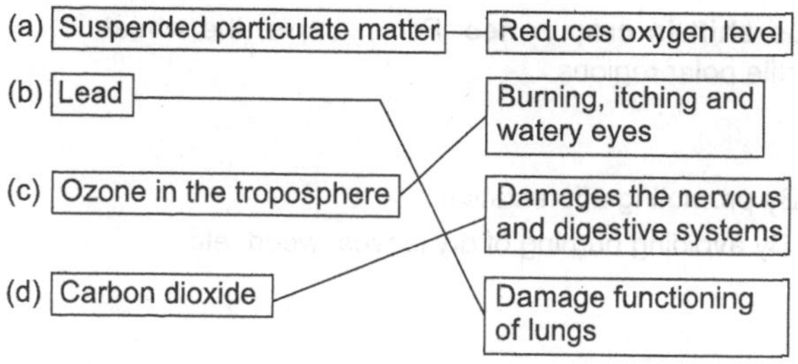

Ans. (c)

Q.3 Examine the image showing air pollution in Delhi. Which of the following best explains the role of burning fossil fuels in contributing to the air pollution depicted in the image?

(a) Burning fossil releases carbon monoxide that traps heat in the atmosphere, causing global warming.
(b) Burning fossil fuels produces large amount of pollutants in the atmosphere that causes air pollution and makes air quality worse.
(c) Burning fossil fuels increases the amount of oxygen in the air, making it fresher and cleaner.
(d) Burning fossil fuels has no impact on air pollution and does not affect air quality.

Ans. (b) Burning fossil fuels produces large amount of pollutants in the atmosphere that causes air pollution and makes air quality worse.

Q.4 The gases coming from a car's exhaust contain oxides of nitrogen. How are these oxides formed?

(a) Nitrogen reacts with carbon dioxide.
(b) Nitrogen reacts with carbon monoxide.
(c) Nitrogen reacts with oxygen.
(d) Nitrogen reacts with petrol.

Ans. (c) In car engines, combustion of fuel produces high temperature that causes nitrogen and oxygen present in air to react. It produces the oxides of nitrogen.

Q.5 The acid which is responsible for the acid rain is

(a) acetic acid (b) citric acid
(c) nitric acid (d) maleic acid

Ans. (c) nitric acid

Q.6 Which of the following reactions is involved in the formation of nitric acid in acid rain?

(a) $2NO_2 + H_2O \longrightarrow HNO_2 + HNO_3$
(b) $NO_2 + O_2 \longrightarrow HNO_3$
(c) $NO + H_2O \longrightarrow HNO_3$
(d) $NO_2 + O_2 \longrightarrow HNO_3$

Ans. (a) $2NO_2 + H_2O \longrightarrow \underset{\text{(Nitric acid)}}{HNO_3} + \underset{\text{(Nitrous acid)}}{HNO_2}$

Q.7 Which of the following is not responsible for acid rain?

(a) Sulphuric acid (b) Formic acid
(c) Sulphurous acid (d) Nitric acid

Ans. (b) Formic acid (It is an organic acid and is not formed in atmosphere).

Q.8 Which shows both the correct source and the correct effect of the pollutant?

	Pollutant	Source	Effect
(a)	Carbon monoxide	Incomplete combustion of carbon-containing materials	Global warming
(b)	Oxides of nitrogen	Decaying vegetable matter	Global warming
(c)	Ozone	Photochemical reactions	Acid rain
(d)	Sulphur dioxide	Volcanoes	Acid rain

Ans. (d) Sulphur dioxide is produced by volcanoes and it causes acid rain.

Q.9 Which of the following in not the impact of acid rain?
(a) Acid rain causes damage to marble, limestone.
(b) Acid rain causes corrosion of metals.
(c) Acid rain affects soil chemistry.
(d) Acid rain increases the temperature of earth.

Ans. (d) Acid rain increases the temperature of earth.

Q.10 Which of the following is a greenhouse gas?
(a) Methane (b) Oxygen
(c) Carbon (d) Nitrogen

Ans. (a) Methane

Q.11 Among the following gases, which is the major contributor towards global warming:
(a) CFC (b) CH_4 (c) CO_2 (d) O_2

Ans. (c) CO_2

Q.12 The major sources of water vapour are
(a) industrial and vehicular exhaust
(b) burning of fuels
(c) volcanic eruptions
(d) All of the above

Ans. (d) All of the above

Q.13 Absence of a greenhouse gas will drop the temperature to about
(a) -15° C (b) 15°C (c) -18° C (d) 18°C

Ans. (c) -18° C

Q.14 Consider the following measures regarding way to reduce global warming.
I. Afforestation
II. Use of solar energy
III. Pooling of cars can be practised

The correct option is
(a) Only I (b) Only II
(c) I and III (d) I, II and III

Ans. (d) I, II and III

Q.15 Ozone layer prevent which harmful radiation from reaching the earth's surface?
(a) Ultraviolet rays (b) Cosmic rays
(c) Alpha rays (d) X-rays

Ans. (a) Ultraviolet rays

Q.16 The carbon compound, that is responsible for ozone hole in atmosphere.
(a) Chlorofluorocarbons (CFCs)
(b) Ethane
(c) Nitrogen oxide
(d) Propane

Ans. (a) Chlorofluorocarbons (CFCs)

Q.17 Which of the following is responsible for depletion of ozone layer?
(a) Nascent oxygen (b) Nascent chlorine
(c) Oxygen gas (d) Fluorine gas

Ans. (b) Nascent chlorine, which is released by decomposition of chlorofluoro carbons by ultraviolet rays is responsible for ozone depletion.

Q.18 The following reaction sequence causes depletion of ozone.

1. $ClO(g) + O(g) \longrightarrow Cl(g) + O_2(g)$
2. $CF_2Cl_2(g) \xrightarrow{\text{Ultraviolet rays}} CF_2Cl(g) + \underset{\text{(Free radical)}}{Cl(g)}$
3. $Cl(g) + O_3(g) \longrightarrow ClO(g) + O_2(g)$

(a) $1 \to 2 \to 3$ (b) $3 \to 2 \to 1$
(c) $2 \to 3 \to 1$ (d) $2 \to 1 \to 3$

Ans. (c) $2 \to 3 \to 1$.

TYPE - 2 — 01 Mark

Assertion-Reason Questions

Direction (Q. Nos. 1-5) In the following questions statement are given Assertion and Reason.
(a) Both (A) and (R) are true and (R) is the correct explanation of (A).
(b) Both (A) and (R) are true but (R) is not the correct explanation of (A).
(c) (A) is true but (R) is false.
(d) (A) is false but (R) is true.

Q.1 **Assertion** (A) pH of acid rain can be as low as 2.
Reason (R) Acid rain contains very high concentration of acids like nitric acid and sulphuric acid.

Ans. (a) pH of acid rain can be as low as 2. It is because of the presence of very high concentration of nitric acid and sulphuric acid.
Therefore, both (A) and (R) are true and (R) is the correct explanation of (A).

Q.2 **Assertion** (A) Acid rain accelerates the degradation of historical monuments such as the Taj Mahal.
Reason (R) The reaction between sulphuric acid and calcium carbonate produces calcium sulphate, which is soluble in water and accelerated the disintegration of marble.

Ans. (a) Sulphuric acid from acid rain reacts with calcium carbonate in marble, forming soluble calcium sulphate. This dissolves in water, leading to erosion and degradation of monuments like the Taj Mahal.
Therefore, both (A) and (R) are true and (R) is the correct explanation of (A).

Q.3 Assertion (A) The increase in average temperature of the earth's surface is called global warming.

Reason (R) Sulphur oxides are the major contributor for global warming.

Ans. (c) The increase in average temperature of the earth's surface is called global warming. CO_2 is the major contributor for global warming.

Therefore, (A) is true but (R) is false.

Q.4 Assertion (A) The name greenhouse comes from glass structure called greenhouses that are used to grow green plants in the colder regions.

Reason (R) CO_2, O_2, SO_2, CH_4, N_2O and H_2O vapour are the greenhouse gases.

Ans. (c) The name greenhouse comes from the glass structure called greenhouses that are used to grow green plants in the colder regions.

CO_2, CH_4, N_2O and H_2O vapour are the greenhouse gases.

Therefore, (A) is true but (R) is false.

Q.5 Assertion (A) Decrease in the quantity of oxygen in the upper layer of atmosphere is called depletion of ozone.

Reason (R) Excessive use of chlorofluorocarbons is one of the cause of ozone depletion.

Ans. (d) Decrease in the quantity of ozone in the upper layer of atmosphere is called depletion of ozone.

Excessive use of chlorofluorocarbons is one of the cause of ozone depletion.

Therefore, (A) is false but (R) is true.

TYPE - 3 — 01 Mark

Fill in the Blanks

Q.1 Natural pollution is caused by .... (forest fires, smoking)

Ans. forest fires

Q.2 Supersonic jets release oxides of .... into the atmosphere. (sulphur, nitrogen).

Ans. nitrogen

Q.3 .... affects yield of crops and cause damage to lungs. (Sulphur dioxide, Ozone layer).

Ans. Sulphur dioxide

Q.4 Rain becomes slightly .... due to dissolution of atmospheric gases in water. (basic, acidic).

Ans. acidic

Q.5 The acid rain results in the damaging of plants and retard the growth of ....(roots, leaves)

Ans. leaves

Q.6 Metals lose their .... because of acid present in rain. (lustre, conductivity).

Ans. lustre

Q.7 Rise in average temperature of the earth's surface is called .... (global warming, ozone layer depletion)

Ans. global warming

Q.8 Carbon dioxide, water vapour, oxides of nitrogen, CH_4, O_3, CFCs, etc., are called .... (noble gases, greenhouse gases)

Ans. greenhouse gases

Q.9 .... is released from degradable matter. (Methane, Carbon monoxide)

Ans. Methane

Q.10 .... are responsible for depletion of ozone layer in upper strata of the atmosphere. (Methane, Freons)

Ans. Freons

TYPE - 4 — 01 Mark

Correct the Incorrect Statement

Q.1 Oxides of nitrogen are produced by burning fuels in furnaces at low temperature.

Ans. Oxides of nitrogen are produced by burning fuels in furnaces at **high** temperature.

Q.2 Smog is a mixture of smoke and air.

Ans. Smog is a mixture of smoke and **fog**.

Q.3 Fall in average temperature of earth's surface is caused by the radiation trapped in the earth's atmosphere.

Ans. **Rise** in average temperature of earth's surface is caused by the radiation trapped in the earth's atmosphere.

Q.4 Due to acid rain, glaciers melt, more water evaporates, and pattern of rainfall changes.

Ans. Due to **global warming**, glaciers melt, water evaporates and pattern of rainfall changes.

Q.5 CFCs are decomposed by X-rays into highly reactive chlorine, which is produced in its atomic form.

Ans. CFCs are decomposed by **UV rays** into highly reactive chlorine, which is produced in its atomic form.

TYPE - 5 01×05=05 Marks

Match the Columns

Q.1 Match the Column I (causes, effects and processes) with Column II (corect terms/descriptions).

Column I	Column II
A. Sulphur dioxide and nitrogen dioxide	1. Toxic to aquatic life.
B. pH lower than 5.6	2. Precursor gases of acid rain.
C. Acidic rain water in lakes	3. Indicator of acid rain.
D. Limestone and marble deterioration	4. Removes gaseous pollutants like sulphur dioxide from smoke.
E. Scrubbers in industries	5. Corrosion of buildings and monuments

Ans. A→2, B→3, C→1, D→5, E→4.

Q.2 Match the reactions given in Column I with the products given in Column II.

Column I	Column II
A. $NO + O_3 \longrightarrow$	1. $2SO_3$
B. $2NO_2 + H_2O \longrightarrow$	2. $NO_2 + O_2$
C. $2SO_2 + O_2 \xrightarrow{\text{Particulate}}$	3. H_2SO_4
D. $SO_3 + H_2O \longrightarrow$	4. O_3
E. $O + O_2 \underset{\text{light}}{\overset{\text{UV}}{\rightleftharpoons}}$	5. $HNO_3 + HNO_2$

Ans. A→2, B→5, C→1, D→3, E→4.

TYPE - 6 01 Mark

Identify the Following

Q.1 Acid rain occurs because of the oxides of mainly two elements, one of which is nitrogen. Name the other element.

Ans. Sulphur

Q.2 Name the reason behind, Taj Mahal in Agra is getting discoloured and lustreless.

Ans. Acid rain

Q.3 Name the device which is used to reduce the impact of acid rain.

Ans. Scrubber

Q.4 Name the term used to denote ozone blanket in the upper atmosphere.

Ans. Ozone layer

Q.5 Which disease can be caused due to the formation of ozone hole?

Ans. Skin cancer

TYPE - 7 02 Marks

Short Answer Type I Questions

Q.1 Answer the following questions.

(i) Name two natural sources of air pollution.

(ii) Name two man-made sources of air pollution.

Ans. (i) Volcanoes and forest fires. **(1)**

(ii) Automobiles and coal power plant. **(1)**

Q.2 Identify the air pollutant from its sources.

(i) By burning of coal.

(ii) By burning of fuel in internal combustion of engine.

Ans. (i) Oxides of sulphur. **(1)**

(ii) Oxides of nitrogen. **(1)**

Q.3 Excessive amount of certain substances in the environment cause pollution. Explain this using hydrogen sulphide and fluoride as examples.

Ans. Excessive concentration of hydrogen sulphide gas reduces growth of crops and causes irritation to human eyes. **(1)**

Excess concentration of fluorides cause destruction of vegetation and affects teeth and bones. **(1)**

Q.4 Explain how carbon monoxide is harmful?

Ans. Affinity of haemoglobin for carbon monoxide is about 200 times more stronger than oxygen. Haemoglobin permanently reacts with carbon monoxide to form carboxy haemoglobin. It reduces the oxygen carrying capacity of blood by an amount equivalent to the amount of haemoglobin converted into carboxy haemoglobin. Thus, a person may die due to deficiency of oxygen. This is called carbon monoxide, poisoning and due to this carbon monoxide is known as silent killer. **(2)**

Q.5 How can carbon monoxide pollution be controlled?

Ans. Carbon monoxide pollution can be controlled by the following ways.

(i) Using substitute fuels for gasoline, such as natural gas, like compressed natural gas (CNG).

(ii) Switching over from internal combustion engine to electrical powered cars. **$(1 \times 2 = 2)$**

Q.6 What do we mean by SPM?

Ans. SPM means suspended particulate matter that is the solid suspended and smoke, dust and vapour. These are very harmful as small particles get deposited in the lungs and gradually damage the functioning of lungs. **(2)**

Q.7 Complete the following reactions:

(i) $N_2(g) + O_2(g) \xrightarrow{\text{Lightning}}$

(ii) $NO(g) + O_3(g) \longrightarrow$

Ans. (i) $N_2(g) + O_2(g) \xrightarrow{\text{Lightning}} 2NO(g)$ **(1)**

(ii) $NO(g) + O_3(g) \longrightarrow NO_2(g) + O_2(g)$ **(1)**

Q.8 **(i) What is the effect of acid rain on the forest growth?**

(ii) A student observed that the iron gates in his locality turned reddish-brown after monsoon season. What could be the reason behind his observation?

Ans. (i) The acid rain damages the leaves of plants and retards the growth of forest. The forest deterioration has already taken place in the world because of acid rain. **(1)**

(ii) The iron gates turned reddish-brown due to the formation of rust on them. The rain in monsoon season is acidic in nature, which causes corrosion of metals. **(1)**

Q.9 **Acid rain damages the structures made up of limestone or marble. The sulphur containing component of acid rain, '*A*' dissolves '*B*', component of marble. Give this reaction and identify *A* and *B*.**

Ans. $\underset{(A)}{H_2SO_4} + \underset{(B)}{CaCO_3} \longrightarrow CaSO_4 + CO_2\uparrow + H_2O$ **(1)**

where, *A* and *B* are

$A = H_2SO_4, B = CaCO_3$ **(1)**

Q.10 **What is the role of CO_2 in the 'greenhouse effect'? Also, write the name of greenhouse gases.**

Ans. Heat from the sun after being absorbed by the earth is re-emitted by the earth. Some heat is absorbed by CO_2 which then radiate it back to the earth, thus, maintaining the constant temperature of the earth. **(1)**

The greenhouse gases are carbon dioxide, methane, water vapour, nitrous oxide, CFCs and ozone. **(1)**

Q.11 **Study the graph given below and answer the following questions.**

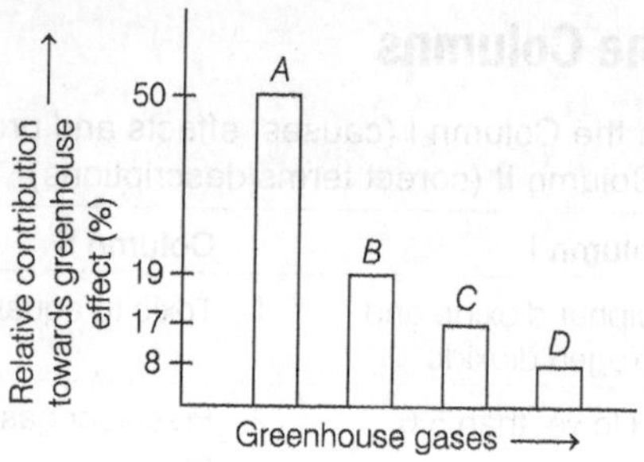

Identify *A*, *B*, *C* and *D*.

Ans. $A = CO_2$ (50%)

$B = CH_4$ (19%)

$A =$ CFCs (17%)

$D = O_3$ (8%) **(½ × 4 = 2)**

Q.12 **Green plants use carbon dioxide for photosynthesis and return oxygen to the atmosphere, even then carbon dioxide is considered to be responsible for greenhouse effect. Explain why?**

Ans. The amount of CO_2 produced due to human activity such as burning of fossil fuels like coal, natural gas, petroleum, etc., and production of lime from limestone, is much more than that consumed during photosynthesis.

The consumption in photosynthesis has further decreased due to deforestation.

So, the amount of carbon dioxide is increasing in the atmosphere.

Thus, carbon dioxide is considered to be responsible for greenhouse effect. **(2)**

Q.13 **The diagram given below represents greenhouse effect.**

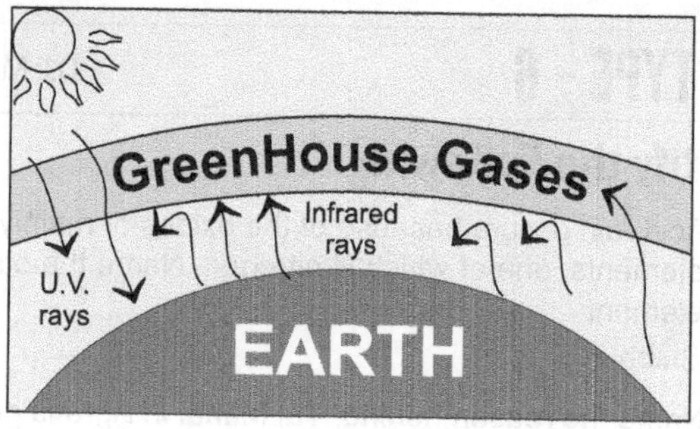

(i) If the concentration of greenhouse gases continues to rise, what would happen?

(ii) How can we mitigate the impact of the enhanced greenhouse effect on ecosystems?

Ans. (i) If greenhouse gases increases, more heat will be trapped in the Earth's atmosphere, leading to higher global temperatures and climate change. **(1)**

(ii) To mitigate the impact, we can protect forests, reduce pollution, use renewable energy and promote sustainable practices to help decrease the amount of greenhouse gases in the atmosphere. **(1)**

Q.14 What would have happened if the greenhouse gases were totally missing in the earth's atmosphere? Discuss.

Ans. Greenhouse gases are useful in keeping the earth warm, with an average temperature of about 15°C. In their absence, average surface temperature will fall to about – 18°C. This temperature will freeze all water and destroy most of the living beings. **(2)**

Q.15 Observe the given picture and answer the following questions.

(i) What does the image depict in relation to global warming? Explain its impact on polar ecosystems.

(ii) Discuss the effect of global warming in rise in sea levels?

Ans. (i) The image depicts the melting of polar ice caps due to global warming. Rising temperatures are causing habitat loss for species like polar bears and threatening their survival. **(1)**

(ii) Due to global warming, glaciers and polar ice caps have started to melt, and gradually this may lead to increase in sea level. This will in turn flood coastal areas in countries like India, Bangladesh, Netherland and Maldives. **(1)**

Q.16 Give reason why chlorofluorocarbons lead to depletion of ozone?

Ans. Chlorofluorocarbons are very light and reach the second layer of atmosphere. When CFCs reach the ozone layer, the UV rays break apart the CFCs and thus release the chlorine atom.

$$CF_2Cl_2(g) \xrightarrow{\text{UV rays}} CF_2Cl(g) + \underset{\text{(Free radical)}}{Cl(g)}$$

Thus, free radical [Cl] reacts with ozone and destroys the ozone layer. **(2)**

Q.17 The table shows pollutants and their possible effect predict the pollutant on the basis of effect given.

Pollutant	Effect
—	Cause destruction of the ozone layer
—	Forms acid rain

Ans.

Pollutant	Effect
CFCs	Cause destruction of the ozone layer
Oxides of N and S	Forms acid rain

(1 × 2 = 2)

Q.18 What do we mean by scavenging?

Ans. Locking of chlorine free radicals and chlorine monoxide radicals is called scavenging. In the atmosphere, nitrogen dioxide scavenges chlorine monoxide and methane scavenges chlorine atoms. These scavengers react with chlorine monoxide and free radicals of chlorine. **(2)**

TYPE - 8

03 Marks

Short Answer Type II Questions

Q.1 The sequence of reactions given below shows the formation of one of the component of acid rain.

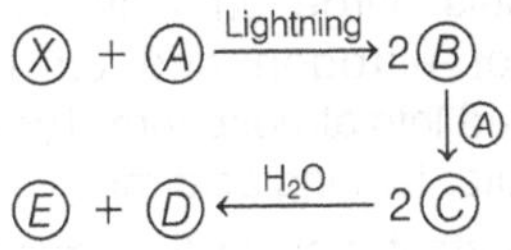

Identify *A*, *B*, *C*, *D* and *E*.

Ans.

$$\underset{(X)}{N_2} + \underset{(A)}{O_2} \xrightarrow{\text{Lightning}} 2NO$$

$$2NO \xrightarrow{O_2(A)} 2NO_2$$

$$\underset{(E)}{HNO_3} + \underset{(D)}{HNO_2} \xleftarrow{H_2O} \underset{(C)}{2NO_2}$$

(3)

Q.2 Statues and monuments in India are affected by acid rain. How?

Ans. The air around the statues and monuments in India contains fairly high levels of oxides of sulphur and nitrogen. It is mainly due to a large number of industries and power plants around the areas.

Oxides of nitrogen and sulphur are acidic in nature. SO_2 and NO_2 after oxidation and reaction with water are major contributors to acid rain.

$$2SO_2(g) + O_2(g) + 2H_2O(l) \longrightarrow 2H_2SO_4(aq)$$

$$2NO_2(g) + H_2O(l) \longrightarrow HNO_3(aq) + HNO_2(aq)$$

This acid rain reacts with marble of statues and monuments causing damage to these.

$$CaCO_3(s) + H_2SO_4(aq) \longrightarrow CaSO_4(s) + H_2O(l) + CO_2(g)$$ **(3)**

Q.3 Answer the following questions based on the picture shown below

(i) What are the main pollutants that cause acid rain, leading to the damage seen on the statue in the picture?

(a) Carbon monoxide and methane

(b) Sulphur dioxide and nitrogen oxides

(c) Ozone and particulate matter

(d) Lead and mercury

(ii) Based on the picture showing the damage caused by acid rain to a statue, can you explain how acid rain is formed?

(iii) What is the one important step that can be taken to reduce the damage caused by acid rain to monuments and statues?

Ans. (i) (b) Sulphur dioxide and nitrogen oxides.

(ii) Fossil fuels contain compounds of nitrogen and sulphur in addition to carbon. Due to combustion of these fuels, large amounts of sulphur dioxide, oxides of nitrogen and carbon dioxide gets discharged into atmosphere. These oxides dissolve in rain water forming acid rain.

(iii) One important step is to reduce the emission of oxides of sulphur and nitrogen by **using fuel with low sulphur content.** **(1 × 3 = 3)**

Q.4 Observe the apparatus shown below and answer the following questions.

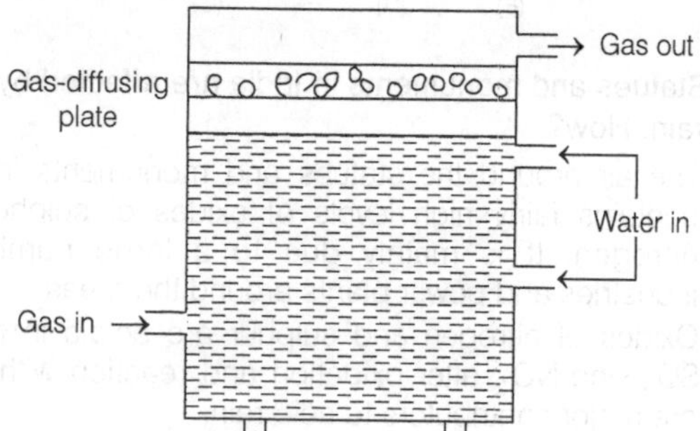

(i) Name the apparatus shown in the figure.

(ii) What is the following apparatus used for? Explain its working.

Ans. (i) The following apparatus is a **scrubber.** **(1)**

(ii) A scrubber is a device which is used to reduce the pollution in the atmosphere. It absorbs gaseous pollutants. It can remove smoke and sulphur dioxide from the atmosphere. It consists of a fine spray of water and gas rising from the stack which is passed through the scrubber. The water in the scrubber absorbs carbon dioxide. This also reduces the formation of acid rain. **(2)**

Q.5 Give any three ways to reduce global warming.

Ans. (i) Minimise the use of automobiles.

(ii) Plant more trees to increase the green cover.

(iii) Avoid burning of dry leaves, wood, etc. **(1 × 3 = 3)**

Q.6 Chlorofluorocarbons, CFCs, are also greenhouse gases.

(i) Name **one** other greenhouse gas found in the atmosphere.

(ii) State the origin of this greenhouse gas, named in part (i).

(iii) Describe how the presence of CFCs in the upper atmosphere increases the amount of ultra-violet rays reaching the Earth's surface.

Ans. (i) Methane

(ii) Decay of vegetation.

(iii) The ozone layer absorbs ultraviolet rays and thus protects the earth from the ultraviolet rays coming from the sun. CFCs go into the upper atmosphere and cause ozone depletion by reacting with ozone making the ultraviolet rays to reach to the earth. **(1 × 3 = 3)**

Q.7 Choose the appropriate option to answer the questions below

Carbon dioxide, Water vapour, Oxides of nitrogen, Methane, CFCs, Ozone

Each option can be used once, more than once, or not at all.

(i) The gas which is released in respiration by animals and human beings.

(ii) Used as refrigerants in refrigerators and air conditioners.

(iii) The gas which is emitted during anaerobic decomposition of organic matter in soil, water and sediments.

Ans. (i) Carbon dioxide (ii) CFCs

(iii) Methane **(1 × 3 = 3)**

Q.8 Give some effects of ozone depletion.

Ans. Following are effects of ozone depletion.

(i) **Skin cancer** Depletion of ozone layer will allow ultraviolet rays to enter the earth atmosphere due to which it affects our skin and causes skin cancer.

(ii) **Effect on immune system** Ultraviolet radiations also suppresses immune system. Due to which immunity against certain diseases decreases.

(iii) **Loss of sight** The depletion of ozone layer result in weakening of eye sight and ultimately to blindness. **(1 × 3 = 3)**

TYPE - 9 — 04/05 Marks

Long Answer Type Questions

Q.1 With respect to acid rain, answer the following questions.

(i) What do you mean by acid rain?

(ii) Name any three acids formed when acidic oxides dissolves in water.

(iii) Which oxides are released by vehicular exhaust?

(iv) Give chemical equation for the formation of the following acids.

(a) Nitric acid (b) Sulphuric acid

Ans. (i) Acid rain is the rain which carries large amount of acid than normal rain. Its pH usually ranges between 5.6 and 3.5. Due to combustion of fuels, large amounts of sulphur dioxide, oxides of nitrogen and carbon dioxide gets discharged into the atmosphere. These oxides dissolve in rain water forming mineral acids. **(1)**

(ii) Carbonic acid, sulphurous acid, nitric acid. **(1)**

(iii) **Oxides of nitrogen** are released by vehicular exhaust. **(1)**

(iv) (a) $\underset{\text{Nitrogen dioxide}}{4NO_2} + \underset{\text{Oxygen}}{O_2} + \underset{\text{Water}}{2H_2O} \longrightarrow \underset{\text{Nitric acid}}{4HNO_3}$ **(½)**

(b) $\underset{\text{Sulphur trioxide}}{SO_3} + \underset{\text{Water}}{H_2O} \longrightarrow \underset{\text{Sulphuric acid}}{H_2SO_4}$ **(½)**

Q.2 Answer the following questions.

(i) From where does the acid comes in rain?

(ii) Explain how acid rain effects soil chemistry.

(iii) List any two methods used to reduce formation of acid rain.

Ans. (i) Due to combustion of fuels, large amounts of sulphur dioxide, oxides of nitrogen and carbon dioxide get discharged into the atmosphere. These oxides dissolve in rain water forming mineral acids. That is how the acids comes in rain. **(1)**

(ii) Acid rain affects soil chemistry. It removes calcium and potassium, both the basic ingredients of soil, thus making it lose its fertility, which ultimately damages forests. Acid rain causes loss of nutrient from plants, thus damaging their leaves. **(1)**

(iii) (a) By using coal or oil with low sulphur content.

(b) By using a scrubber, a device that absorbs gaseous pollutants. **(2)**

Q.3 What do you mean by global warming? State the causes and effects of global warming.

Ans. The gradual and continuous rise in average temperature of the earth's surface is called global warming. **(1)**

Causes of Global Warming

(i) High levels of gases, such as carbon dioxide (CO_2), methane (CH_4), ozone (O_3), nitrous oxide (N_2O), chlorofluorocarbons (CFCs) are responsible for global warming.

(ii) Burning of fossil fuels in homes and industries, deforestation, etc., increases the level of carbon dioxide and methane in atmosphere. **(2)**

Effects of Global Warming

(i) An increase in temperature would lead to melting of polar ice caps and consequent rise in sea levels.

(ii) Increase in temperature of earth can cause change in weather and precipitation patterns on the earth. **(2)**

Q.4 What is greenhouse effect and what are the sources of greenhouse gases?

Ans. Heating of earth and its environment due to solar radiation trapped by greenhouse gases such as carbon dioxide and water vapour in the atmosphere is called **greenhouse effect**.

In the absence of greenhouse effect, the average temperature of earth would have been fall to – 18°C rather than the present average temperature of 15°C. **(1)**

Various sources of green house gases are as follows.

(i) **Water vapours** The main sources of water vapour are industrial exhaust, vehicular exhaust, burning of fuels and volcanic eruptions. **(1)**

(ii) **Carbon dioxide (CO_2)** Photosynthesis, respiration, burning of fossil fuels for energy, decomposition of limestone, volcanic eruptions, etc., all processes proceed with the evolution of carbon dioxide into the atmosphere. **(1)**

(iii) **Hydrocarbons (Methane, CH_4)** These are obtained by the incomplete combustion of fossil fuels in the automobile engines and by anaerobic decomposition of organic matter or vegetation. **(1)**

(iv) **Oxides of nitrogen** These are produced by the reaction of dinitrogen and dioxygen at higher altitudes when lightning strikes in atmosphere. Other sources are combustion of fossil fuels, automobile engines, tobacco smoke, denitrifying bacteria and other industrial processes. **(1)**

Q.5 Answer the following question.

(i) Explain the term smog.

(ii) Give two harmful effects of oxides of nitrogen.

(iii) Give two harmful effects of oxides of sulphur.

Ans. (i) It is a combination of oxides of nitrogen and sulphur and of partially-oxidised hydrocarbons and their derivatives which forms a dark, thick, dust and soot laden fog. **(1)**

(ii) (a) It causes irritation in mucous membrane.

(b) Its large concentration causes serious lung diseases. **(2)**

(iii) (a) It causes headache, vomiting and even death due to respiratory failure.

(b) It destroys vegetation and weakens building materials. **(2)**

Q.6 Explain the following

(i) How scrubber reduces the impact of acid rain?

(ii) Depletion of ozone layer.

(iii) How the gases emitted from the supersonic jet aeroplanes causes depletion of ozone layer?

(iv) Explain how chemicals used in industries are responsible for destruction of ozone layer.

(v) Depletion of ozone layer leads to formation of which one.

Ans. (i) A scrubber consists of a fine spray of water and when a smoke stack is passed through the scrubber, the water in it absorbs sulphur dioxide. Thus, the formation of this constituent of acid rain is reduced. **(1)**

(ii) The decrease in the quantity of ozone in upper layer of the atmosphere is called **depletion of ozone layer**. **(1)**

(iii) Nitric oxide emitted from the supersonic jet aeroplanes reacts with ozone to form nitrogen dioxide, nitrogen trioxide and oxygen. This causes depletion of ozone layer. **(1)**

(iv) The chemicals used in industries such as methyl chloride (CH_3Cl), methyl bromide (CH_3Br), carbon tetrachloride (CCl_4), etc., are responsible for destruction of ozone layer. These chemicals decomposed by ultraviolet rays to give highly reactive species which deplete ozone layer by reacting with it. **(1)**

(v) Depletion of ozone layer leads to the formation of an ozone hole. **(1)**

TYPE - 10

03 Marks

Case - Based Questions

Q.1 Ankit is studying air pollution caused by the release of harmful gases into the atmosphere. He notices that carbon monoxide (CO), nitrogen oxides (NO_x), and sulphur dioxide (SO_2) are commonly released by automobiles and industrial activities.

Ankit is concerned about the health effects of these pollutants and their impact on the environment.

(i) How is carbon monoxide released in the air as a pollutant?

(ii) What is the harmful effect of carbon monoxide if inhaled?

(iii) Give any two ways to control the release of carbon monoxide in the air.

Ans. (i) Carbon monoxide (CO) is released into the air as a pollutant mainly through the incomplete combustion of fuels in homes, factories and automobiles. **(1)**

(ii) Carbon monoxide (CO) permanently binds with haemoglobin in the blood to form carboxy-haemoglobin. This blocks the haemoglobin and reduces the blood's ability to carry oxygen. This causes symptoms like headache, dizziness, nausea, and in high concentrations, can lead to death. **(1)**

(iii) Two ways to control the release of carbon monoxide in the air is

- Use of catalytic converters in vehicle exhaust systems to convert carbon monoxide into carbon dioxide and water.
- Regular maintenance of vehicles to ensure proper combustion of fuels and reduce the emission of carbon monoxide. **(1)**

Q.2 Priya is studying the environmental impact of acid rain. She learns that acid rain is caused by the release of sulphur dioxide (SO_2) and nitrogen oxides (NO_x) into the atmosphere, primarily from vehicle exhausts, factories, and power plants. Priya is concerned about the damage acid rain can cause to life and environment.

(i) What is acid rain, and how is it formed?

(ii) What are the harmful effects of acid rain on the environment?

(iii) Give two ways to reduce the formation of acid rain.

Ans. (i) Acid rain is rain water that has a pH of less than 5.6 due to the presence of sulphuric acid (H_2SO_4) and nitric acid (HNO_3), carbonic acid, (H_2CO_3) and nitrous acid (HNO_2), etc. These acids form when sulphur dioxide (SO_2) and nitrogen oxides in the atmosphere react with water vapour or rain water. **(1)**

(ii) Acid rain can damage buildings, plants and aquatic life. It damages limestone and marble structures, harms soil quality and can lead to the death of fish and other aquatic organisms by lowering the pH of water bodies. **(1)**

(iii) Two ways to reduce the formation of acid rain are

- Use of low-sulphur content fuels in power plants and vehicles to reduce the emission of sulphur dioxide (SO_2).
- Installation of scrubbers in industrial chimneys to remove sulphur dioxide (SO_2) before it is released into the atmosphere. **(1)**

Sample Question Paper

SAMPLE QUESTION PAPER
CHEMISTRY

General Instructions

Maximum Marks : 80

Time allowed : Two hours

- You will not be allowed to write during the first **15** minutes. This time is to be spent in reading the question paper.
- The time given at the head of this paper is the time allowed for writing the answers. **Section A** is compulsory. Attempt **any four** questions from **Section B**.
- The intended marks for questions or parts of questions are given brackets [ ].

Section A

(Attempt **all** questions from this section) **(40 Marks)**

Question 1

Select the correct answers to the questions from the given options. **(15)**

(Do not copy the question, write the correct answers only)

(i) Which of the following represents the formula of sodium hypochlorite?

(a) $NaClO$ (b) $NaClO_2$ (c) $NaClO_3$ (d) $NaClO_4$

(ii) Which of the following is not a balanced equation?

(a) $Ca(OH)_2 + CO_2 \longrightarrow CaCO_3 + H_2O$

(b) $Fe + Cl_2 \longrightarrow FeCl_3$

(c) $Zn + H_2SO_4 \longrightarrow ZnSO_4 + H_2$

(d) $2KBr + Cl_2 \longrightarrow 2KCl + Br_2$

(iii) Which of the following is a deliquescent substance?

I. $NaOH$ II. KOH III. $MgCl_2$ IV. $ZnCl_2$

(a) I and II (b) III and IV (c) II and IV (d) All of these

(iv) If the volume of gas at 27°C is doubled at constant pressure. What is the new temperature?

(a) 327°C (b) 255°C (c) 300°C (d) 450°C

(v) $$H_2S + Cl_2 \longrightarrow 2HCl + S$$

In the above reaction, the substance shows reduction is

(a) H_2S (b) S (c) HCl (d) Cl_2

(vi) **Assertion** (A) The volume of gas decreases when the pressure is decreased.

Reason (R) According to Boyle's law, pressure and volume are inversely proportional.

(a) Both A and R are true and R is the correct explanation of A.

(b) Both A and R are true but R is not the correct explanation of A.

(c) A is true but R is false.

(d) A is false but R is true.

(vii) The lightest alkali metal is

(a) potassium (b) sodium (c) lithium (d) rubidium

(viii) The correct order regarding size of atom is

(a) $Li \approx Be > C \approx O$ (b) $Li > Be > C \approx O$ (c) $Li > Be > C > O$ (d) $Be > Li > C > O$

(ix) Which of the following isotope is used for determination of age of fossil fuels?

(a) ${}^{12}_{6}C$ (b) ${}^{14}_{6}C$ (c) ${}^{14}_{7}N$ (d) ${}^{13}_{6}C$

(x) **Assertion** (A) When silver chloride (AgCl) is exposed to sunlight at turns grey.

Reason (R) This happens because silver chloride decomposes into silver and chlorine gas in the presence of sunlight.

(a) Both A and R are true and R is the correct explanation of A.

(b) Both A and R are true but R is not the correct explanation of A.

(c) A is true but R is false.

(d) A is false but R is true.

(xi) Which formula represents the water gas?

(a) $CO_2 + H_2$ (b) $CO + H_2O$ (c) $CO + H_2$ (d) $CO + O_2$

(xii) Which of the following is an example of greenhouse gas?

(a) Oxygen (b) Ammonia (c) Methane (d) Nitrogen

(xiii) An element *X* has atomic mass 40, while the element *Y* has atomic mass 137. Then, the atomic mass of the intermediate element *Z* is nearly equal to

(a) 88 (b) 128 (c) 62 (d) 84

(xiv) What is the percentage composition of hydrogen in water? (Relative atomic mass of $H = 1, O = 16$)

(a) 22.7% (b) 18.4% (c) 11.1% (d) 16.2%

(xv) Which of the following is an ionic compound?

(a) C_2H_4 (b) $MgCl_2$ (c) NH_3 (d) CCl_4

Question 2

(i) The following diagram illustrates the process of reduction of copper from its oxide. **[5]**

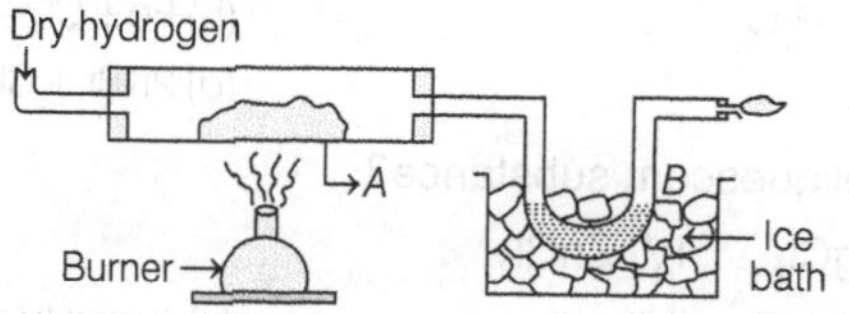

A black coloured substance '*A*' was taken in the combustion tube and heated strongly with H_2 gas, then pinkish red residue was left in the combustion tube and a colourless liquid '*B*' was collected in the *U* tube. Answer the following questions based on the above experiment

(a) Identify *A* and *B*.

(b) How will you support your answer for *B*?

(c) What is the nature of hydrogen gas ?

(d) Give the chemical reaction taking place.

(ii) What do you observe, when **[5]**

(a) mercuric chloride and potassium iodide are crushed together in a mortar?

(b) electric current is passed through acidulated water?

(c) crystals of hydrated copper (II) sulphate are heated strongly in a test tube?

(d) sodium hydrogen carbonate is heated strongly?

(e) barium chloride is added to sodium sulphate solution?

(iii) Complete the following sentences by choosing the correct word(s) from the brackets? **[5]**

(a) Atoms of different elements may be similar in terms of mass number are called............ . (isotopes/isobars)

(b) .... is the strong reducing agent present in activity series. (Potassium/Copper).

(c) The molecular formula of potassium *meta*-aluminate is............ ($KAlO_2$ / $KAlO_4$)

(d) The reaction of lead sulphide with oxygen to form lead sulphate shows .... (combination/decomposition) reaction.

(e) The atomic number of atom of an element has three electrons in the *M*-shell is.......... (13/14)

(iv) Match the column A with Column B **[5]**

	Column A		Column B
(a)	Boyle's law	1.	373 K
(b)	Charle's law	2.	$V \propto T$
(c)	Boiling point of water	3.	$pV = K$
(d)	Freezing point of water	4.	$-273°$ C
(e)	Absolute zero	5.	273 K

(v) (a) Answer the following question based on the given diagram. **[5]**

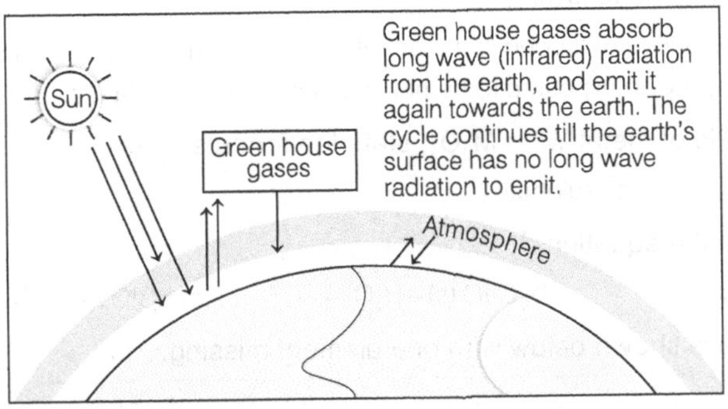

1. Name the effect described in the diagram.
2. Name a major green house gas that is released by excessive burning of fossil fuels.

(b) Explain the following.

1. Mass of an atom is concentrated inside the nucleus of the atom.
2. Atoms combine by transfer and sharing of electron(s).
3. Element has atoms with different mass number.

Section B

(Attempt **any four** questions from this section) **(40 Marks)**

Question 3

(i) Identify the element in each of the following case. **[2]**

(a) An element *A* has 2 electrons in its fourth shell.

(b) Element *B* having zero valency and 10 protons.

(ii) Observe the two test tubes *A* and *B* in the diagram given below and answer the following questions. **[2]**

(a) In which test tube, reaction will take place?

(b) Name the type of reaction.

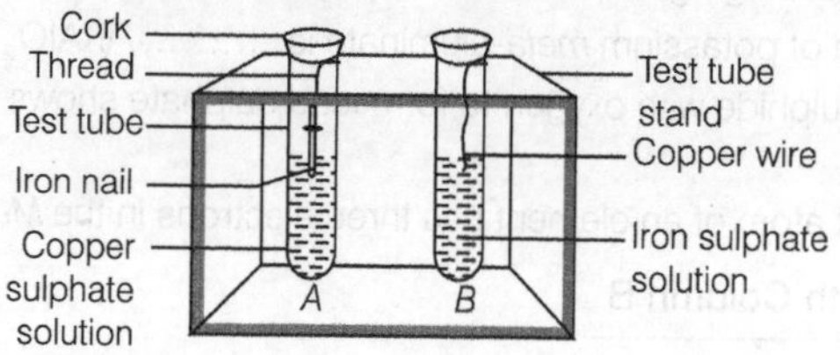

(iii) Write the relative molecular mass of each of the following. **[3]**

(a) Magnesium nitrate $Mg(NO_3)_2$

(b) Zinc sulphate $ZnSO_4$ [S = 32, O = 16, Mg = 24, N = 14, Zn = 65]

(iv) Arrange the following as per the instructions gives in the brackets. **[3]**

(a) Cl, Na, Mg (decreasing order of reducing character)

(b) Li, Be, F, N (decreasing order of atomic radii)

(c) Na, P, S, Cl (increasing order of metallic character)

Question 4

(i) Give a reason for each of the following: **[2]**

(a) Though lead is placed above hydrogen in the activity series, it is not used to prepare hydrogen.

(b) Table salt becomes sticky on exposure to humid air during the rainy season.

(ii) The formula of the oxide of metal '*M*' is M_2O_3, state the formula of its **[2]**

(a) sulphide (b) sulphate

(iii) Complete and balance the equation. **[3]**

(a) $AgNO_3(aq) + NaCl\ (aq) \longrightarrow$ (b) $CaO\ (s) + H_2O \longrightarrow$ (c) $KClO_3(s) \xrightarrow{\Delta}$

(iv) A part of periodic table is shown below with one element missing. **[3]**

H												He
Li	Be											Ne
Na	Mg											Ar
K	Ca	Sc	Ti	V	Cr	Mn	—	Co	Ni	Cu	Zn	—
Rb	Sr											
Cs	Ba											

Based on the above table, answer the following questions.

(a) Name one element that has, octet structure.

(b) Name the alkali metal present in third period.

(c) Identify the two missing elements.

Question 5

(i) Identify the charge in each of the following cases: **[2]**

(a) When the number of electrons is less than the number of protons, the atom carries *X* charge.

(b) When the number of electrons is greater than the number of protons, the atom carries *Y* charge.

(ii) Answer the following questions based on the figure given below. **[2]**

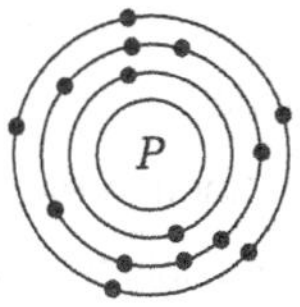

(a) What charge would be attained by the ion of the element *P* during a reaction?

(b) Write the number of electrons present in the element *P*.

(iii) Write balanced equations for each of the following: **[3]**

(a) Reaction of potassium with cold water.

(b) Reaction of magnesium sulphate with sodium hydroxide.

(c) Heating of iron with sulphur.

(iv) When hydrogen is passed over a black solid compound *X*, the products are a colourless liquid and a reddish brown metal *Y′*. Metal *Y′* is divided into two parts and each placed in separate test tubes. Dilute HCl is added to one part of substance and dilute HNO_3 to the other. **[3]**

(a) Write the name of substances *X* and *Y*.

(b) Write one test for the colourless liquid formed in the experiment.

(c) What happen to substances *X* when it reacts with hydrogen?

Question 6.

(i) Answer the following question with reference to table. **[3]**

Group 1	Group 2	Group 16	Group 17	Group 18
—	—	—	*D*	—
—	*B*	*C*	—	—
A	—	—	—	*E*

(a) State which are metals, non-metals and noble gas in the above table.

(b) Which type of ion will be formed by element *A*, *B* and *C*?

(c) Which element is larger in size *D* or *E*?

(ii) (K, Na, Ca, Mg, Al, Zn, Fe, Sn, Pb, H, Cu, Hg, Ag and Au).

Choose the answers from list which fits in the description. **[3]**

(a) The metal which does not react with cold water, but reacts with boiling hot water slowly.

(b) A metal which displaces hydrogen very slowly from dilute HCl.

(c) The metal which on heating reacts with steam, but reaction is reversible.

(iii) The capacity of one cylinder is 4 dm^3 and that of the other is 1 dm^3; their are pressure 560 mm Hg and 1000 mg Hg respectively. Both of these cylinders, containing carbon dioxide, are connected together by a tube fitted with a tap. What will be the final pressure in either cylinder on opening the tap if the temperature remains constant? **[4]**

Question 7

(i) Identify the substance which matches the description given below: **[2]**

(a) Gas which is also called inflammable air.

(b) Two metals which react with dilute nitric acid to liberate hydrogen.

(ii) The elements *X* and *Y* have electronic configuration (2, 8, 18, 2) and (2, 6) respectively, then **[2]**

(a) in which period *X* and *Y* belong? (b) in which group *X* and *Y* belong?

(iii) State, if the solubility increases, decreases or remains the same with rise in temperature for each of the following compounds: **[3]**

(a) Potassium nitrate (b) Sodium chloride (c) Hydrated calcium sulphate

(iv) Identify the type of chemical reaction taking place in each of the following: **[3]**

(a) Barium chloride solution is mixed with copper sulphate solution and a white precipitate is observed.

(b) On heating copper powder in air in a china dish, the surface of copper powder turns black.

(c) On heating white crystals of ferrous sulphate, reddish brown solid is left and smell of a gas having odour of burning sulphur is experienced.

Question 8

(i) (a) State Charle's law. **[2]**

(b) Define anhydrous substance.

(ii) Differentiate between the following pairs. **[2]**

(a) Silver nitrate and zinc sulphide (using HCl).

(b) Copper and magnesium [using dil. H_2SO_4]

(iii) Classify the following reaction by choosing the reactions given in the box below: **[3]**

(combination, decomposition, displacement or double displacement)

(a) $2AgCl(s) \xrightarrow{\text{Sunlight}} 2Ag(s) + Cl_2(l)$

(b) $2Fe(s) + 3Cl_2(g) \longrightarrow 2FeCl_3(s)$

(c) $AgNO_3 + NaCl \longrightarrow AgCl\downarrow + NaNO_3$

(iv) The position of three elements *A*, *B* and *C* in the periodic table are shown below **[3]**

Group 16	Group 17
—	—
—	*A*
—	—
B	*C*

(a) State whether *A* is a metal or non-metal.

(b) State whether *C* is more reactive or less reactive than *A*.

(c) Will *C* be larger or smaller in size than *B*?

Answers

1. (i) (a) The formula of sodium hypochlorite is NaClO.

(ii) (b) $Fe + Cl_2 \longrightarrow FeCl_3$

The following equation is not a balanced equation as the total number of atoms each element on the left side of the equation is not same as the number of atoms on the right side of the equation.

(iii) (d) NaOH, KOH, $MgCl_2$, and $ZnCl_2$ all of these are the examples of deliquescent substances.

(iv) (a) Given, $T_1(°C) = 27°C \Rightarrow T_1(K) = 27 + 273 = 300$ K

$$V_2 = 2V_1$$

By applying Charle's law, $\frac{V_1}{T_1} = \frac{V_2}{T_2}$ (at constant pressure)

$$\therefore \quad \frac{V_1}{300} = \frac{2V_1}{T_2} \Rightarrow T_2(K) = 600$$

$\therefore T_2(°C) = T_2(K) - 273 = 600 - 273$

$T_2(°C) = 327°C$

(v) (d) In the given reaction, **chloride** (Cl_2) is reduced to hydrogen chloride by gain of hydrogen and thus, it shows reduction.

(vi) (d) A is false, but R is true.

According to Boyle's law volume of a given mass of a dry gas in inversely proportional to its pressure at constant temperature. Thus, the volume of gas **increases** when the pressure is decreased.

(vii) (c) The lightest alkali metal is **lithium**.

(viii) (c) Since, the size of an atom decreases on moving left to right in a period, therefore, the correct, decreasing order of the size of atom is Li > Be > C > O.

(ix) (b) ${}^{14}_{6}C$ is used for determining the age of fossil fuels.

(x) (a) Both A and R are true and R is the correct explanation of A.

When silver chloride (AgCl) is exposed to sunlight, it undergoes photochemical decomposition, to form a grey metal, silver and a greenish yellow gas, chlorine.

$$\underset{\text{Silver chloride (white)}}{2AgCl} \xrightarrow{\text{Sunlight}} \underset{\text{Silver (grey)}}{2Ag(s)} + \underset{\text{Chlorine (greenish yellow gas)}}{Cl_2(l)}$$

(xi) (c) **($CO + H_2$)** represent the formula of the water gas.

(xii) (c) **Methane (CH_4)** is an example of greenhouse gas.

(xiii) (a) According to Dobereiner's traid the atomic mass of the intermediate element Z is nearly equal to the average of the atomic masses of the element X and Y.

$$\therefore \text{ Atomic mass of Z} = \frac{40 + 137}{2} = 88.5 \simeq 88$$

(xiv) (c) 11.1%

Relative molecular mass of $H_2O = (1 \times 2) + (16) = 18$

Since, 18g of water contains 2 g of hydrogen

$\therefore$ 100g of water contains $\frac{2}{18} \times 100 = 11.11$ g of Hydrogen

$\therefore$ Percentage composition of hydrogen in water is 11.1%.

(xv) (b) **$MgCl_2$** is an ionic compound, whereas C_2H_4, NH_3 and CCl_4 are the examples of covalent compounds.

2. (i) (a) The substance 'A' is CuO and 'B' is H_2O.

(b) When hydrogen gas is passed over the strongly heated copper oxide it reduces the copper oxide to copper and itself gets oxidised to water.

(c) Hydrogen gas acts as strong **reducing agent** as it itself gets oxidised to water and reduce copper oxide to copper.

(d) The chemical reaction taking place is as follows:

$$\underset{\text{(Black)}}{CuO(s)} + H_2(g) \xrightarrow{\Delta} \underset{\text{Pinkish red residue}}{Cu(s)} + H_2O(l)$$

(ii) (a) When mercuric chloride ($HgCl_2$) and potassium iodide (KI) are rushed together in a mortar, they will react to give a **scarlet-coloured** called mercuric iodide (HgI_2)

$$HgCl_2 + 2KI \longrightarrow HgI_2 + 2KCl$$

(b) Acidulated water breaks into hydrogen and oxygen when electric current is passed through it.

$$2H_2O \xrightarrow[\text{current}]{\text{electric}} 2H_2 + O_2$$

(c) When the blue crystals of hydrated copper (II) sulphate are heated strongly in a test tube they will turn into a white powder of anhydrous copper sulphate.

$$\underset{\text{Hydrated blue colour salt}}{CuSO_4 \cdot 5H_2O} \underset{\text{Cool}}{\overset{\text{Heat}}{\rightleftharpoons}} \underset{\text{Anhydrous white colour salt powder}}{CuSO_4} + 5H_2O$$

(d) When sodium hydrogen carbonate is heated strongly, it decomposes to give sodium carbonate, water vapour and carbon dioxide gas.

$$\underset{\text{Sodium hydrogen carbonate}}{2NaHCO_3} \xrightarrow{\Delta} \underset{\text{Sodium carbonate}}{Na_2CO_3} + H_2O + CO_2\uparrow$$

(e) When barium chloride is added to sodium sulphate solution, a white precipitate of barium sulphate is formed.

$$BaCl_2(aq) + Na_2SO_4(aq) \longrightarrow \underset{\text{white ppt.}}{BaSO_4(s)} + 2NaCl(aq)$$

(iii) (a) Isobars (b) Potassium (c) $KAlO_2$ (d) Combination (e) 13

(iv) (a) → (3), (b) → (2), → (c) → (1), (d) → (5), (e) → (4)

(v) (a) 1. Greenhouse effect. 2. Carbon dioxide (CO_2) gas.

(b) 1. The mass of an atom is concentrated inside the nucleus of an atom due to the presence of protons and neutrons into it.

2. Atoms combine by transfer and sharing of electron (s) so that the combination atom can gain the stable electronic configuration (octet) is completed.

3. Atoms of the same element can have different numbers of neutrons, leading to different mass numbers. These atoms with the same atomic number but different mass numbers are called isotopes.

3. (i) (a) The number of electrons in fourth, N-shell = 2

Hence, the number of electrons in the K, L and M shells will be = 2, 8, 8

∴ Atomic number = 2 + 8 + 8 + 2 = 20

Thus, the element A having 2 electrons in its fourth shell is **calcium**.

(b) Since, Atomic number = Number of proton = 10

Thus, the element B having zero valency and 10 protons is **neon**.

(ii) (a) The reaction will take place in the **test tube** A, because iron lies above the copper in metal activity series and thus, it displaces copper from its copper sulphate solution.

(b) Displacement reaction

(iii) (a) Atomic mass of Mg = 24, N = 14, and O = 16

$\therefore$ Relative molecular mass of $Mg(NO_3)_2 = 24 + (2 \times 14) + (6 \times 16) = 24 + 28 + 96 = 148$ amu

(b) Atomic mass of Zn=65, S = 32 and O = 16

$\therefore$ Relative molecular mass of $ZnSO_4 = 65 + 32 + (4 \times 16) = 65 + 32 + 64 = 161$ amu

(iv) (a) On moving left to right across a period, the reducing character decreases because the effective nuclear charge increases and due to which the ability of losing electron decreases. Therefore, the decreasing order of reducing character is Na > Mg > Cl.

(b) On moving left to right across a period, the atomic radii of an atom decreases due to increase in nuclear charge. Therefore, the decreasing order of atomic radii is **Li > Be > N > F**.

(c) On moving left to right across a period, the metallic character or the ability to lose electrons decreases. Therefore, the increasing order of metallic character is **Cl < S < P < Na**.

4. (i) (a) Lead is placed above hydrogen in the activity series, though it is not used to prepare hydrogen because it reacts with acids like hydrochloric acid or dilute sulphuric acid to form an **insoluble coating** of lead chloride or lead sulphate which prevents further reaction.

(b) Table salt contains deliquescent impurities like **magnesium chloride** and **calcium chloride**. These impurities absorb moisture from atmospheric air and makes table salt moist and sticky.

(ii) Since, the formula M_2O_3 represents that the valency of M is 3.

(a) Formula of sulphide of metal 'M' is M_2S_3.

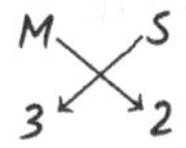

(b) Formula of sulphate of metal 'M' is $M_2(SO_4)_3$.

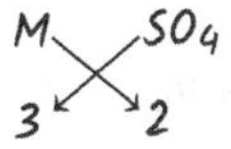

(iii) (a) $AgNO_3(aq) + NaCl(aq) \longrightarrow AgCl(s)\downarrow + NaNO_3$

(b) $CaO(s) + H_2O(l) \longrightarrow Ca(OH)_2(aq)$

(c) $2KClO_3(s) \xrightarrow{\Delta} 2KCl + 3O_2$

(iv) (a) **Ne (Neon)** is the element that has octet structure.

(b) **Na (Sodium)** is an alkali metal present in third period.

(c) The two missing elements are Fe (Iron) and Kr (Krypton).

5. (i) (a) When the number of electrons is less than the number of protons the atom carries **positive** (X) charge.

(b) When the number of electrons is greater than the number of protons, the atom carries **negative** (Y) charge.

(ii) (a) The ion of element P and would attain a **(-3) charge** during a reaction. This is because it needs to gain 3 electrons to complete its octet in the outermost shell and achieve a stable electronic configuration.

(b) The number of electrons present in the element P is **15**.

(iii) (a) $2K + 2H_2O \longrightarrow 2KOH + H_2$
Potassium Water Potassium hydroxide

(b) $MgSO_4 + 2NaOH \longrightarrow Mg(OH)_2 + Na_2SO_4$
Magnesium sulphate Sodium hydroxide Magnesium hydroxide Sodium sulphate

(c) $Fe + S \xrightarrow{Heat} FeS$
Iron Sulphur Iron sulphate

(iv) (a) The substance X is copper oxide (CuO) and Y is copper (Cu).

(b) **Test for the colourless liquid formed** (water) Adding calcium chloride to the liquid will result in a white precipitate, indicating the presence of water.

(c) When hydrogen gas is passed over heated copper oxide (CuO), the copper oxide is reduced to copper (Cu), and the hydrogen is oxidised to form water (H_2O).

$$\underset{\text{Black solid}}{CuO} + H_2 \xrightarrow{\Delta} \underset{\text{(Reddish-brown)}}{Cu} + H_2O$$

6. (i) (a) **Metals** A and B

Non-metals C and D

Noble gas E

(b) Ion formed by the element A and B is cation and by the element C is anion.

(c) **Element** E is larger in size than the element D due to presence of more number of shells and larger atomic radii.

(ii) (a) **Mg (Magnesium)** does not react with cold water but reacts slowly with boiling hot water.

(b) **Sn (Tin)** displaces hydrogen very slowly from dilute HCl.

(c) **Fe (Iron)** reacts with steam on heating and the reason is reversible.

(iii) Total volume of carbon dioxide (after opening the top) = $(4 + 1)\ dm^3 = 5\ dm^3$

For the first cylinder

$$p_1V_1 = p_2V_2$$

$$560 \times 4 = p_2 \times 5$$

$$\therefore \quad p_2 = \frac{560 \times 4}{5} = 448 \text{ mmHg}$$

For the second cylinder

$$p_1V_1 = p_2V_2$$

$$1000 \times 1 = P_2 \times 5$$

$$\therefore \quad p_2 = \frac{1000 \times 1}{5} = 200 \text{ mm Hg}$$

$\Rightarrow$ Final pressure = 448 + 200 = 648 mm Hg.

7. (i) (a) **Hydrogen (H_2)** is also known as inflammable air because it easily ignites and burns in the presence of oxygen.

(b) **Magnesium (Mg)** and **manganese (Mn)** react with very dilute nitric acid to produce hydrogen gas.

(ii) (a) Element x having electronic configuration (2, 8, 18, 2) belongs to **period 4** as it has 4 shells.

Element y having electronic configuration (2, 6) belongs to **period 2** as it has 2 shells.

(b) Element x (2, 8, 18, 2) have 2 valence electrons, so it belongs to **group 2.**

Element y have 6 valence electrons, so it belongs to **group 16.**

(iii) (a) Solubility of sodium nitrate **increases** with rise in temperature.

(b) Solubility of sodium chloride **increases** with rise in temperature.

(c) Solubility of hydrated calcium sulphate **decreases** with rise in temperature.

(iv) (a) Precipitation reaction (a type of double displacement reaction).

$$BaCl_2(aq) + CuSO_4(aq) \longrightarrow \underset{\text{White ppt.}}{BaSO_4(s)\downarrow} + CuCl_2$$

(b) Combination reaction

$$\underset{\text{(Reddish brown)}}{2Cu(s)} + O_2(g) \longrightarrow \underset{\text{Black}}{2CuO(s)}$$

(c) Decomposition reaction

$$\underset{\text{(White)}}{2FeSO_4(s)} \xrightarrow{\text{Heat}} \underset{\text{(Reddish brown)}}{Fe_2O_3(s)} + SO_2(g) + SO_3(g)$$

8. (i) (b) Charle's law states that the volume of a given mass of a dry gas is directly proportional to its absolute temperature, if the pressure remains constant.

(b) Substances which do not contain any water molecules along with their salts are called as anhydrous substance.

(ii) (a) On reaction with HCl silver nitrate ($AgNO_3$) gives curdy white precipitate whereas, with zinc sulphide a rotten egg smelling gas is evolved.

$$AgNO_3 + HCl \longrightarrow \underset{\text{(white ppt.)}}{AgCl\downarrow} + HNO_3$$

$$ZnS + 2HCl \longrightarrow ZnCl_2 + H_2S\uparrow$$

(b) Since, magnesium (Mg) lies above hydrogen in reactivity series, so it displaces hydrogen from dil. H_2SO_4 whereas copper lies below hydrogen in the reactivity series hence it does not displace hydrogen and no reaction will be observed.

$$Mg + \underset{\text{Dil.}}{H_2SO_4} \longrightarrow MgSO_4 + H_2$$

$$Cu + \underset{\text{Dil.}}{H_2SO_4} \longrightarrow \text{No reaction}$$

(iii) (a) Decomposition reaction (b) Combination reaction (c) Double displacement reaction

(iv) (a) Since, A belongs to group 17 and has 7 valence electrons, so, it is a **non-metal** and it will gain electrons to complete its octet.

(b) Since, C lies below A in the same group so, as we go down the group size of element increases and the ability of accepting electrons decreases. Thus, reactivity decreases. Therefore, C is less reactive than A.

(c) C is smaller in size than B because as when we move from left to right across a period, the atomic size decreases due to increases effective nuclear charge.